THE "S" WORD

THE "S" WORD

A Short History of an American
Tradition ... Socialism

John Nichols

VERSO

London • New York

This edition first published by Verso 2011
© John Nichols 2011

All rights reserved

The moral rights of the author have been asserted

1 3 5 7 9 10 8 6 4 2

Verso
UK: 6 Meard Street, London W1F 0EG
US: 20 Jay Street, Suite 1010, Brooklyn, NY 11201
www.versobooks.com

Verso is the imprint of New Left Books

ISBN-13: 978-1-84467-679-8

British Library Cataloguing in Publication Data
A catalogue record for this book is available from the British Library

Library of Congress Cataloging-in-Publication Data
A catalog record for this book is available from the Library of Congress

Typeset in Minion Pro by MJ Gavan, Truro, Cornwall
Printed in the US by Maple Vail

Contents

Whitman, Sylvie and the Emmas

On a cloudless day in the second summer of Barack Obama's presidency—when even the children who were so enamored of his election had begun to ask: "When is the president going to end the war?"—my daughter Whitman and I boarded the ferry that would deliver us to a place where it was still possible to believe in the very best of America's promise. I had been to the island in New York harbor before, but this was Whitman's first visit to the Statue of Liberty. We would, of course, climb as high as permitted, purchase modestly absurd souvenirs and sample the various ice creams proffered by the National Park Service and its assigns. But our primary purpose was a more patriotic one. Whitman is, by virtue of her name and parentage, of a literary bent. And we were inclined this day to read one of America's finest poetic expressions in the setting where the author intended.

Every child should know America not as the foreboding behemoth a succession of misguided and ill-intended presidents have sought to make it but in the light that Emma Lazarus saw it, as the great and welcoming land that would proudly take upon herself the title: "Mother of Exiles."

"Keep ancient lands your storied pomp ..."

And, yes: "Give me your tired, your poor, your huddled masses yearning to breathe free, the wretched refuse of your teeming shore, Send these, the homeless, tempest-tost to me, I lift my lamp beside the golden door!"

With those thrilling lines—still possessing "the power to raise goose-bumps" that author Caleb Crain heard—Lazarus transformed what was to have been a monument to those ideals of international republicanism that linked the American and French revolutions—"La Liberté Eclairant le Monde" (Liberty Enlightening the World) is the actual name of the copper statue—into something altogether more radical and egalitarian. It was not the sculptor Frédéric Auguste Bartholdi who made the Statue of Liberty into what Paul Auster properly proclaimed to be "a symbol of hope to the outcasts and downtrodden of the world." It was Emma Lazarus who would imagine the "beacon-hand" that "Glows world-wide welcome ..." and who would inspire the rest of us to do the same.

That Lazarus, with her poem written in the service of a fund-raising drive to erect the statue's pedestal, gave the great lady of New York harbor her "raison d'etre"—as James Russell Lowell mused a century ago—is no longer questioned by any but the most crudely unwelcoming of Americans (an unsettling number of whom, with supreme irony, now refer to themselves as "Republicans"). Lazarus's poem, "The New Colossus," has entered the pantheon of American statements—a part of National Public Radio's "credo of America"—along with Tom Paine's hope that this experiment might "begin the world over again," Abraham Lincoln's promise that "all men are created equal" and the Rev. Martin Luther King, Jr.'s call to bend the arc of history toward the realization of that promise with a civil rights revolution sufficient that all Americans might declare themselves to be "free at last."

All of the words in the credo are radical. And so it should come as no surprise that Emma Lazarus was a radical. Nor should it come as any surprise that, like Paine, Lincoln and King, Lazarus was an American who entertained and advocated ideas that can reasonably be described as "socialist."

This fact, while self evident in her time, and historically evident to this day, is a neglected chapter of the story of Emma Lazarus, of one of our nation's most enduring tribunes and, indeed, of the credo of America.

Just as the rough and revolutionary edges of Paine, Lincoln and King have been buffed away by time, public relations and a dumbing down of our history that makes them over as temperate men of limited imagination and capacity to inspire, so the memory of Emma Lazarus has been robbed of meaning by those who would have America be something it was never intended to be: a conservative land ever at odds with a forward march of human progress from the enlightenment to liberation to the cooperative commonwealth. There is an imagining now of Lazarus as a sort of uptown do-gooder, penning kind words with regard to the less fortunate. But that crude characterization would have horrified the poet.

Emma Lazarus was a radical reformer who sought out and embraced socialists, communists and others who proposed transformational responses to the economic and social disparities that diminished not just "ancient lands" with their "storied pomp" but the "New World" of America. She recognized in the tenements of Manhattan and Brooklyn of the 1870s and 1880s a circumstance of inequality that doomed both new immigrants and the descendents of the slaves, indentured servants and religious dissenters who had arrived long before the republican revolt of 1776 to experience a wrenching poverty that, when companioned with racial and ethnic discriminations, made the promise of "life, liberty and the pursuit of happiness" seem vague at best, and at worst empty.

In her poem "Progress and Poverty," written several years before "The New Colossus," Lazarus challenged the elites of the Gilded Age to recognize that their wealth was forged through the exploitation of impoverished laborers. Imagining America as a "vessel, manned by demigods, with freight of priceless marvels," she asked,

> But where yawns the hold
> In that deep, reeking hell, what slaves be they
> Who feed the ravenous monster, pant and sweat,
> Nor know if overhead reign night and day?

"Progress and Poverty" was penned as a paean to the political economist and social philosopher Henry George, whose book of the same title inspired an international movement to reorder property relations so that the earth's resources would no longer be the possession of wealthy and powerful elites. Arguing that the "fundamental mistake" of capitalism was "treating land as private property," George declared: "We must make land common property." George became a hero to the urban radicals of the 1880s through his advocacy for taxing the rich and his campaigns for public ownership of communications and transportation systems and for municipal control of water supplies and delivery of basic services. Lazarus and her circle embraced George's conviction that: "The progress of civilization requires that more and more intelligence be devoted to social affairs, and this not the intelligence of the few, but that of the many. We cannot safely leave politics to politicians, or political economy to college professors. The people themselves must think, because the people alone can act." George's followers became popular educators. In Lazarus's case, her poetry was not merely a vehicle for vibrant wordplay but a tool for transforming the politics of her native New York, America and the world. "For Emma Lazarus, George's utopian vision had the force of a revelation," observed her biographer, Esther Schor. "It showed her both her complicity in exploiting the poor and her ethical responsibility to remedy it. 'Your work is not so much a book as an event,' she wrote, 'the life & thought of no one capable of understanding it can be quite the same after reading it ...'" Embracing the "indisputable truth" of George's arguments, Lazarus told the author: "No one who prizes justice or common honesty can dine or sleep or read or work in peace until the monstrous wrong in which we are all accomplices be done away with ..."

A secular Jew haunted by the news of pogroms abroad and addressable grievances at home, Lazarus would, as Schor observed, use "the model of a Jewish duty to repair the world," to conceive "of a mission for America"—a mission emphasizing that "when you have the benefits of freedom, you had more than rights; you had duties." To that end, Lazarus published essays, articles and poems—earning considerable recognition in the US and Europe—that marked her in her time as a political activist who would be celebrated not merely as the author of a sonnet associated with the Statue of Liberty but, in the words of a contemporary, Rev. Dr. H. P. Mendes, as "a voice against all injustice."

Lazarus wrote before Eugene Victor Debs and Victor Berger imagined a Socialist Party, even before a campaigner for Henry George's 1886 New York mayoral campaign, Daniel DeLeon, began in the early 1890s to popularize the Marxist platform of the Socialist Labor Party. That we know of, she never carried the card of a party or declared a political preference. While socialists and communists would eventually claim her, Lazarus was not a political joiner. Yet, she acknowledged the influence of socialist ideas on her writing and set out to popularize those notions that inspired her. She penned manifestos that were determinedly progressive in their sympathy for workers and immigrants. She traveled to Europe to meet and interview the most radical thinkers of the day—fellow Zionists, literary adventurers and Marxists of varying creeds. One of her most widely circulated essays was a portrait of author and utopian socialist William Morris, whose "extreme socialistic convictions" the poet presented as an understandable response to "glaring" social and economic inequalities on display in his native Britain.

Though she would wrestle with and reject some radical ideas, Lazarus recognized their power and urged that they be included in the great debates about America's future. In this, she was a true child of the enlightenment, a believer in the very American precept that the radical ideas of one moment could become the common-sense solutions of the next.

For much of the twentieth century, before the beneficial influence of feminist and people's history projects opened up our past, Lazarus was a relatively neglected figure. When she was all but forgotten by genteel society, however, the poetry of Emma Lazarus was reintroduced to America by left-wing groups such as the American Committee for the Foreign Born and the Emma Lazarus Federation of Jewish Women's Clubs, a radical organization that began as the Women's Division of the Jewish People's Fraternal Order of the International Workers Order. The "Emmas," as these activists were known, celebrated Lazarus's birthday each year on Liberty Island, urged New York and other cities to declare "Emma Lazarus Days," and campaigned for economic and social justice "in our own time in the same spirit as Emma Lazarus did in her day." They experienced their share of political persecution—in 1960, June Gordon, the executive director of the Emma Lazarus Federation, was threatened with deportation because of challenges to her immigration status (more than three decades after her arrival in the country) and her long involvement with left-wing causes—yet they persevered. There is a lovely photograph from the 1963 March on Washington for Jobs and Freedom, in which a few dozen Emmas are seated beneath their banner on the grounds of the Lincoln Memorial. What image could possibly have made their mentor more proud?

The Emmas did not just honor the memory of Emma Lazarus, however. They kept it alive and vibrant. Today, Lazarus is an iconic figure. Yet, the "spirit" of which the Emmas spoke is not so well understood as it should be.

The story of Emma Lazarus, the whole story, is an important one for contemporary Americans. It reminds us that the authors of "the American credo" were not free-market capitalists preaching laissez-faire mantras of "eat or be eaten," "survival of the fittest," "close the borders" or "government is the problem." In fact, this country, founded in radical opposition to monarchy, colonialism and empire, has from its beginning been home to socialists, social democrats, communists and radicals of every variation. Criticisms of capitalism were not "imports" brought to our shores by the tired, the poor, the huddled masses of ancient lands. They were conceived of, written about and spoken by Americans long before Karl Marx or Fidel Castro or Nelson Mandela or Hugo Chavez put pen to paper or grasped the sides of a lectern. Emma Lazarus was not, as is often thought, an immigrant; she was a fourth-generation American with family roots planted in the soil of America before the signing of the Declaration of Independence.

Socialist ideas, now so frequently dismissed not just by the Tories of the present age but by political and media elites that diminish and deny our history, have shaped and strengthened America across the past two centuries. Those ideas were entertained and at times embraced by presidents who governed a century before Barack Obama was born.

That does not mean that America is a socialist country, nor even the "social democracy that does not speak its name" that author Michael Harrington once imagined. But it does mean that, to know America, to understand and appreciate the whole of this country's past, its present and perhaps its future, we must recognize the socialist threads that have been woven into our national tapestry.

This book traces those threads, not with the narrow purpose of producing a simple history of American socialist or social democratic enterprise but with the broader purpose of producing a whole history of the American experiment—a history that reflects all of the influences and ideals that inspired the development of a nation that I love in the way that Emma Lazarus did.

This book has been on my mind for more than a decade, going back to the closing years of Bill Clinton's wasted presidency. I toyed for many years with a different title, *The Need of Socialism*, as a frame for arguing that America needed to at the very least consider socialist alternatives to free market fundamentalism in order to have a full and functional debate. But that was when socialism was neglected. Now, it is the subject of daily derision, a derision that is at once more intense and more ignorant than at any point in the long history of the United States—with the possible exceptions of the few years after World War I when America experienced its first "red scare," although even then Socialists were still being elected to Congress, and the dark age of the 1950s and the second "red scare," although even then Socialists were still serving as mayors of major American cities.

The intensity of the current anti-socialist fervor on the right has surely been enhanced by a 24/7 news cycle that always needs something to shout about. But the shouters have been more successful at frightening the political class than the people, as polling suggests that the constant referencing of the "S" word has created more interest in—and support for—socialist ideas than at any time in recent American history. That interest is a healthy thing, not merely because it has the potential to free up the debate and introduce new and useful ideas to a national discourse that has grown gaunt and pale, but also because it invites a robust exploration of where we come from and who we are.

Americans are disconnected from their history now, and they run the risk of becoming more disconnected. It is not so much a matter of specific details—dates, names, outlines of old debates—as it is one of basic understanding. That basic understanding helps us to respond rationally to challenges: to recognize that an oil spill may call for nationalization of an energy company's US assets, to understand that real health-care reform should replace insurance companies rather than enrich them, to know that a no-strings-attached bailout of big banks will not cause bankers to make more loans to small businesses or to forego foreclosures. These are basic premises not merely for socialists but for citizens whose recognition of economic and political reality is broader and healthier when it is informed by a range of ideas that includes a socialist critique.

My dear friend and frequent co-author Bob McChesney and I have talked about this notion for years. Many of the core ideas of this book are rooted in our conversations. He is the wisest and best of public intellectuals (and friends) and this book would not have been possible without his counsel, questioning and constant encouragement. The same goes for my longtime editor Andy Hsiao, who jumped at the idea of doing this book; how he remains so enthusiastic and yet so rational is a marvel and a delight. Andy and I have done a number of books together, but this one is our truest collaboration. I am proud to be associated with Andy and the folks at Verso, including my friend Tom Penn, along with the original street-fighting man, Tariq Ali. My editors at *The Nation*, especially Katrina vanden Heuvel, Roane Carey, Richard Kim and Betsy Reed give me the time, space and encouragement a writer needs to explore the American experiment in ways that few writers can. I cherish our relationships. That is also true of the people I work with at *The Capital Times* newspaper, an old progressive daily, in Madison, Wisconsin, where Dave Zweifel, Paul Fanlund, Chris Murphy, Judie Kleinmaier and Lynn Danielson are grand colleagues. Matt Rothschild of *The Progressive* is a great friend and editor who asks the right questions and guides me to the right answers, as do Ruth Conniff and Amitabh Pal. Amy Goodman, Juan Gonzalez and the *Democracy Now!* crew have given me great forums for broader political discussions and continue to give me hope for independent and adventurous journalism, as do my hosts on the BBC, RTE, Al Jazeera, MSNBC, and public and community radio stations in the US and abroad, especially Jon Wiener and Sonali Kolhatkar at KPFK, Mitch Jeserich, Philip Maldari, Aimee Allison and Brian Edwards-Tiekert at KPFA, Norm Stockwell at WORT, John "Sly" Sylvester at WTDY, Joy Cardin, Jean Feraca and Ben Merens at Wisconsin Public Radio, as well as Rick Perlstein, Dave Zirin, Bill Lueders, Jeremy Scahill, Chris Hayes, Ari Berman, Alex Cockburn and dozens of other wise and supportive colleagues in print and online.

I owe an immense debt to the many historians I cite in the source notes, but I want to pay particular tribute to Paul Buhle, whose talent for combining scholarship and warm humanity matches that of our late friend Howard Zinn. This book benefited from his insights and those of Tony Benn, Bernie Sanders, Gore Vidal, Medea Benjamin, Billy Bragg,

Gary Lucas, Barbara Lawton, Bob Kimbrough and Phyllis Rose, Ben and Sarah Manski, Allen Ruff, Inger Stole, John Stauber, David Panofsky, Patti Smith, Sharon Lezberg, Brian Yandell, Nikki Anderson, Lee Cullen, the baristas at Ancora, the rockers at B-Side, the crowd behind the counter at Cork and Bottle and hundreds of other friends and neighbors, as well, of course, as the remarkable Mary Bottari.

Writers work best when they are part of a community, or communities, and I am blessed by mine in Madison, Milwaukee, New York, Washington, San Francisco (hey Sue and Leah), London and beyond. I am especially indebted to my fellow Tom Paine enthusiasts, as well as the media reformers and independent bookstore owners who make me welcome wherever I travel. The soundtrack for this book was provided by Mr. Dave Alvin; Tom Robinson; Billy Bragg, who sang about a "socialism of the heart"; Max Romeo, who sang that "socialism is love"; and Patti Smith, who taught us: "People Have the Power."

People do have the power. Whitman's great aunt, Carolyn Fry, taught me that. Aunt Cary was not a socialist. She was a Wisconsin Progressive, of the old-school Robert M. La Follette breed. She knew that La Follette sought the presidency in 1924 with the endorsement of the Socialist Party of Eugene Victor Debs and Norman Thomas. And that the Wisconsin Progressive Party—which governed the state in the 1930s—was a coalition of rural Republicans and Milwaukee Socialists. She also knew that the Milwaukee Socialists ran a clean, corruption-free city that was prosperous, debt-free and enlightened. So the "S" word did not frighten her. She could take socialist ideas or leave them, depending on their relevance to the debate at hand.

Whitman's friend, Sylvie Panofsky, had a grandmother, Gianna Sommi Panofsky, who knew far more about socialism than Aunt Cary. Gianna was a native of Parma, Italy, whose sensibilities were framed by the partisans who battled fascism before and during World War II. She laughed at the ignorance of contemporary conservatives who conflated fascism and socialism as the same thing; her experience told her that they were opposites. And she knew which side she was on—not just in Italy but in Chicago, where she threw herself into campaigns on behalf of civil rights, economic and social justice and peace and international solidarity.

It happened that, during the writing of this book, both Aunt Cary and Gianna passed away. Neither death was entirely unexpected, but each was deeply felt. I spoke at both memorial services. And, one day, when I was volunteering in the lunchroom at Lapham Elementary School, Whitman and Sylvie asked me to talk about the book I was working on. I told them it was about America. Aunt Cary, a Daughter of the American Revolution, and Gianna, an Italian immigrant who knew more about her adopted land than most natives, would have understood that a book about socialism could indeed be a book about America. It would not have surprised either of them to think that Emma Lazarus kept company with socialists, that she popularized socialist proposals, and that her loveliest poetry was informed by socialist ideals and hopes for America and the world. Indeed, it would have surprised them had Lazarus not been so fully engaged with and inspired by the great ideas and ideals of her time.

This book is written in the hope that Whitman and Sylvie will know as much about America as their ancestors did, and that they will act as well and wisely on its behalf. As such, it is dedicated to four women, two now gone and two coming on, and a country still bold enough to tell ancient lands to keep their pomp while she lifts her lamp beside the golden door.

CHAPTER ONE

"More of a Socialist Than I Thought": Walt Whitman and a Very American Ism

Come, I will make the continent indissoluble,
I will make the most splendid race the sun ever shone upon,
I will make divine magnetic lands,
    With the love of comrades,
      With the life-long love of comrades …

For you these from me, O Democracy, to serve you ma femme!
For you, for you I am trilling these songs.
        —Walt Whitman, "For You, O Democracy," 1855

The fellowship that you celebrate is the finest that ever filtered through the ages. It is the quintessence of human kinship, born of freedom, consecrated to brotherhood, and expressed in love. It is immortal and eternal. Its power is omnipotent. It changes beasts into gods, and hells of anguish and despair into heavens of peace and joy. In grateful, loyal, loving memory of Old Walt, I am yours.
        —Eugene Victor Debs to the Walt Whitman Fellowship, 1907

On a hot July afternoon in 1888, Horace Logo Traubel hurried along an indistinct avenue in his native city of Camden, New Jersey, to a small Greek Revival home at 328 Mickle Street. There, as he did each day, the young writer, reformer and socialist sat in conversation with the "good gray poet" who had, using royalties from an 1882 edition of his most popular collection, purchased a home on a street populated according to city records by "laborers, roofers, carpenters, railroad workers, a dentist and a physician, a baker, painters, clerks, sawyers, dressmakers, designers, a minister, machinists, an iron moulder, a blacksmith, a publisher, salespeople, and milk dealers."

Though he was by then one of the world's most well-known and well-regarded literary figures, Walt Whitman spent the last years of his long life on and around the "teeming cities' streets" of a working-class neighborhood in a working-class town. The poet was attended to by bohemian radicals and outliers in whose disdain for aristocracy and airs he found far more communal connection than he ever had in the salons of his more elite enthusiasts. Chief among them was Traubel, the son of a Jewish immigrant who like "Old Walt" had quit school early and gained his informal education as a typesetter, printer and eventual journalist for daily newspapers. Introduced to Whitman shortly after the poet's 1873 arrival in Camden, Traubel revered Whitman and paid little mind to the neighbors who "protested against my association with the 'lecherous old man.'" Like his mentor, Traubel moved comfortably and respectfully among "the drunken gentlemen and respectable toughs" of Camden and nearby Philadelphia. By that summer of 1888, the younger man, now thirty, had determined to become Boswell to the sixty-nine-year-old Whitman's Dr. Johnson. At the poet's urging, the younger man started in the spring of that year to "jot down" what would, in the words of the literary lion's biographer, Jerome Loving, become Traubel's "greatest contribution to world literature … a day-to-day summary with quotations of his generally half-hour meetings with the aging poet."

Traubel's *With Walt Whitman in Camden* is remarkable not merely for its detail but also for the insight it provides into the late-in-life understandings of one of the most historically expansive of American writers, a man who was born when the former presidents Thomas Jefferson and James Madison remained active citizens and who would die some years after the births of the future presidents Franklin Roosevelt and Harry Truman. On the day of our particular interest, July 16, 1888, Whitman and Traubel engaged in a sort of Socratic dialogue about the literary life. "Are you the last of your race?" asked the younger man. "Neither the first nor the last," replied the elder. "Will there be more poets or less?"

"More—more: and greater poets than there have ever been." "What kind? Your kind?" "I don't know about that: some free kind, sure: they are bound to come—to come soon." Whitman bemoaned lesser poets who "talk about form, rule, canons, and all the time forget the real point, which is the substance of poetry." "But," he continued, "here and there, every now and then, one, several, will raise the standard. *Leaves of Grass* will finally make its way."

When a great poet gets to discussing his craft and legacy, especially when the soliloquy references his greatest work, it is easy to lose sight of the rest of the conversation. But Traubel was at least as interested in Whitman's politics as his poetry. And, this afternoon, there was much to discuss. In the post, Whitman had received a copy of the British radical journal *Today*, which described itself as "the exponent of scientific Socialism, and the unsparing assailant of all our modern forms of competitive anarchy," and to which George Bernard Shaw, Eleanor Marx (Karl's daughter and tribune), Annie Besant and James Ramsey Macdonald, who in 1924 would become Britain's first Labour Party prime minister, were contributors. Whitman's articles and poetry appeared in *Today* as well, along with pieces by the American poet's most enthusiastic British champion, socialist agitator, poet and gay rights pioneer Edward Carpenter. The July 1888 edition featured a lengthy extract from Marx's *Capital* and a piece by a British essayist and contemporary of William Morris, Reginald A. Beckett, titled "Walt Whitman as a Socialist Poet."

Had Whitman read the piece, inquired Traubel. "Yes, I read every word of it—not, however, because of its literary quality (though that is respectable enough) but just to see how I look to one who sees all things from the standpoint of the socialist. Of course, I find I am a good deal more of a socialist than I thought I was: maybe not technically, politically, so, but intrinsically, in my meanings."

"A good deal more of a socialist than I thought"?

Could Walt Whitman have known what he was saying? This is the writer whose *Leaves of Grass* was described by no less a critic than Ralph Waldo Emerson as "indisputably American," who John Burroughs hailed as "our poet of democracy," who inspired everyone from Carl Sandburg (admittedly, a socialist, but a socialist who saw "America in the crimson light of a rising sun fresh from the burning, creative hand of God") to

Woody Guthrie (admittedly, another socialist, but one who wrote what ought to be the national anthem), who Ronald Reagan and Allen Ginsberg and every schoolchild has quoted from memory. That Whitman might have been red or, at the least, a little bit pink twists the national narrative.

Everything that there is about America is, we are frequently informed, supposed to be at odds with socialism. Everyone who ever mattered, or ever could matter, to America must be a true believer in the free-enterprise system, in no-holds-barred capitalism, in a patriotism that attaches the dollar sign to the flag and preaches the necessity of invading oil-rich lands while dismissing environmental necessities at home because—to quote the supposedly wiser of the two Presidents Bush—"the American way of life is not negotiable."

If we have been led to believe anything by the current discourse, it is the basic premise that America was founded as a capitalist country and that socialism is a dangerous foreign import best barred at the border. The increasingly if not quite wholly accepted "wisdom" holds that everything public is inferior to anything private; that corporations are always good and unions always bad; that progressive taxation is inherently evil and the best economic model is the one that avoids the messiness of equity by allowing the extremely wealthy to skim off their share before letting what remains trickle down to the great mass of Americans. No less a historian than Rush Limbaugh informs us with some regularity that proposals to tax people as rich as he is in order to provide health care for sick kids and jobs for the unemployed are "antithetical to the nation's founding." Limbaugh, the loudest voice in an anti–Barack Obama echo chamber, says that the president is "destroying this country as it was founded."

The shrillest of Limbaugh's flattering imitators, Fox News's Sean Hannity, charged when Obama offered tepid proposals to organize a private health-care system in a modestly more humane manner, that "the Constitution was shredded, thwarted, the rule of law was passed aside ..." Hannity got no argument from his guest on the day he assessed the damage done to the Constitution by those who would care for our own: former speaker of the US House of Representatives Newt Gingrich. "This is a group prepared to fundamentally violate the Constitution," the former congressional leader who fancies himself a future president said of an Obama administration that he argued was playing to the "30 percent of the country [that] really is [in favor of] a left-wing secular socialist system." Then, for good measure, Gingrich compared Obama with Venezuelan President Hugo Chávez—an actual and ardent socialist who, though the former speaker apparently missed the report, had recently referred to the American president as "a poor ignoramus [who] should read and study a little to understand reality"—with a crack about Obama's previous employment as a constitutional law professor. "Which constitution was he teaching? Venezuelan constitutional law?" opined Gingrich. "I mean, you know, I can't imagine how he could have actually taught American constitutional law and be this wrong this often."

The former speaker, who swore more than a few oaths to "support and defend the Constitution of the United States ... without any mental reservation or purpose of evasion," surely knows that the document makes no reference to economic systems, to capitalism, to free enterprise or to corporations or business arrangements. Unfortunately, as James Madison warned, partisan excess can cause even former history professors at West Georgia College to lose their bearings. The same can be said for former heads of the Fellowship of Christian Athletes at Wasilla High School.

Though Sarah Palin famously struggled to name a "favorite founder" when asked to do so by Glenn Beck, and though she made remarks about the role of the vice presidency that provoked a lively national debate about whether she had ever read the nation's founding document, that did not in the spring of 2009 prevent the former governor of Alaska from raising constitutional concerns about Obama's proposal to develop a system of "universal building codes" in order to promote energy efficiency. "Our country could evolve into something that we do not even recognize, certainly that is so far from what the founders of our country had in mind for us," a gravely concerned Palin informed a nodding Sean Hannity on the Fox News Channel.

Hannity had an idea about the direction in which Obama was evolving the country.

Arching an eyebrow and leaning forward with all the "I play an anchorman on TV" sincerity of someone who had recently volunteered to be waterboarded for charity, he interrupted Palin with a one-word question.

"Socialism?"

"Well," the immediate former vice-presidential nominee of the second-oldest political party in the nation responded, "that's where we are headed."

Actually, it's not.

Palin is wrong about the perils of energy efficiency. And she is wrong about Obama.

That is no cover for the president. This book is not written as a defense of Barack Obama against any charge. In fact quite the opposite, as the closing chapter will detail. What is important for the purposes of introduction is that the president says he is not a socialist. And the country's most outspoken socialists heartily agree with him on that point. Indeed, the only people who seem to think Obama displays even minimally social-democratic tendencies are those pundits, politicos and pretenders to concern about the republic who imagine—out of sincere if misguided faith, or for the purposes of crude electioneering—that the very mention of the word "socialism" should inspire in Americans a reaction not unlike that of a vampire confronted with the Host.

It is arguable, if we take seriously Obama's own reactions to questions about his ideological bent indicate, that he may be more frightened by the "S" word than Palin.

When a *New York Times* reporter asked the president during a ninety-minute interview on Air Force One in March of 2009 whether his domestic policies suggested that he was a socialist, as had by that point become something akin to gospel truth in the precincts of right-wing talk radio and its congressional hallelujah chorus, Obama chuckled. "The answer would be no," replied a relaxed chief executive, who asserted that he was simply taking criticism because he was "making some very tough choices" on the budget. (In fact, the president was avoiding tough choices and erring on the side of compromises, with an eye toward drawing Republican support for an economic stimulus proposal that—in reflection of those compromises—would ultimately spend more money on Republican-favored tax cuts than on the New Deal–style job creation initiatives that progressive Democrats favored.)

Once Obama had returned to the circle of his hyper-cautious political counselors, however, he was no longer relaxed. The president who is arguably more familiar with socialist theories and actual socialists than any commander in chief since Franklin Roosevelt, and whose monitoring of the print, broadcast and digital discourse is the most sophisticated of any chief executive in history, was worried. Had he been too casual in his chatter about socialism? He called *Times* reporter Jeff Zeleny from the Oval Office. "It was hard for me to believe that you were entirely serious about that socialist question," Obama said. Then, as if reading from talking points, he declared: "It wasn't under me that we started buying a bunch of shares of banks. And it wasn't on my watch that we passed a massive new entitlement, the prescription drug plan, without a source of funding."

"We've actually been operating in a way that has been entirely consistent with free-market principles," said Obama, who concluded with the kicker: "Some of the same folks who are throwing the word 'socialist' around can't say the same."

Nice spin. And, as with any good spin, there's more than a kernel of truth at the heart of the statement.

Obama really is avoiding consideration of socialist, or even mildly social-democratic, responses to the "very tough choices" that confront him. He took the single-payer "Medicare for All" option off the table at the start of the health-care reform debate, rejecting the approach chosen by other countries that have provided quality care to all citizens while dramatically reducing costs. His supposedly "socialist" response to the collapse of the auto industry was to provide tens of billions in bailout funding to General Motors and Chrysler, multinational corporations that used the money to lay off tens of thousands of auto workers and mechanics in the US while relocating work to new plants to Mexico and China—about as far as a country can get from the social-democratic model of using industrial policy to promote job creation and the renewal of depressed communities and neglected regions. And when BP's Deepwater Horizon well exploded and threatened the entire Gulf Coast, instead of seizing control of the crisis by putting the Army Corps of Engineers and other government agencies in charge of capping the well, Obama left the job to a foreign corporation that lied about the extent of the spill, made decisions based on its own corporate well-being rather than environmental and human needs, and failed at even the most basic tasks.

In every instance, Obama rejected sound socialist or social-democratic solutions in favor of private-sector fantasies. So perhaps we should take Obama at his word when he says he is "operating in a way that has been entirely consistent with free-market principles." The problem, of course, is that Obama's rigidity in this regard is causing him to dismiss ideas that are often sounder than the "free-market fixes" presented by a self-interested private sector. Borrowing ideas and approaches from socialists would not make Obama any more of a socialist than Abraham Lincoln, Teddy Roosevelt, Franklin Roosevelt or Dwight Eisenhower, all of whom sampled suggestions from Marxist tracts or picked pieces from Socialist Party platforms with a frequency that ultimately caused the *New York Times* to note in a 1954 profile of an aging Norman Thomas, the steadiest of Socialist presidential contenders, that "he had made a great contribution in pioneering ideas that have now won the support of both major parties"—ideas like, and this is the *Times*'s list: "Social Security, public housing, public power developments, legal protection for collective bargaining and other attributes of the welfare state [that] were anathema to Democrats and Republicans when Mr. Thomas abandoned the Presbyterian ministry to become an apostle of pacifism and social reform" forty years earlier.

To the extent that Obama is bent on remaining consistent with "free-market principles"—even when those principles require him to reject the sounder solutions and superior ideas contributed to the current debate by socialist and social-democratic thinkers of the twenty-first century, many of whom are our most visionary and innovative academics, policy analysts and on-the-ground activists—Obama is a very different American president from predecessors who read Marx and were conversant with the career of the author of *The Communist Manifesto*, who consulted with Socialist candidates and writers, who invited prominent Socialists to serve in their administrations, who forged whole policy initiatives based on books written by socialists and who recognized that the embrace and implementation of sound socialist or social-democratic solutions did not put them at odds with the American experiment or constitution.

So, while this book is not a defense of Obama, nor necessarily a defense of socialism, it is a defense of history—of American history, with its rich and vibrant hues, some of them red.

America has always suffered fools who would narrow the nation's range of options so that the debate might begin and end on the right. But the real history of America, the history that matters because it empowers rather than constricts, tells us that the only thing unique about our present station on the national journey is that we have suffered the fools so thoroughly by now that a good many Americans—not just Tea Partisans or Rush Limbaugh "Dittoheads," but citizens of the great middle—might actually take Sarah Palin seriously when she gets to ranting and raving about how socialism, in the form of building regulations, is antithetical to Americanism.

Palin is not the first of her kind. While consistent construction codes have never before been seen as quite so serious a threat, there is nothing new about the charge that a president who is guiding "big government" toward endeavors other than the invading and occupying of foreign countries is a "socialist." What is new is the cautious response of more serious citizens to the fools and fearmongers who abandon Tom Paine's imagining of an American as one who "by casting their eye over a large field, takes in likewise a larger intellectual circuit, and thus approaching nearer to an acquaintance with the universe, their atmosphere of thought is extended, and their liberality fills a wider space."

In the spring of 2009, just months after Barack Obama and a Democratic Congress took office—with the most sweeping mandate afforded the party since 1964, the year when Lyndon Johnson and his Democratic administration called upon one of the leading lights of American socialism, Michael Harrington, to help frame a "war on poverty"—twenty-three political professionals of the highest order, members of the Republican National Committee, proposed that the party of Obama, House Speaker Nancy Pelosi and Senate Majority Leader Harry Reid be formally rebranded as "the Democrat Socialist Party."

An RNC resolution, advanced by top Republican leaders from every region of the country—including Ron Kaufman, who served as White House Political Director for former President George Herbert Walker

Bush and a top political adviser to President George Walker Bush—proposed to put Palin's "logic" into the practice of the Republican Party and, by extension, into the national political discourse:

> WHEREAS, the American Heritage Dictionary defines socialism as a system of social organization in which the means of producing and distributing goods is owned by a centralized government that often plans and controls the economy; and
>
> WHEREAS, the Democratic Party has outlined their plans to nationalize the banking, financial and health care industries; and
>
> WHEREAS, the Democratic Party has proposed massive government bailouts for the mortgage and auto industries; and
>
> WHEREAS, the Democratic Party has passed trillions of dollars in new government spending, all with strings attached in order to control nearly every aspect of American life; and
>
> WHEREAS, the Democratic Party and its leadership have dedicated themselves to a new taxing objective of direct income redistribution which takes additional taxes from one group of people and gives it in direct cash transfers to another group of people who pay no federal income taxes at all; and
>
> WHEREAS, the American people are crying out for truth, honesty and integrity in politics; therefore be it
>
> RESOLVED, that we the members of the Republican National Committee recognize the Democratic Party's clear and obvious purpose in proposing, passing and implementing socialist programs through federal legislation; and be it further
>
> RESOLVED, that we the members of the Republican National Committee recognize that the Democratic Party is dedicated to restructuring American society along socialist ideals; and be it further
>
> RESOLVED, that we the members of the Republican National Committee call on the Democratic Party to be truthful and honest with the American people by acknowledging that they have evolved from a party of tax and spend to a party of tax and nationalize and, therefore, should agree to rename themselves the Democrat Socialist Party.

Cooler heads prevailed. Sort of.

At an "emergency" meeting of the RNC—an august body that traces its history to the first Republican National Convention in 1856, where followers of the French socialist Charles Fourier, Karl Marx's editor and their abolitionist comrades initiated what was the most radical restructuring of American political parties in the nation's history—it was suggested by a group of senior Republicans that included Mississippi Governor Haley Barbour, a former RNC chair and rumored presidential prospect, that the proposal to impose a new name on the Democrats might make "the Republican party appear trite and overly partisan."

In a compromise, the suggestion that the opposition should "agree to rename themselves the Democrat Socialist Party" was dropped. But the "march toward socialism" language remained. Thus, the members of the Republican National Committee now officially "recognize that the Democratic Party is dedicated to restructuring American society along socialist lines" and that the Democrats have as their "clear and obvious purpose ... proposing, passing and implementing socialist programs through federal legislation."

Seeking to calm the more fevered of his compatriots, the chairman of the group's resolutions committee, Mississippi Republican National Committeeman Henry Barbour (Haley's nephew) "denied that the final resolution was markedly different from what had originally been proposed" in an interview with the New York Times. The younger Barbour explained that it was only a shift in "tone": "We wanted to be respectful but we wanted to be firm."

In fact, the Republican Party is now firmer in its assertion that the Democratic Party is steering the nation "toward socialism" than it was during Joe McCarthy's "red scare" of the 1950s, when the senator from Wisconsin accused another Democratic president of harboring Communist Party cells in the federal government. That president, Harry Truman, had stirred the outrage of conservatives by arguing that the federal government had the authority to impose anti-lynching laws on the states and by proposing a genuine national health-care plan. (Ultimately, Truman would go even further: seizing control of a major industry—steel mills—in an exercise of his commander-in-chief powers that would have made George W. Bush drool with envy.) But what really bugged the Republicans of 1950 was that Truman, who was supposed to lose in 1948, had not just won the election but restored Democratic control of the House and Senate.

To counter this ominous electoral trend, Republicans, led by Ohio Senator Robert Taft, announced early in 1950 that their campaign slogan in the year's congressional elections would be "Liberty Versus Socialism." To that end, they produced a 1,950-word addendum to their national platform, much of which was devoted to a McCarthyite rant that began: "The major domestic issue today is liberty versus socialism." The statement proceeded to charge that Truman's Fair Deal program "is dictated by a small but powerful group of persons who believe in socialism, who have no concept of the true foundation of American progress and whose proposals are wholly out of accord with the true interests and real wishes of the workers, farmers and businessmen."

But the Republicans of the Cold War era backed off the "Liberty Versus Socialism" line after they were called out by President Truman, who reminded his critics that his Fair Deal policies were outlined in the 1948 Democratic platform, which had proven to be wildly popular with the electorate. "If our program was dictated as the Republicans say, it was dictated at the polls in November, 1948. It was dictated by a 'small but powerful' group of 24,000,000 voters," said Truman, adding: "I think they knew more than the Republican National Committee about the real wishes of the workers, farmers and businessmen."

Truman did not cower at the mention of the word "socialism," which in those days was well distinguished in the minds of most Americans from the Stalinism of the Soviet Union, with which the president—a mean Cold Warrior—was wrangling. Nor did the president, who counted among his essential political allies trade unionists like David Dubinsky, Jacob Potofsky and Walter Reuther, all of whom had in the none too distant past allied with socialist causes and in many cases with the Socialist Party of Eugene Victor Debs and Norman Thomas, rave about the evils of social democracy. Rather, he joked: "Out of the great progress of this country, out of our advances in achieving a better life for all, out of our rise to world leadership, the Republican leaders have learned nothing. Confronted by the great record of this country and the tremendous promise of its future, all they do is croak—socialism."

Duly chastened, savvy Republicans moved to abandon the whole "Liberty Versus Socialism" campaign. The return to realism was led by Maine Senator Margaret Chase Smith, who feared that her party was harming not just its electoral prospects but the country. That same spring she would issue her "Declaration of Conscience"—the first serious challenge to McCarthyism from within the Republican party—in which she rejected the anti-communist hysteria of the moment and declared:

> Those of us who shout the loudest about Americanism in making character assassinations are all too frequently those who, by our own words and acts, ignore some of the basic principles of Americanism—
> The right to criticize;
> The right to hold unpopular beliefs;
> The right to protest;
> The right of independent thought.

Republicans might be determined to end Democratic control of the Congress, Smith suggested in her declaration:

> Yet to displace it with a Republican regime embracing a philosophy that lacks political integrity or intellectual honesty would prove equally disastrous to this nation. The nation sorely needs a Republican victory. But I don't want to see the Republican Party ride to political victory on the Four Horsemen of Calumny—Fear, Ignorance, Bigotry and Smear.
> I doubt if the Republican Party could—simply because I don't believe the American people will uphold any political party that puts political exploitation above national interest.

Most Republicans lacked the courage to so directly confront McCarthy. But Smith's wisdom prevailed among leaders of the RNC and the chairs of the Republican Senatorial Committee and the Republican Congressional Committee, who ditched the "Liberty Versus Socialism" slogan and reduced Taft's 1,950-word manifesto to a ninety-nine-word digest that Washington reporters explained had been cobbled together in order to "soft-pedal" the whole "showdown on 'liberty against socialism'" thing. Pennsylvania Congressman James Fulton, who like many other Republican moderates of the day actually knew and worked with Socialist Party members and radicals of various stripes in groups such as the United World Federalists, was blunter. The cheap sloganeering of the "Liberty Versus Socialism" wing steered his party away from what should be the fundamental question for Republicans in the post-war era: "whether we go back to Methuselah or offer alternative programs for social progress within the framework of a balanced budget."

Imagine if today a prominent Republican were to make a similar statement. The wrath of Limbaugh, Hannity, Palin and the Tea Party movement would rain down upon him. The Club for Growth would organize to defeat the RINO ("Republican-In-Name-Only") and the ideological cleansing of the party of Lincoln, Teddy Roosevelt, Dwight Eisenhower and Margaret Chase Smith would accelerate. Some of my Democratic friends are quite pleased with the prospect; as the Republicans of the current moment approach cliffs of extremism that they avoided even in the days of Joe McCarthy, these Democrats suggest, the high ground will be cleared for candidates of their liking. The results of the November 2010 mid-term elections cast doubt upon this assumption. And even if this theory eventually proves electorally sound, it neglects the damage done to democracy and to democratic governance when the popular discourse collapses, when ideas are subsumed beneath personalities and slogans, and when the only real fights are between a party that positions itself on the fringe and another that positions itself slightly closer to the twenty-first century—with the expectation, now common among Democratic strategists, that the way to a win on election day is to troll the center right for the votes of the old "Main Street Republicans" and then presume that fear of a totalitarian right will keep everyone who stands to the left of center on board.

If universal building codes and protections for children with pre-existing conditions can be presented as assaults on American values and the rule of law—and reported upon as such in major media that turn a promise of balance into an excuse for airing nonsense—then the debate has been dumbed down to such an extent that the right has already won, no matter what the result on election day. And a nation founded in revolutionary revolt against empire, a nation that nurtured the radical Republican response to the original sin of slavery, a nation that confronted economic collapse and injustice with a New Deal and a "war on poverty," a nation that spawned a civil rights movement, and that still recites a Pledge of Allegiance—penned by the great socialist preacher Edward Bellamy in 1892—to the ideal of an America "with liberty and justice for all," is bereft not merely of the prospect for meaningful change, but also of what has so often in our history been the essential element of progress.

That element—a social-democratic critique combined, frequently, with pressures from an active Socialist Party and Communist Party, along with independent socialist activism in labor and equal rights campaigns for women, racial and ethnic minorities, immigrants, gays and lesbians and people with disabilities—has from the first years of the American journey been a part of our public debate and our political life. It has influenced, shaped and advanced the cause of a more perfect union. One need not be a Socialist, nor the follower of any tendency or party of the left, to recognize the contribution made by socialists to America. This country would not be what it is today, indeed it might not even *be*, were it not for the positive influence of social democrats, socialists, communists and their fellow travelers. The great political scientist Terence Ball reminds us that "at the height of the Cold War a limited form of socialized medicine—Medicare—got through the Congress over the objections of the American Medical Association and the insurance industry, and made it to President Johnson's desk."

That did not just happen by chance. A young writer who, in the depths of the Cold War, had recognized that it was entirely possible to reject the totalitarianism of the Stalinist Soviet Union and its satellites while still learning from Marx and embracing a "democratic socialism," left the fold of Dorothy Day's Catholic Worker movement to join the Young People's Socialist League. Michael Harrington wanted to change the nature of the debate about poverty in America, and, perhaps remarkably or perhaps presciently, he presumed that attaching himself to what was left of the once muscular but at that point ailing American Socialist Party was the way to do so. In a 1959 article for the American Jewish Committee's then-liberal magazine *Commentary*, Harrington sought, in the words of his biographer, Maurice Isserman, "to overturn the conventional wisdom that the United States had become an overwhelmingly middle-class society. Using the poverty-line benchmark of a $3,000 annual income for a family of four, he demonstrated that nearly a third of the population lived below those standards which we have been taught to regard as the decent minimums for food, housing, clothing and health."

He succeeded beyond his wildest dreams.

The article led to a book, *The Other America: Poverty in the United States*. The book became required reading for American policymakers, selling more than 70,000 copies in its first year of publication. "Among the book's readers, reputedly, was John F. Kennedy, who in the fall of 1963 began thinking about proposing anti-poverty legislation," recalls Isserman. "After Kennedy's assassination, Lyndon Johnson took up the issue, calling in his 1964 State of the Union address for an 'unconditional war on poverty.' Sargent Shriver headed the task force charged with drawing up the legislation, and invited Harrington to Washington as a consultant."

Harrington's proposals—made in conjunction with his friend and drinking pal Daniel Patrick Moynihan—for the renewal of New Deal public works projects with the purpose of improving infrastructure and renewing communities, ending unemployment and redistributing wealth, were never fully embraced. America did not "abolish poverty." But Harrington's advocacy, and that of others who adopted the view that the government of the world's wealthiest nation could and should intervene to address the suffering of those who lacked the resources to care for themselves or their families, underpinned the rapid advance of what the author described as the necessary work of "completing Social Security" by providing health care for the aged. It cheered on the Johnson administration's "Great Society," including enactment of the Social Security Act of 1965 establishing Medicare. Johnson took his hits—his 1964 Republican challenger, Barry Goldwater, objected: "Having given our pensioners their medical care in kind, why not food baskets, why not public housing accommodations, why not vacation resorts, why not a ration of cigarettes for those who smoke and of beer for those who drink"—but Americans agreed with their president (and with Michael Harrington): "The Social Security health insurance plan, which President Kennedy worked so hard to enact, is the American way. It is practical. It is sensible. It is fair. It is just."

Could a plan decried as "socialized medicine" by the American Medical Society because it was, in fact, socialized medicine, really be "the American way"? Practically, of course, it is just that. During the Medicare debate in the early 1960s, Texas US Senate candidate George H. W. Bush may have denounced the proposal as creeping "socialism," and Ronald Reagan may have warned that if it became a reality citizens would eventually find themselves "telling our children and our children's children what it once was like in America when men were free." Yet, Bush and Reagan managed the program during their presidencies and Tea Party activists now show up at Town Hall meetings to threaten any congressman or woman who would dare to tinker with their beloved Medicare.

Americans would not have gotten Medicare if Harrington and the socialists who came before him—from Socialist Party presidential candidates such as Eugene Victor Debs and Norman Thomas, to organizers such as Mary Marcy and Margaret Sanger, and the Communist Elizabeth Gurley Flynn—had not for decades been pushing the limits of the debate about health care to the left. No less a player in the national health-care debate than the late Senator Edward Kennedy declared: "I see Michael Harrington as delivering the Sermon on the Mount to America." The same was true in abolitionist days, when socialists—including friends of Marx who had immigrated to the United States after the crushing of the 1848 revolutions in Europe—energized the movement against slavery and helped to give it political expression in the form of the Republican Party. The same was true in the early years of the twentieth century, when radical editors—especially the Socialist Victor Berger—battled attempts to crush civil liberties and defined our modern understanding of freedom of speech, freedom of the press and the right to petition for the redress of grievances. The same was true when a lifelong Socialist, A. Philip Randolph, called the March on Washington for Jobs and Freedom and asked a young preacher named Martin Luther King, Jr., who had surrounded himself with socialist counselors, to deliver what would come to be known as the "I Have a Dream" speech.

Again and again across the great arc of American history, at the critical junctures in our national journey, socialist citizens, thinkers and organizers, supported by Socialist candidates and elected officials (at the federal, state and local levels), have provoked and prodded the body politic in progressive directions. Despite their determined efforts, America is not a socialist country—at least not in any formal sense. It may be true, as historian Patrick Allitt suggests, that "millions of Americans, including many of these critics [of the Obama administration], are ardent supporters of socialism, even if they don't realize it and even if they don't actually use the word" to describe public services that are "organized along social-ist lines," like schools and highways. In fact, contemporary American socialists and Tea Partiers might reach unexpected, not to mention uncomfortable, agreement with Allitt's argument that "socialism as an organizational principle is alive and well here just as it is throughout the industrialized world"—even as they would disagree on whether that's a good thing.

Even if programs "organized along socialist lines" do not make a country socialist, and even if America's relationship with social democ-racy is more nuanced and more complicated than that of many other nations, the United States is a country that has always been and should continue to be informed by socialists, socialist ideals and a socialist critique of public policies.

That may read to some as a radical statement.

It's not, at least for those who choose to be realistic about our history, about our moment and about the future that has yet to be written.

We live in complex times, when profound economic, social and environmental challenges demand a range of responses, not merely those calculated to protect the economic advantages of some very, very wealthy men (and a few women) who have over the past quarter century, through Republican and Democratic administrations, mar-shaled sufficient campaign contributions, lobbying muscle, spin and media acquiescence to assure that public policies are made in the name of the American people but without our informed consent and against our best interests. Socialists may not have all the answers that the American people are seeking, even if polls suggest that more Americans find appeal in the word "socialist" today than at any time in decades. Indeed, social-ists of different tendencies and traditions are not even in agreement among themselves. This book does not seek to sort out specific ideo-logical, tactical and historical debates. What it does seek is a broader recognition that, without socialist ideas and advocacy of many kinds and characters, there is an insufficient counterbalance to the pull of an anti-government impulse that has less to do with classic libertarianism than with the manipulation of the debate by corporations that do not wish to be regulated, taxed or otherwise governed.

Which returns us to our friend Walt Whitman, who preached that "the genius of the United States is not best or most in its executives or legislatures, nor in its ambassadors or authors or colleges or churches or parlors, nor even in its newspapers or inventors ... but always most in the common people."

Just as America is not a socialist country, Whitman was not a socialist poet—at least not in any pure or political sense. Whitman was not a joiner, and despite the encouragement of his compatriots in later years, he did not carry the card of any socialist or social-democratic tendency. This was in character for a poet who celebrated the "varied carols" he heard America singing and who delighted in contradicting himself. But Whitman was a determined egalitarian, a small-"d" democrat who spent a lifetime evolving and expanding his understanding of what these words meant, not merely for the white male sons of Paumanok but for sons of slaves, for women, for new immigrants and first Americans. His was a conscious poetry that said of America: "Other lands have their vitality in a few, a class, but we have it in the bulk of our people." So it is not really so shocking that, in old age, Whitman recognized himself as "a good deal more of a socialist" than he had earlier imagined. The man who spoke those words was surrounded late in life by socialists who had read in his poetry the truth of their convictions. Some, like Horace Traubel, were American-born and, in fact, from just around the corner in Camden. Others came from around the world. Several of the most revealing books on Whitman's last years were written by British socialists who traveled to the United States with the specific purpose of meeting the sage. Among Whitman's most frequent correspondents in the late 1880s and early 1890s was J. W. Wallace, an architect from Bolton, near Manchester in the north of England, who found in the poet's celebration of comradeship and democracy the ideal language of romantic socialist commitment. Wallace made the pilgrimage to Camden to meet Whitman in 1891, a year after another Bolton radical, Dr. John Johnson, had paid a similar visit. Together they penned a lovely book, *Visits to Walt Whitman in 1890–1891*. The radical reformer Edward Carpenter, whose Whitman-steeped writing would inspire and influence both the British socialist and gay rights movements, was another visitor, as was Oscar Wilde, whose 1891 pamphlet *The Soul of Man Under Socialism* expressed a libertarian socialist perspective that seemed to merge Whitman and Kropotkin in its declaration that: "With the abolition of private property, then, we shall have true, beautiful, healthy Individualism. Nobody will waste his life in accumulating things, and the symbols for things. One will live. To live is the rarest thing in the world. Most people exist, that is all."

What was it that so many socialists found so very satisfying in the words of the poet whom Emerson hailed as the author of "the most extraordinary piece of wit & wisdom that *America* has yet contributed"?

What they detected in *Leaves of Grass* was something Whitman had understood from his youth: that the "roughness and spirit of defiance" of the American people, the supreme safeguard against that "hour when tyranny may ... enter upon this country," had first been expressed by the most radical of its founders. As a champion of the writings of Tom Paine, the "citizen of the world" pamphleteer whose calls for revolution and ultimately for economic justice would so inspire the socialists of early nineteenth-century Europe and America, Whitman had few competitors. Paine was widely dismissed and denigrated by the political and intellectual elites of the mid-nineteenth century. Yet, as a young man, Whitman sought out New Yorkers who had known Paine, with the purpose of imbibing as much of the pamphleteer's spirit as he could. As an old man, he would declare, on the 140th anniversary of Paine's birth:

> That he labor'd well and wisely for the States in the trying period of their parturition, and in the seeds of their character, there seems to me no question. I dare not say how much of what our Union is owning and enjoying today—its independence—its ardent belief in, and substantial practice of, radical human rights—and the severance of its government from all ecclesiastical and superstitious dominion—I dare not say how much of all this is owing to Thomas Paine, but I am inclined to think a good portion of it decidedly is.

Chapter 2 of this book will sojourn with Paine, whose outsized role in the shaping of social-democratic theory has yet to be fully appreciated by the likes of Glenn Beck or, for that matter, Paine enthusiast Barack Obama. It is enough to note here that Whitman associated Paine with the cause of "radical human rights." So too did Fanny Wright, the daughter of a Scottish acolyte of Paine's, who would become in the words of her conservative detractors "the great red harlot" of American radicalism in the late 1820s and early 1830s. An ardent abolitionist and feminist, Wright was the first woman to edit an American journal of opinion and the first to regularly lecture before audiences of men and women. Her following was so immense that candidates who championed her utopian socialist views, while officially running on the ticket of the Working Men's Party—which identified itself as the political voice of "the working class of society"—were frequently described as campaigning on "the Fanny Wright ticket."

Whitman adored Fanny Wright, who was promoting the radical Popular Health Movement when he was a young "scribbler" for the newspapers of Long Island, Brooklyn and eventually Manhattan. As he told Horace Traubel fifty years later:

In those days I frequented the anti-slavery halls, in New York—heard many of their speakers—people of all qualities, styles—always interesting, always suggestive. It was there I heard Fanny Wright ... a woman of the noblest make-up whose orbit was a great deal larger than theirs—too large to be tolerated for long by them: a most maligned, lied-about character—one of the best in history though also one of the least understood. [My] remembrance of her all centers about New York. She spoke in the old Tammany Hall there, every Sunday, about all sorts of reforms. Her views were very broad—she touched the widest range of themes—spoke informally, colloquially. She published while there the *Free Inquirer*, which my daddy took and I often read. She has always been to me one of the sweetest of sweet memories: we all loved her: fell down before her: her very appearance seemed to enthrall us.

Wright was not the only socialist the young Walt Whitman would encounter. He was surrounded by radical reformers in the New York City of the 1840s and 1850s, a time when Horace Greeley's *New York Tribune* was running columns by Karl Marx, when back-to-nature experiments in communal living were all the rage, and when a young New York lawyer named Alvan Bovay, having recently promoted the free-soil agenda with a campaign that urged newly-enfranchised workers to "Vote Yourself a

Farm," was beginning to conceive of a new political party that he and his compatriots would dub "Republican."

The young Walt Whitman embraced elements of the radicalism that was all around him—unsettled by the slave auctions he had witnessed while visiting New Orleans, he returned to New York in 1848 to launch the *Freeman*, a newspaper supporting the Free Soil Party that briefly became the vehicle of the anti-slavery and economic justice campaigners who would eventually reconfigure as Republicans. But more often than not, the poet endeavored to "be curious, not judgmental" as he moved among "the gangs of kosmos and prophets" that populated his "Mannahatta." He would emerge, in the words of the trenchant *New York Times* reviewer Ralph Thompson, as "essentially a man of the broadest social, political and moral capacities." Thompson was, of course, correct when he observed that "Whitman is too complex to be ticketed Type A, B or C." But equally correct was the great literary historian of the mid-twentieth century, Newton Arvin, who used Whitman's words themselves, the poems and the prose, to argue: "Enough and more than enough remains to fortify the writers and the men of our time in their struggles against a dark barbarian reaction, and to interest and animate the peoples of a near future in their work of building a just society."

Not a socialist poet, then, but a poet with room for socialism—containing multitudes, as does America—Walt Whitman provides enough and more than enough of a touchstone for this book's essential argument: that American history is more socialist than Sarah Palin, or perhaps even her most ardent detractors, dares imagine. Eugene Victor Debs spoke of how he would "feast" and "refresh myself at Old Walt's flowing fountain of inspiration." This was not idle referencing. As Newton Arvin reminds us, "We inherit no fuller or braver anticipatory statement than 'Leaves of Grass' of a democratic and fraternal humanism."

And so we begin, as every American journey should, with Tom Paine, Fanny Wright and Walt Whitman, a copy of *Leaves of Grass* and a charge from the poet that refreshed Debs a century ago and refreshes radicals to this day—not merely as a personal manifesto, but in the language of the political platform that is yet to be:

This is what you shall do: Love the earth and sun and the animals, despise riches, give alms to every one that asks, stand up for the stupid and crazy, devote your income and labor to others, hate tyrants, argue not concerning God, have patience and indulgence toward the people, take off your hat to nothing known or unknown or to any man or number of men, go freely with powerful uneducated persons and with the young and with the mothers of families, read these leaves in the open air every season of every year of your life, re-examine all you have been told at school or church or in any book, dismiss whatever insults your own soul; and your very flesh shall be a great poem and have the richest fluency not only in its words but in the silent lines of its lips and face and between the lashes of your eyes and in every motion and joint of your body ...

CHAPTER TWO

"A Broader Patriotism": Thomas Paine and the Promise of Red Republicanism

The rugged face of society, checkered with the extremes of affluence and want, proves that some extraordinary violence has been committed upon it, and calls on justice for redress.

—Thomas Paine, *Agrarian Justice,* 1797

[The] many socialist Paineites … and their affiliation to every species of radicalism in the land boded evil to the future of our Republic.

—*New York Times,* 1856

Thomas Paine said that "one just man deserves more respect than a rogue with a crown." The people's right to rebel has been opposed only by reactionaries …

—Fidel Castro, 1953

Tom Paine experienced poverty, banishment from one profession and then another, frequent bouts of unemployment, severe disease, broken marriage, the perils of the immigrant, exile, another exile and still another exile, arrest, trials in person and in absentia, imprisonment and an appointment with the guillotine. He was decried in the popular press as a threat to decency and a dangerous influence upon women and children, reproached by the church, abandoned by revolutionary comrades gone respectable and, in a final indignity, denied the right to cast a ballot at the polling place of the nation he called into being.

But nothing prepared Paine for the indignities of the afterlife. For Paine, what began with an ill-noted death and a sparsely attended funeral degenerated into infamy—and then worse.

Paine died in a borrowed room at 59 Grove Street in New York City's Greenwich Village, late in the spring of the first year of the presidency of James Madison, who fifteen years earlier as the American minister to revolutionary France had declared the pamphleteer a US citizen and secured his freedom from Luxembourg Prison. It was around the time of his release that Paine published *The Age of Reason*, with its denunciation of "the general wreck of superstition, of false systems of government and false theology" and its declaration that: "All national institutions of churches, whether Jewish, Christian or Turkish, appear to me no other than human inventions, set up to terrify and enslave mankind, and monopolize power and profit." John Adams, ever ready to advance his own career at the expense of the founding ideals, attacked Paine as an "insolent Blasphemer of things sacred and transcendent, Libeler of all that is good," as part of a guilt-by-association campaign organized to defame Thomas Jefferson, who had maintained a friendship with the writer who Adams dismissed as "a mongrel between pig and puppy, begotten by a wild boar on a bitch wolf." The attacks by Adams and his Federalist allies carried the day, redefining the author of the essential tract of the Revolutionary canon, *Common Sense*, as persona non grata in the nation they were evolving—or, Paine would argue, devolving—from the "spirit of '76." As Henry Adams, John's great-grandson, would observe: Paine came in the last years of his life to be "regarded by respectable society, both Federalist and Republican, as a person to be avoided, a person to be feared." Even Madison, who as a young man had observed that "ecclesiastical establishments tend to great ignorance and corruption, all of which facilitate the execution of mischievous projects," chose political ambition over association with the author of *The Age of Reason*. By the time Paine breathed his last he was, in the words of the great Republican radical and proselytizer of free thought and humanism Ralph Ingersoll: "Maligned on every side, execrated, shunned and abhorred— his virtues denounced as vices—his services forgotten—his character blackened. He was a victim of the people, but his convictions remained unshaken. He was still a soldier in the army of freedom, and still tried to enlighten and civilize those who were impatiently waiting for his death. Even those who loved their enemies hated him, their friend—the friend of the whole world—with all their hearts."

Paine's passing brought no official proclamations from the White House or the Capitol. Flags did not drop to half staff. The obituaries were not kind; the most widely circulated, that of the *New York Citizen*, served up less than a half-compliment: "He had lived long, did some good and much harm." At the funeral, such as it was, six mourners were in attendance, including a pair of African-American freedmen who were reportedly "filled with gratitude" for Paine's outspoken if then still-lonely advocacy on behalf of the abolition of slavery.

Needless to say, Paine was not accorded a Christian burial. Rather, his remains were interred at the corner of the farm where he had lived in New Rochelle, New York, a spot from whence the British radical William Cobbett and his compatriots removed the pamphleteer's bones in 1819. The plan to rebury Paine in England, with hopes that this presence would inspire popular upheaval, went awry when Cobbett became otherwise occupied: so vociferously condemning the massacre of campaigners for parliamentary reform at Peterloo that he was sued for libel and threatened with jail. After Cobbett's death in 1835, Paine's bones were lost to history.

Were it left to the emerging political establishment of the United States, which an aging Jefferson warned was making useless the "sacrifice of ... the generation of '76" and committing "treason against the hopes of the world," Paine would have been dismissed altogether. Indeed, as Mark Twain noted, "It took a brave man before the Civil War to confess he had read *The Age of Reason*."

But history has an odd way of rewarding those who are on the right side of its arc. When it becomes necessary to find nobility in the past of a nation embarrassed, for instance, by a previous embrace of human bondage, even the most disregarded founder can be restored to a pedestal. So it has been with Paine, whose twentieth century proved to be far more generous than his nineteenth. The face of the British immigrant who within months of his arrival at Philadelphia had made himself the tribune of the American Revolution even found its way onto a US postage stamp, issued, long after the other founders had been so honored, in the turbulent year of 1968. The fortunate side of history is that it ultimately finds the good guys and gives them a posthumous pat on the back; the unfortunate side is that, in the process of re-veneration, sharp edges are often buffed away, precise details are forgotten and we lose sight of what made the good guys good. Poor Paine, finally readmitted to the circle of founders, was reduced in the soft focus of contemporary tribute to a forty-seven-page pamphlet, *Common Sense*, and a few good lines about "the times that try men's souls." So it was that, 171 years after Paine's sparsely attended funeral, Ronald Reagan would accept the Republican nomination for president of the United States with a rousing if vaguely heretical referencing of Paine and the greatest liberal president of the twentieth century, Franklin Delano Roosevelt:

> Everywhere we have met thousands of Democrats, Independents and Republicans from all economic conditions and walks of life bound together in that community of shared values of family, work, neighborhood, peace and freedom. They are concerned, yes, but they are not frightened. They are disturbed, but not dismayed. They are the kind of men and women Tom Paine had in mind when he wrote—during the darkest days of the American Revolution—"We have it in our power to begin the world over again."
>
> Nearly 150 years after Tom Paine wrote those words, an American president told the generation of the Great Depression that it had a "rendezvous with destiny." I believe that this generation of Americans today has a rendezvous with destiny.

Presumably, if Roosevelt was turning in his grave, Paine would have been spinning—had he found a final resting place.

At least Reagan was a former liberal Democrat who had come of age in the period during the 1930s and 1940s when radicals such as Howard Fast—a member of the American Communist Party who during World War II penned the best-selling *Citizen Tom Paine*, which imagined a vaguely fictionalized hero telling Ben Franklin that he intended to go to America to write "what a man can't say because he's got no guts in him to say it!"—were engaged in the heavy lifting of resurrecting Paine's memory. The future president had read Paine in those days and, as a far more intellectually agile student of history than his detractors and some of his friends have ever cared to admit, Reagan undoubtedly recognized at least a measure of the irony and the power of using Paine to propose a conservative "revolution." He even got the reference to the closing lines of *Common Sense* right—no small feat, as another Paine-quoting president, Barack Obama, has, like so many others, stumbled over Paine's artful wordplay and ended up describing a "power to make the world anew."

So if Paine might have been discomfited at the prospect of being called into the service of Reagan's political (and, eventually, territorial) ambitions, he was at least somewhat understood—and arguably respected, as was surely the case when Obama regularly quoted the founder on the campaign trail in 2008 before slipping a few lines from *The Crisis* into his January 20, 2009, inaugural address.

The same will not be said of Glenn Beck's employment of Paine in the work of dismantling Obama's presidency, a project that has seen the Fox News program host speculate about "the odds that Barack Obama is the Antichrist." Beck's real theme, of course, is that Obama is the "anti-American." This is about a lot more than the "birther" nonsense that Beck's followers so enthusiastically entertain, with regard to the settled "question" of whether the president can produce a Hawaiian birth certificate. Beck claims that Obama has "contempt" for America and that the president does not "respect" the Constitution—despite having taught the details of the document for many years as a law school instructor. Obama and his allies have, Beck tells his audiences, developed an "almost-complete plan" to "destroy the Constitution, destroy the founders, and destroy our faith."

And what will the Manchurian president and his henchmen replace them with? Why, socialism, of course.

Obama, says Beck, "intends to transform America from Madison to Marx."

How so?

"Apart from his childhood teenage years and adult childhood spent with radicals, Marxists and communists and then attending a Marxist church for twenty years with a Marxist pastor, what has he done lately?" asks Beck, who then tells his Fox viewers:

Well, there is the tiny matter of taking over the auto industry. No big deal: GM is just, has been taken over, 61 percent and then, of course, the nagging little detail of the government now controls much of America's banking industry. We have that.

Then, of course, there is AIG insurance, the insurance giant. We also took those over. Those are fantastic.

Yes, he has taken the first step towards socialization—total government control of our health care system. I had an appointment with my doctor today, he was thrilled about that. Controlling the entire health care industry, it's only one-sixth. Don't worry about that.

He's also seized control of the entire student loan industry—just wipe the industry out.

Far from celebrating capitalists and capitalism, he demonized the wealthy dating back to the early days of his campaign …

So, while many of the mentioned policy offenses began with the administration of George Bush and Dick Cheney, and while they all gave federal dollars *to* corporations as opposed to taking money *from* them, we have Beck's "case for why Barack Obama might be considered a socialist."

Clearly, this is a host who could use all the help he can find to peddle an argument that suffers so many deficits of fact and logic.

Which brings Glenn Beck to Tom Paine.

In March of 2009, less than two months into Obama's presidency, Beck revealed on his radio show that he had a favored founder—at least for the moment.

"I might as well tell you. I'm rewriting *Common Sense*. I'm rewriting Thomas Paine's *Common Sense*, and I have been working on it since December and I have really been studying it and quite honestly the first time I read it, I thought, oh, my gosh, I can't rewrite this. And this came to me. I just had this feeling that I need to get *Common Sense* and read some more Thomas Paine and I think maybe I should rewrite it," he explained.

Now, there will be those who wonder about a timeline that seems to begin with a decision to rewrite a pamphlet and then proceeds to reading it. But let's cut Beck some slack, on the theory that anyone who is promoting Paine ultimately does service—whether they intend it or not—to "the cause of all mankind," a cause that has as its end a cooperative commonwealth discerned by the author in *The Rights of Man* as arriving: "When it shall be said in any country in the world, my poor are happy; neither ignorance nor distress is to be found among them; my jails are empty of prisoners, my streets of beggars; the aged are not in want, the taxes are not oppressive; the rational world is my friend, because I am the friend of its happiness: when these things can be said, then may that country boast its constitution and its government." That this is a radically different endgame from the one pursued by Beck—whose tear-stained and emotionally overwrought worldview tends toward a frequently articulated anxiety about the dangers of democracy, a fear of all things "progressive" and an over-arching disdain for arrangements that seek to achieve the dreaded "social justice"—would seem to be a given. But it is also a given that there are limits to the amount of historical precision that can be demanded of a TV personality who promises "the fusion of entertainment and enlightenment."

Here's Beck on the radio, back in the spring of 2009:

> [In] one day three people that I really respect called me and emailed me and said, Glenn, you know, I've been thinking, have you thought about rewriting *Common Sense*. And we were on the book tour and I said, the next bookstore we go to, you know, would one of you guys go and get Thomas Paine's *Common Sense*. And I read it and it is some of the most powerful writing you have ever seen. It's quite amazing. Absolutely amazing. But the secret of it is there's no shame in it. There is no second thought of, well, I don't know, this party says this or this party. This was *Common Sense*. And everybody says, "Oh, you're trying to be a populist" or whatever. No. The populist sentiment is *Common Sense*! We have just moved so far away from *Common Sense* and we need to see it again. We need to see it again. So we'll give you that in our free email newsletter … And pass it on to all of your friends and then connect. Please, connect. Go to The912Project.com and connect with other people that are thinking like you … Please. *Common Sense* tells you that we're in trouble. *Common Sense* tells you that we the people are responsible for it and we the people are the only ones to fix it. Not those people that we are paying and overpaying in Washington on both sides of the aisle, but we the people.

In June of 2009, just in time for the Tea Party movement's arrival at that summer's congressional town hall meetings about health-care reform, there came *Glenn Beck's Common Sense: The Case Against an Out-of-Control Government, Inspired by Thomas Paine*—not to be confused with Glenn Beck's *Arguing with Idiots: How to Stop Small Minds and Big Government* or Glenn Beck's *America's March to Socialism: One Small Step Toward Big Government, One Giant Leap Toward Missile Parades ...*

It happens that I have written a number of books that explore the contributions made by sincere conservatives and libertarians—especially "old right" anti-interventionists and Constitutionalists such as Howard Buffett, John Flynn and the good Murray Rothbard—to national discourses about war and peace, presidential accountability and the role played by mass media in democracy. While I'm on the left, I've been proud to participate in forums at the libertarian Cato Institute and have delighted in appearing on national television programs in conjunction with thoughtful conservatives such as Bruce Fein. So I was vaguely hopeful about Beck's book. And, as someone who had been arguing for a number of years that, because the pamphleteer was so far ahead of his time, the twenty-first century would be the true "age of Paine," I was excited by the prospect that a leading light on the right would be wrestling with Paine's legacy.

But Beck did not wrestle with Paine. He barely paid attention. I have to admit that I am not in the habit of relying on Amazon reviews, but I was struck by one of the first online assessments of *Glenn Beck's Common Sense*, which explained: "As a fan of Thomas Paine (especially *Common Sense* and *Age of Reason*), I was very much excited to read Beck's book. After the first few chapters, I realized there is almost NO connection at all to Paine's work. It seems that it is more of a marketing ploy to attach one's name to Paine and use a famous title of Paine's work that inspired a nation, to generate book sales ... This book should be called *Beck's Sense*."

Beck's Sense is about right. With its lengthy ruminations on "the cancer of progressivism" and a chapter on the millionaire author's problems with the US tax code, *Glenn Beck's Common Sense* is heavy on the Beck and light, very light, on the Paine. Even when he does address the founding moment, Beck imagines a Paine who never existed, making the great questioner of religious orthodoxy over as part of a circle that "understood our rights and liberties are gifts from God." And he repositions the man who penned the words: "The *world* is my *country*, all *mankind* are my brethren, and to do good is my religion…" as an isolated American who would be much concerned about "transnationalism." But you have to search for these assertions, as vast sections of the book pass without mention of Paine. To the extent that Beck does make any connection, it is in the title, the "tattered" cover, a reprint of the original pamphlet, and a claim to having been "inspired by Thomas Paine." The packaging—physical and intellectual—might lead not just Beck fans but less Fox-inclined Americans passing casually through airport bookstalls to imagine Paine as a proto-libertarian critic of all (or at least most) things governmental—along the lines of the far more Beckish John Randolph of Roanoke, the traditionalist congressman from Virginia who in the early years of the nineteenth century would declare: "I am an aristocrat. I love liberty, I hate equality."

But Paine was nothing of the sort.

Paine did not love government, but he saw it as a necessity that could be evil or good, depending on the relative power of elites versus the power of the people. He was a proponent of taxation, especially progressive taxation for the purpose of redistributing wealth to the poor and the dispossessed. His ideas about guaranteed incomes, national health care and social-welfare schemes earned him recognition as the first great proponent of old-age pensions; indeed, the author is so associated with the cause of providing governmental aid to the elderly, the young and the disabled that no less an authority than the Social Security Administration recalls: "One of the first people to propose a scheme for retirement security that is recognizable as a forerunner of modern social insurance was Revolutionary War figure Thomas Paine."

In the broadest sense, the brilliant historian and Paine biographer Harvey Kaye has refuted the argument that contemporary conservatives have a serious claim on Paine, writing:

> For all their citations of Paine and his lines, conservatives do not—and truly cannot—embrace him and his arguments. Bolstered by capital, firmly in command of the Republican Party, and politically ascendant for a generation, they have initiated and instituted policies and programs that fundamentally contradict Paine's own vision and commitments. They have subordinated the Republic—the *res publica*, the commonwealth, the

public good—to the marketplace and private advantage. They have furthered the interests of corporations and the rich over those of working people, their families, unions, and communities and overseen a concentration of wealth and power that, recalling the Gilded Age, has corrupted and enervated American democratic life and politics. And they have carried on culture wars that have divided the nation and undermined the wall separating church and state. Moreover, they have pursued domestic and foreign policies that have made the nation both less free and less secure politically, economically, environmentally, and militarily. Even as they have spoken of advancing freedom and empowering citizens, they have sought to discharge or at least constrain America's democratic impulse and aspiration. In fact, while poaching lines from Paine, they and their favorite intellectuals have disclosed their real ambitions and affections by once again declaring the "end of history" and promoting the lives of Founders like John Adams and Alexander Hamilton, who in decided contrast to Paine scorned democracy and feared "the people."

But for the purposes of this particular query, it is most relevant to consider the startling misread of Paine by the Tea Partisan-in-chief, as it reveals much about the extent to which our contemporary debate has been strangled by ignorance—be it genuine or manufactured—with regard to the richest chapters of American history. Important as this consideration may be, it is, as well, amusing, since in their attempt to link their narrow worldview with Paine's expansive one, Beck and his associates have made common cause with the one founder who really can be—and, in fact, is—identified as a forefather of socialism. Famously, when the British Labour Party was advancing an energetically socialist agenda in platforms that were considered radical even in the context of the late twentieth century, its Paineite leader, Michael Foot, declared: "International arbitration, family allowances, maternity benefits, free education, prison reform, full employment; much of the future later offered by the British Labour Party was previously on offer, in better English, from Thomas Paine."

Foot, who with Bertrand Russell and historians E. P. Thompson and Christopher Hill participated in the formation of the British Thomas Paine Society, and then served for forty-seven years as its president, had already been reading Paine for six decades when he became my finest guide to the pamphleteer. He always cautioned against trying to wedge Paine into a "proto-socialist" box. The distinction is a subtle one, as we will see that Paine was a pioneering exponent of ideas that were more than sufficiently socialistic to cause Glenn Beck's head to explode. But Foot was wise to recognize Paine's broader contribution as a radical respondent to the demands of his age, able, because of his genius for communicating, to become an ageless role model for the nascent rebels and reformers who would as socialists challenge the aristocracy of wealth in the nineteenth, twentieth and twenty-first centuries.

What radical would not choose as a motto Paine's pronouncement: "Let them call me rebel and welcome, I feel no concern from it; but I should suffer the misery of devils, were I to make a whore of my soul by swearing allegiance to one whose character is that of a sottish, stupid, stubborn, worthless, brutish man"? Who would not want to attach themselves and their cause to lines so stirring as: "The Sun never shined on a cause of greater worth. 'Tis not the affair of a City, a County, a Province, or a Kingdom; but of a Continent—of at least one-eighth part of the habitable Globe. 'Tis not the concern of a day, a year, or an age; posterity are virtually involved in the contest, and will be more or less affected even to the end of time, by the proceedings now. Now is the seed-time of Continental union, faith and honor"? Or "a new era for politics is struck—a new method of thinking hath arisen. All plans, proposals, &c. prior to the nineteenth of April, i.e. to the commencement of hostilities, are like the almanacks of the last year; which tho' proper then, are superseded and useless now"? Or the contemporary favorite: "We have every opportunity and every encouragement before us, to form the noblest, purest constitution on the face of the earth. We have it in our power to begin the world over again. A situation, similar to the present, hath not happened since the days of Noah until now. The birthday of a new world is at hand, and a race of men, perhaps as numerous as all Europe contains, are to receive their portion of freedom from the event of a few months"? And even if events have a tendency to keep suggesting that the *Age of Reason* has not quite arrived, there was—and still is—something appealing about the prospect that the reforms, rebellions and revolutions of a particular moment might finally induce the grand mingling of optimism and enthusiasm that could justify the declaration that "the present age will hereafter merit to be called the *Age of Reason*, and the present generation will appear to the future as the Adam of the new world."

Sign me up. Sign us all up.

It was not just that Paine wrote in better English. He connected in a more deeply-rooted, more intellectually and emotionally fundamental manner than did other writers of his time with the sense, or at least with the hope, that we might yet "clear away the rubbish of errors, into which the subject of government has been thrown" and proceed toward a representative system where "every man is a proprietor in government, and considers it a necessary part of his business to understand." It would take a little more than two centuries for protestors outside the 1999 World Trade Organization ministerial summit in Seattle to put the final touches on the theme—with the slogan: "This is what democracy looks like!"—but Paine started the discussion. And he advanced it with a language that remained as urgent and alive in 1848 and 1932 and 1963 and 2008 as it had been in 1776. Paine compelled engagement, not of a casual or solely intellectual character, but of an immediate and visceral nature. Long before the words "socialist" or "communist" entered the popular parlance, years before Karl Marx or Frederick Engels were born, the cultural historian Catherine Hall reminds us: "It was the writings of Tom Paine and the revolutionary ideals of liberty, equality and fraternity that inspired the ... creation of new traditions of Radicalism and protest."

Historians of radical movements, from E. P. Thompson to Eric Hobsbawm to Howard Zinn, all point to Paine as a touchstone for what would become the clearly identifiable left—be it called "liberal," "progressive" or "socialist"—across the decades and now centuries since the passing of the pamphleteer. As Hall explains, "Paineite Radicalism was central to the political discourses of working people ... With its stress on Radical egalitarianism, its rejection of the traditions of the past, its convention that the future could be different, its belief in natural rights and the power of reason, its questioning of established institutions and its firm commitment to the view that government must represent the people, it gave a cutting thrust to radical demands." So it was that when, twenty-two years after Paine's death, William Lloyd Garrison launched his radical abolitionist newspaper, *The Liberator*, he did not simply declare: "I am in earnest—I will not equivocate—I will not excuse—I will not retreat a single inch—AND I WILL BE HEARD." He confirmed the point by adopting as the newspaper's permanent motto a paraphrase of Paine: "Our country is the world—our countrymen are mankind." Julius Wayland's socialist "agitation sheet" of the late nineteenth and early twentieth century, *The Appeal to Reason*—which would publish Upton Sinclair's *The Jungle*, Joe Hill's poems and Mother Jones's calls to action —was reputedly named in Paine's honor. Wayland's People's Pocket Series circulated tens of thousands of copies of the eighteenth-century author's books in 3 1/2" x 5" paperbacks that sold for twenty-five cents apiece. A young Eugene Victor Debs came upon Paine during a period of youthful self-education in which "everything that was revolutionary appealed to me." As the Socialist Party's frequent nominee for the presidency would explain it: "The revolutionary history of the United States and France stirred me deeply and its heroes and martyrs became my idols. Thomas Paine towered above them all."

Paine's language, "dictated by no passion but that of humanity," did not merely provide what E. P. Thompson described as "a new rhetoric of radical egalitarianism." There was more than mere rhetoric in his later books and pamphlets, especially *The Rights of Man* and the last of his major works, *Agrarian Justice*. Both contained content that provided, if not quite a Socialist Party platform, then surely the rough outlines for a social-democratic response to inequality.

Our friend Glenn Beck declared in one of his rants regarding creeping socialism, "I'm not asking you to go out on a limb with me. I am asking you to discover it for yourself. I'm asking you to do your own homework. I'm asking you to question with boldness. I'm asking you to 'Read It!' Read the words yourself … I am asking you to find the truth in these things."

Fair enough.

Let's read what Paine wrote.

Let's recognize that *Common Sense* was a call to revolution against hereditary monarchy, nobility and tradition, which inspired a rejection of the established order with a charge that: "A long habit of not thinking a thing wrong, gives it a superficial appearance of being right, and raises at first a formidable outcry in defense of custom."

Let's accept that *The Crisis* was Paine's call to carry through to its end an American Revolution that took as its premise: "We fight not to enslave, but to set a country free, and to make room upon the earth for honest men to live in."

But how would those men (and women)—and the men and women of any state forged in revolution—organize their affairs? How would they conjure what Paine envisioned as a new sort of government that reflected not the dictates of a powerful few, but the multitude? Though Paine was often critical of governments, he did not imagine a modern state without government. The problem was not government, Paine argued by the time that the United States got around to approving a Constitution, but rather the denial of popular will and wisdom by "a false system of government." In his last years, Paine made his great contributions to political science, particularly in *The Rights of Man*, with its pioneering yet precise deconstruction of governmental forms. He feared government that "operates to benumb." "When the mind of a nation is bowed down by any political superstition in its government, such as hereditary succession is, it loses a considerable portion of its powers on all other subjects and objects," observed Paine, who rejected as intolerable any and all governmental forms that demanded blind allegiance or the empty "patriotism" of "my country right or wrong." Paine disdained: "the same obedience to ignorance, as to wisdom; and when once the mind can bring itself to pay this indiscriminate reverence, it descends below the stature of mental manhood. It is fit to be great only in little things. It acts a treachery upon itself, and suffocates the sensations that urge the detection."

The writer's counter to such a circumstance was never to romanticize the disconnected libertarian living in individualist isolation. Rather, it was the communal contract of representative government which he saw as "always parallel with the order and immutable laws of nature, and meets the reason of man in every part." "Like the nation itself, it possesses a perpetual stamina, as well of body as of mind, and presents itself on the open theater of the world in a fair and manly manner," he explained in *The Rights of Man*. "Whatever are its excellences or defects, they are visible to all. It exists not by fraud and mystery; it deals not in cant and sophistry; but inspires a language that, passing from heart to heart, is felt and understood."

Paine was not a pure democrat. He believed in constitutions, rules and structures that replaced the whim of the potentate or property owner with an understanding that "the law is king." But those constitutions, rules and structures were constructed—if we might paraphrase an American president who said he never tired of reading Paine—not to cage the better angels of democracy but to harness their power, and focus it on the pursuit of a more perfect union.

Paine's passion for engaged citizenship was—and is—radical. Long before the other founders, he fully recognized and celebrated the merit and the power of broad suffrage. "The right of voting for representatives is the primary right by which other rights are protected," Paine wrote in his *First Principles of Government.* "To take away this right is to reduce a man to slavery, for slavery consists in being subject to the will of another, and he that has not a vote in the election of representatives is in this case." Paine was equally ardent in his rejection of the class divisions that even the liberals of the enlightenment accepted, arguing in his *Letter to the Addressers*: "When the qualification to vote is regulated by years, it is placed on the firmest possible ground, because the qualification is such as nothing but dying before the time can take away; and the equality of Rights, as a principle, is recognized in the act of regulating the exercise. But when Rights are placed upon, or made dependent upon property, they are on the most precarious of all tenures. 'Riches make themselves wings, and fly away,' and the rights fly with them; and thus they become lost to the man when they would be of most value."

But Paine did not end there. He had from his earliest writings recognized, as he explained in *Common Sense*, that what was truly foul and anti-democratic in the "composition of monarchy" was a calculus that "first excludes a man from the means of information ..." Like Jefferson and Madison at their most democratic—and it can fairly be noted that they were not always at their most democratic—Paine abhorred the secrecy and official conniving not just of kings and czars but of petty royalists who, despite their affiliation with a particular revolution, endeavored ultimately to produce a rule that was of, by and for the propertied and powerful elites. It was not a personal feud that led John Adams to attack Paine's "career of mischief," and to argue that there was "no severer satyr on the age" than the pamphleteer. Adams, with his attachment to British forms and practices—he proposed that America's executive be referred to by regal titles such as "His Majesty the President" or "His High

Mightiness"—and general distrust of democracy, made no secret of his belief that there was a "natural aristocracy among mankind." Arguing that America should nurture its aristocracy with a system that assured that these "brightest ornaments" of the nation might always enjoy "the greatest blessings of society," Adams emerged as an arch-elitist who feared frequent elections and popular agitation. As president, he sought to constrain the freedom of the press with a Sedition Act that made it a crime to publish "false, scandalous, and malicious writing" against the government or its officials. This was antithetical to Paine's proposals to develop the infrastructure of democracy and citizenship so that:

> [The] representative system diffuses such a body of knowledge through-out a nation, on the subject of government, as to explode ignorance and preclude imposition. The craft of courts cannot be acted on that ground. There is no place for mystery; nowhere for it to begin. Those who are not in the representation, know as much of the nature of business as those who are. An affectation of mysterious importance would there be scouted. Nations can have no secrets; and the secrets of courts, like those of individuals, are always their defects.
>
> In the representative system, the reason for everything must publicly appear. Every man is a proprietor in government, and considers it a nec-essary part of his business to understand. It concerns his interest, because it affects his property. He examines the cost, and compares it with the advantages; and above all, he does not adopt the slavish custom of follow-ing what in other governments are called Leaders.

Adams feared what he derisively referred to as "the age of Paine," and rightly so. The combination of information and the right to act on it was, as the Paineite Eugene Victor Debs explained at the opening of his 1904 presidential campaign on the Socialist Party ticket, a powerful threat to old orders. "Ignorance alone stands in the way of socialist success. The capitalist parties understand this and use their resources to prevent the workers from seeing the light. Intellectual darkness is essen-tial to industrial slavery," declared Debs, adding: "The very moment a workingman begins to do his own thinking he understands the para-mount issue, parts company with the capitalist politician and falls in line with his own class on the political battlefield."

Fourteen years later, addressing the jury that convicted him of violating a new Sedition Act that was rhetorically and ideologically indebted to Adams, Debs would invoke the name of Paine, and the memory of how "A century and a half ago, when the American colonists were still foreign subjects, and when there were a few men who had faith in the common people and believed that they could rule themselves without a king, in that day to speak against the kings was treason. If you read Bancroft or any other standard historian, you will find that a great majority of the colonists believed in the king and actually believed that he had a divine right to rule over them. They had been taught to believe that to say a word against the king, to question his so-called divine right, was sinful. There were ministers who opened their bibles to prove that it was the patriotic duty of the people to loyally serve and support the king. But there were a few men in that day who said, 'We don't need a king. We can govern ourselves.' And they began an agitation that has been immortalized in history."

The greatest Socialist agitator of his age would then explain:

I believe in the Constitution of the United States. Isn't it strange that we Socialists stand almost alone today in defending the Constitution of the United States? The revolutionary fathers who had been oppressed under king rule understood that free speech and the right of free assemblage by the people were the fundamental principles of democratic government. The very first amendment to the Constitution reads: "Congress shall make no law respecting an establishment of religion or prohibiting the free exercise thereof; or abridging the freedom of speech, or of the press; or the right of the people peaceably to assemble, and to petition the government for a redress of grievances." That is perfectly plain English. It can be understood by a child. I believe that the revolutionary fathers meant just what is here stated—that Congress shall make no law abridging the freedom of speech or of the press, or of the right of the people to peaceably assemble, and to petition the government for a redress of grievances.

That is the right that I exercised [by delivering an anti-war speech] at Canton on the 16th day of last June; and for the exercise of that right, I now have to answer to this indictment. I believe in the right of free speech, in war as well as in peace. I would not, under any circumstances, gag the lips of my bitterest enemy. I would under no circumstances suppress free speech. It is far more dangerous to attempt to gag the people than to allow them to speak freely of what is in their hearts. I do not go as far as [the abolitionist, social reformer and proponent of a moral "Godly Common-wealth"] Wendell Phillips did. Wendell Phillips said that the glory of free men is that they trample unjust laws under their feet. That is how they repeal them. If a human being submits to having his lips sealed, to be in silence reduced to vassalage, he may have all else, but he is still lacking in all that dignifies and glorifies real manhood.

Now, notwithstanding this fundamental provision in the national law, Socialists' meetings have been broken up all over this country. Socialist speakers have been arrested by hundreds and flung into jail, where many of them are lying now. In some cases not even a charge was lodged against them—guilty of no crime except the crime of attempting to exercise the right guaranteed to them by the Constitution of the United States.

I have told you that I am no lawyer, but it seems to me that I know enough to know that if Congress enacts any law that conflicts with this provision in the Constitution, that law is void. If the Espionage Law finally stands, then the Constitution of the United States is dead. If that law is not the negation of every fundamental principle established by the Constitution, then certainly I am unable to read or to understand the English language.

It is not surprising that Socialist Party leaders such as Debs, who embraced both industrial organization and the ballot box as tools for achieving radical change, would celebrate Paine as a pioneering small-"d" democrat. As they advocated for expanding the franchise to the poor, women and minorities, they could point to a founder who understood, as they did, that: "The right of voting for representatives is the primary right by which other rights are protected."

This is not exactly the same line adopted by Glenn Beck, who after "rewriting *Common Sense*" used his television program to claim not once, not twice, but repeatedly, that "democracy does not work." "We're not a democracy," Beck argued in June 2010, before warning, ominously, that "there is a concerted effort by the progressives to make us a democracy."

Conservative commentator Matthew Continetti—author of no less than *The Persecution of Sarah Palin: How the Elite Media Tried to Bring*

Down a Rising Star—characterizes Beck's regular ranting as a "nonsense" of "paranoid scenarios" proffered by a "former Top 40 DJ who was addicted to alcohol and drugs before bottoming out, converting to Mormonism, and retooling his radio skills to a new format—conservative talk." The *Weekly Standard* associate editor worries, with good reason, about an increasingly prominent right-leaning "thinker" who invites his audience to imagine Woodrow Wilson (No. 1) and FDR (No. 3) as higher rank-holders on the list of the "Top Ten Bastards of All Time" than Pontius Pilate (No. 4), Adolf Hitler (No. 6) or Pol Pot (No. 10). But Continetti, like many other thinking conservatives, gives Beck credit for "introducing new thinkers to the reading public" and argues: "By attacking progressivism, Beck is taking on a big idea. He is forcing people to question their assumptions."

Perhaps it is out of deference to Tom Paine's memory that I find it impossible to fully accept Continetti's assessment of Beck. I'd like to give the television host credit for "forcing people to question their assumptions" or "introducing new thinkers to the reading public" or, to turn a Beck phrase on Beck, "taking on history." But this seems a rather too generous calculus. My suspicion is that Beck hasn't gotten beyond the Cliffs Notes version of American history. And I am not sure he's even past the "Wikiquotes" compendium when it comes to Paine. Beck's book on Paine quotes sparingly from *Common Sense*, often failing to get far beyond the title—as in "Is common sense completely dead in America?" Or "Common sense still lives in my house and it's about time it is applied again in Washington!" Or, in a section on entitlements, "Common sense tells us that this is national suicide."

Were Beck to delve a little deeper in the canon, however, he would quickly recognize that, like any and every great thinker, Paine evolved. The pamphleteer—who remarked in 1776 that "it is pleasant to observe by what regular gradation we surmount the force of local prejudice as we enlarge our acquaintance with the world"—learned from the experience of two "successful" revolutions, and several failed ones, that "the moral principle of revolutions is to instruct, not to destroy." In other words, there had to be more to the revolt against a "bad king's" tyranny than the hope that the new monarch might be good.

Paine was a proud revolutionary. But what marked him as a rabble-rouser of historic proportions was that he distinguished between upheavals. He rejected the rebellions of old as pointless. Like Pete Townsend two centuries later, Paine chose to "take a bow for the new revolution":

> The revolutions which formerly took place in the world had nothing in them that interested the bulk of mankind. They extended only to a change of persons and measures, but not of principles, and rose or fell among the common transactions of the moment. What we now behold may not improperly be called a "counter-revolution." Conquest and tyranny, at some earlier period, dispossessed man of his rights, and he is now recovering them. And as the tide of all human affairs has its ebb and flow in directions contrary to each other, so also is it in this. Government founded on a moral theory, on a system of universal peace, on the indefeasible hereditary Rights of Man, is now revolving from west to east by a stronger impulse than the government of the sword revolved from east to west. It interests not particular individuals, but nations in its progress, and promises a new era to the human race.

In his seminal work *The Rights of Man*, written in 1791 as a rebuke to the cautious reformer Edmund Burke's reactionary tract *Reflections on the Revolution in France*, Paine made the case for revolt against governments that were not of, by and for the people—especially monarchies, but also aristocratic "republics" and military dictatorships. What is most vital for our endeavor here is his argument regarding the point and purpose of these revolts. "It is not worth making changes or revolutions," Paine argued, "unless it be for some great national benefit."

What sort of benefit?

In the final sections of *The Rights of Man*, the ones surely read by Eugene Victor Debs if perhaps not by Glenn Beck, Paine began to outline the welfare state that is properly associated with, if not full-fledged socialism, then at least social democracy as it has come to be understood. By ending the economic abuses of the monarchy, the nobility and "national religions," by cutting the size of the army and pursuing relations with other republics based on diplomacy rather than military might ("to unite nations that have hitherto been enemies, and to extirpate the horrid practice of war …") and by abolishing the "the aristocratical system" of large estates and inherited wealth, Paine argued, republics could free up immense amounts of money to aid the poor.

Glenn Beck may claim, with regard to redistribution of the wealth, that: "Our Founders all warned against that. They didn't think it was better to 'spread the wealth around.'" Actually, they did. No less a founding father than Benjamin Franklin wrote to Robert Morris in 1783:

> All the Property that is necessary to a Man, for the Conservation of the Individual and the Propagation of the Species, is his natural Right, which none can justly deprive him of: But all Property superfluous to such purposes is the Property of the Publick, who, by their Laws, have created it, and who may therefore by other Laws dispose of it, whenever the Welfare of the Publick shall demand such Disposition. He that does not like civil Society on these Terms, let him retire and live among Savages. He can have no right to the benefits of Society, who will not pay his Club towards the Support of it.

The founder Beck has chosen to affiliate himself with, indeed to "rewrite" for the twenty-first century, went even further than Franklin. Specifically, Paine favored a "Plan of a progressive tax, operating to extirpate the unjust and unnatural law of primogeniture, and the vicious influence of the aristocratical system." As well, he outlined models for inheritance taxes, arguing that "there ought to be a limit to property or the accumulation of it by bequest." He proposed "taxing luxuries," on the theory that: "Admitting that any annual sum, say, for instance, one thousand pounds, is necessary or sufficient for the support of a family, consequently the second thousand is of the nature of a luxury, the third still more so, and by proceeding on, we shall at last arrive at a sum that may not improperly be called a prohibitable luxury." And, for good measure, he advanced plans for taxes on speculation, investments and interest, suggesting that "it would be good policy in the stockholders themselves to consider it as property, subject like all other property, to bear some portion of the taxes."

Glenn Beck may warn that terms such as "social justice and economic justice" are foreign constructs that are associated—on the cards he holds up on his cable television program—with the hammer and sickle. He may counsel against making common cause with those who have "talked about economic justice, rights of the workers, redistribution of wealth," and surprisingly, "democracy." But Paine devoted most of his writing in later years to addressing what he referred to as "the claims of justice." And he did so largely in a social—arguably social-democratic—context.

It is certainly true that Franklin Roosevelt's New Deal-era responses to economic injustice drew inspiration from the platforms of the Socialist Party that Debs handed off to Norman Thomas. But Roosevelt, a lifelong reader of Paine who quoted the pamphleteer in his fireside chats ("So spoke Americans in the year 1776. So speak Americans today!"), borrowed at least as much from the distant revolutionary's canon.

In the conclusion to *The Rights of Man*, Paine imagined, and in the context of the times actually outlined budgets for:

- Social Security: an "Annuity of six pounds (per annum) each for all poor persons, decayed tradesmen, and others (supposed seventy thousand) of the age of fifty years, and until sixty," and an "Annuity of ten pounds each for life for all poor persons, decayed tradesmen, and others (supposed seventy thousand) of the age of sixty years."
- Child Welfare Programs: "Provision for two hundred and fifty-two thousand poor families, at the rate of four pounds per head for each child under fourteen years of age; which, with the addition of two hundred and fifty thousand pounds, provides also education for one million and thirty thousand children."
- Public Housing: "The plan will then be: First, To erect two or more buildings, or take some already erected, capable of containing at least six thousand persons, and to have in each of these places as many kinds of employment as can be contrived, so that every person who shall come may find something which he or she can do."
- Massive Public Works Programs: "To receive all who shall come, without enquiring who or what they are. The only condition to be, that for so much, or so many hours' work, each person shall receive so many meals of wholesome food, and a warm lodging, at least as good as a barrack. That a certain portion of what each person's work shall be worth shall be reserved, and given to him or her, on their going away; and that each person shall stay as long or as short a time, or come as often as he choose, on these conditions."

- Earned-Income Tax Credits: "By remitting the taxes of the poor, they will be totally relieved ..."

The purpose, Paine explained, was to achieve an end that might, by most reasonable definitions, be described as "social justice." Indeed, he was just getting started on the path that would lead him to instruct the republics of the world: "Let us then do honor to revolutions by justice, and give currency to their principles by blessings."

Throughout the 1790s, Paine would dig deeper into economic debates, continually revisiting issues of wealth and poverty, fair distribution of income and the establishment of a state akin to what the socialists of the late nineteenth and early twentieth centuries would refer to as the "cooperative commonwealth." He would observe economic inequality and recognize it not as "God's plan" or "fate." Rather, Paine asserted: "The rugged face of society, checkered with the extremes of affluence and want, proves that some extraordinary violence has been committed upon it, and calls on justice for redress." The old revolutionary's writing and lecturing would culminate in the publication, in 1797, of his last widely-circulated pamphlet, *Agrarian Justice*.

More detailed and radical than *The Rights of Man*, *Agrarian Justice* would advocate taxing the wealthy in order to raise a fund sufficient to establish:

- Fixed payments—of an amount equal to roughly two-thirds of the annual wage for an agricultural laborer—to be paid to every man and woman in a country upon their reaching the age of majority (twenty-one).
- Annual pension payments for every person over age fifty.
- Generous disability pensions for "the lame and blind" that anticipated both Social Security and national health-care plans.

Paine would make his case for this economic revolution with the same language and energy that he brought to his previous calls to begin the world over again. Applying the template of the radical pamphleteer, he explained *The Crisis*, outlined a *Common Sense* solution and then called his enlightened comrades into battle on behalf of reason and *The Rights of Man*.

First came the indictment, not this time of a King George or a corrupt church, but of an unnatural economic order that permitted great wealth to reside in close proximity to abject poverty:

> Whether that state that is proudly, perhaps erroneously, called civilization, has most promoted or most injured the general happiness of man is a question that may be strongly contested. On one side, the spectator is dazzled by splendid appearances; on the other, he is shocked by extremes of wretchedness; both of which it has erected. The most affluent and the most miserable of the human race are to be found in the countries that are called civilized.

> To understand what the state of society ought to be, it is necessary to have some idea of the natural and primitive state of man; such as it is at this day among the Indians of North America. There is not, in that state, any of those spectacles of human misery which poverty and want present to our eyes in all the towns and streets in Europe.

> Poverty, therefore, is a thing created by that which is called civilized life. It exists not in the natural state. On the other hand, the natural state is without those advantages which flow from agriculture, arts, science and manufactures.

> The life of an Indian is a continual holiday, compared with the poor of Europe; and, on the other hand, it appears to be abject when compared to the rich. Civilization, therefore, or that which is so-called, has operated two ways: to make one part of society more affluent, and the other more wretched, than would have been the lot of either in a natural state.

> It is always possible to go from the natural to the civilized state, but it is never possible to go from the civilized to the natural state. The reason is that man in a natural state, subsisting by hunting, requires ten times the quantity of land to range over to procure himself sustenance, than would support him in a civilized state, where the earth is cultivated.

> When, therefore, a country becomes populous by the additional aids of cultivation, art and science, there is a necessity of preserving things in that state; because without it there cannot be sustenance for more, perhaps, than a tenth part of its inhabitants. The thing, therefore, now to be done is to remedy the evils and preserve the benefits that have arisen to society by passing from the natural to that which is called the civilized state.

> In taking the matter upon this ground, the first principle of civilization ought to have been, and ought still to be, that the condition of every

person born into the world, after a state of civilization commences, ought not to be worse than if he had been born before that period.

But the fact is that the condition of millions, in every country in Europe, is far worse than if they had been born before civilization began, had been born among the Indians of North America at the present.

Those with property, Paine argued, owed a debt to society, a debt that should be collected and then redistributed to those lacking property. To wit:

It is a position not to be controverted that the earth, in its natural, uncultivated state was, and ever would have continued to be, the common property of the human race. In that state every man would have been born to property. He would have been a joint life proprietor with the rest in the property of the soil, and in all its natural productions, vegetable and animal.

But the earth in its natural state, as before said, is capable of supporting but a small number of inhabitants compared with what it is capable of doing in a cultivated state. And as it is impossible to separate the improvement made by cultivation from the earth itself, upon which that improvement is made, the idea of landed property arose from that parable connection; but it is nevertheless true, that it is the value of the improvement, only, and not the earth itself, that is individual property.

Every proprietor, therefore, of cultivated lands, owes to the community a ground-rent (for I know of no better term to express the idea) for the land which he holds; and it is from this ground-rent that the fund proposed in this plan is to issue.

Paine was no fool, and no more of a utopian pleader than he had been in the day when his cool assessments of the circumstance of the colonials inspired an outmanned and outgunned Continental Army to fight with such vigor that Benjamin Franklin would tell him: "You, Thomas Paine, are more responsible than any other living person on this continent for the creation of what are called the United States of America." The writer who had employed "simple facts, plain arguments, and *Common Sense*" to spark a revolution against empire now employed the same incendiary weapons to spark a revolution against economic injustice:

It is not charity but a right, not bounty but justice, that I am pleading for. The present state of civilization is as odious as it is unjust. It is absolutely the opposite of what it should be, and it is necessary that a revolution should be made in it. The contrast of affluence and wretchedness continually meeting and offending the eye, is like dead and living bodies chained together. Though I care as little about riches as any man, I am a friend to riches because they are capable of good.

I care not how affluent some may be, provided that none be miserable in consequence of it. But it is impossible to enjoy affluence with the felicity it is capable of being enjoyed, while so much misery is mingled in the scene. The sight of the misery, and the unpleasant sensations it suggests, which, though they may be suffocated cannot be extinguished, are a greater drawback upon the felicity of affluence than the proposed ten per cent upon property is worth. He that would not give the one to get rid of the other has no charity, even for himself.

There are, in every country, some magnificent charities established by individuals. It is, however, but little that any individual can do, when the whole extent of the misery to be relieved is considered. He may satisfy his conscience, but not his heart. He may give all that he has, and that all will relieve but little. It is only by organizing civilization upon such principles as to act like a system of pulleys, that the whole weight of misery can be removed.

The plan here proposed will reach the whole. It will immediately relieve and take out of view three classes of wretchedness—the blind, the lame, and the aged poor; and it will furnish the rising generation with means to prevent their becoming poor; and it will do this without deranging or interfering with any national measures.

To show that this will be the case, it is sufficient to observe that the operation and effect of the plan will, in all cases, be the same as if every individual were voluntarily to make his will and dispose of his property in the manner here proposed.

But it is justice, and not charity, that is the principle of the plan. In all great cases it is necessary to have a principle more universally active than charity; and, with respect to justice, it ought not to be left to the choice of detached individuals whether they will do justice or not. Considering, then, the plan on the ground of justice, it ought to be the act of the whole growing spontaneously out of the principles of the revolution, and the reputation of it ought to be national and not individual.

A plan upon this principle would benefit the revolution by the energy that springs from the consciousness of justice. It would multiply also the national resources; for property, like vegetation, increases by offsets. When a young couple begin in the world, the difference is exceedingly great whether they begin with nothing or with fifteen pounds apiece. With this aid they could buy a cow, and implements to cultivate a few acres of land; and instead of becoming burdens upon society, which is always the case where children are produced faster than they can be fed, would be put in the way of becoming useful and profitable citizens. The national domains also would sell the better if pecuniary aids were provided to cultivate them in small lots.

It is the practice of what has unjustly obtained the name of civilization (and the practice merits not to be called either charity or policy) to make some provision for persons becoming poor and wretched only at the time they become so. Would it not, even as a matter of economy, be far better to adopt means to prevent their becoming poor? This can best be done by making every person when arrived at the age of twenty-one years an inheritor of something to begin with.

This was the language of the next revolution, the next revolutions, which Paine would not witness. Ailing physically, he was at odds with George Washington—whom he rebuked in 1795 as an "apostate" who had "abandoned good principles [if] you ever had any"—and estranged from Jefferson, who might have shared Paine's views regarding religion but not the fervency with which the pamphleteer had advanced them in the *Age of Reason*. Even the French legislators—to whom he addressed *Agrarian Justice* for their "safeguard" while pointing out that "this work is not adapted for any particular country alone: the principle on which it is based is general"—were no longer Paineites.

Paine would die in the worst of circumstances and, perhaps, the best. His name and most of his writings had ceased to be well regarded by the elites. Of his old comrades, only Jefferson—perhaps prodded by his long conversations late in life with the young utopian socialist and Paineite Fanny Wright—would return to the radical camp in old age. The former president issued as his epitaph a suitably revolutionary rebuke to the compromises of the cautious administrators who had assumed the power, if surely not the mantle, of the "generation of '76." The constant reader if inconstant supporter of Paine had absorbed the message of the writer's later and more incendiary pronouncements, especially *The Rights of Man*, which in the early 1790s he hailed—in a none-too-subtle jab at John Adams—for pushing back "against the political heresies which have sprung up against us." Finally, from his deathbed, he would cite it again in what Jefferson biographer Willard Sterne Randall describes as both "the last letter he ever wrote" and a "reaffirmation" of the ideals of his younger years. In 1826, as the fiftieth anniversary of America's revolution against colonialism and the divine right of kings approached, the author of the rebellion's founding document—now aged eighty-three—was asked to attend a Fourth of July celebration in Washington. Jefferson could not make the journey from his beloved Monticello. The infirmity that had narrowed the great traveler's range would claim him (and Adams), with an irony the most romantic of the founders would have appreciated, on the anniversary itself. But the invitation to the celebration gave Jefferson an opportunity to speak one last time to the nation he and Paine had forged with their remarkable words.

In a public letter to the *National Intelligencer* newspaper, Jefferson urged not only that the spirit of '76 be maintained but that a new generation might raise even higher the banner of liberty:

> May [July 4] be to the world, what I believe it will be, to some parts sooner, to others later, but finally to all: the signal of arousing men to burst the chains under which monkish ignorance and superstition had persuaded them to bind themselves, and to assume the blessings and security of self-government.
>
> That form [of government] which we have substituted, restores the free right to the unbounded exercise of reason and freedom of opinion.
>
> All eyes are opened, or opening, to *The Rights of Man*.

Then, recalling Paine's line about how peoples ought "not be governed like animals, for the pleasure of their riders," Jefferson observed: "The general spread of the light of science has already laid open, to every view, the palpable truth [that] the mass of mankind has not been born with saddles on their backs, nor a favored few booted and spurred, ready to ride them legitimately, by the Grace of God."

The palpable truth of that egalitarian principle was not well received by the "respectable" classes of an America that still accepted both slavery in the south and wide disparities between rich and poor in the growing cities of the north. The old plantation owners and the new merchant elites might acknowledge for historical purposes that Paine had benefited the Revolutionary cause in his youth. But they bemoaned his questioning of religion and feared his influence on economic debates to such an extent that the *New York Times* would at mid-century editorialize about the dangerous influence of the "many socialist Paineites," with their "theoretical dreams of false liberty" and "their affiliation to every species of radicalism in the land."

At the heart of the Paineite agitation by Burke's despised "several petty cabals," which continued spreading the radical gospels of *The Rights of Man* and *Agrarian Justice* far beyond the borders of the United States and the United Kingdom, was an economic populism that the conservative *Times* of 1856 feared "boded evil for the future welfare of our Republic." While much has been made, and appropriately so, of the influence Paine's *Age of Reason* had on free-thinking, deist and atheist movements in the years after his death, historians such as Eric Foner and Harvey Kaye have well noted the pamphleteer's parallel influence on economic and political debates. *Agrarian Justice*, though too rarely mentioned in contemporary discussions of Paine's canon, had a dramatic and long-lasting impact on the broad debate about land reform, which was closely linked with the rise of explicitly socialist and proto-communist movements in Europe and the United States.

Many of the campaigners, Paine's contemporaries and those who came after him, would vary and extend his arguments, as did the French utopian socialist Charles Fourier with his assertion that: "The first right of men is the right to work and the right to a minimum [income]." The radical British land-use reformer Thomas Spence would wrestle with Paine's proposals in pamphlets of his own, such as 1793's *The Real Rights of Man* and 1801's *The Restorer of Society to Its Natural State*. Even those who disagreed with Paine's precise provisions hailed his influence, as did the Welsh utopian socialist Robert Owen, who expounded on his theories about communal living in addresses to the US Congress before launching his New Harmony experiment in Indiana in the 1820s. The New York labor organizer and editor Thomas Skidmore, who outlined a theory of wage slavery and formed the radical Working Men's Party, would object to Paine's cooperation with the businessmen and bankers of the Revolutionary era while borrowing premises from the pamphleteer in his combative 1829 book, *The Rights of Man to Property!*

Skidmore's New York political activism intersected with that of the remarkable Fanny Wright, "the female Tom Paine," whose social and political radicalism cut a swath across Europe and her adopted United States. Born into a Scottish Paineite household in 1795, Wright inherited great wealth, used it to tour the States as a young woman, and then wrote a well-received book about the experience. This led to a correspondence with the Marquis de Lafayette, the French hero of the American Revolutionary War and comrade of Paine's who traveled always with a tattered copy of *Common Sense*. Lafayette invited Wright to join him on his triumphal return to the United States, almost fifty years after the Revolution, and together they visited Jefferson at Monticello. There, the young woman and the aging author of the Declaration of Independence reportedly debated the issue of slavery—as Jefferson and Paine had so many years earlier. Jefferson passed several months later, but Wright would go on to join the broader public debate on that issue and virtually every other major social and economic concern of the moment.

A pioneering feminist who would be hailed at the National Woman's Rights Convention of 1858 as "the first woman in this country who spoke on the equality of the sexes," Wright was also, in the words of the founder of the utopian Oneida Community, John Humphrey Noyes, an essential figure in the "socialist revival" of the 1820s and "the leading woman in the communistic movement of that period." An uncompromising abolitionist, who would speak of her sorrow that the United States had not followed Paine's counsel of the 1770s and abolished slavery, Wright became an American citizen and poured her fortune into a failed attempt to develop a multiracial communal farming experiment in Tennessee, before heading to New York. Here she began a broader agitation on behalf of economic justice, declaring: "Equality is the soul of liberty; there is, in fact, no liberty without it." So popular did her preachments become that the term "Fanny Wrightism" entered popular parlance.

In particular, Wright aligned with the New York Working Men's Party campaigns of 1829 and 1830, writing in the Paineite weekly newspaper, the *Free Enquirer*: "What distinguishes the present from every other struggle in which the human race has been engaged is that the present is, evidently, openly and acknowledgedly, a war of class and that this war is universal ..." Borrowing language from both Paine and her friend Jefferson's final statement, she thundered: "it is the ridden people of the earth who are struggling to throw from their backs the 'booted and spurred' riders whose legitimate title to starve as well as work them to death will no longer pass current ..."

Attacked in the conservative press as a "blaspheming party" that carried "the mark of Cain," the Working Men's Party proved to be electorally muscular, sending the head of the carpenters' union to the state legislature and attracting large votes in working-class wards of New York City for a class-conscious program that one of its founders, the crusading editor of the *Working Man's Advocate* newspaper, George Evans, outlined in a paraphrase of the Declaration of Independence and *Common Sense*:

"When, in the course of human events, it becomes necessary" for one class of a community to assert their natural and unalienable rights in opposition to other classes of their fellow men, "and to assume among" them a political "station of equality to which the laws of nature and of nature's God," as well as the principles of their political compact "entitle them; a decent respect to the opinions of mankind," and the more paramount duty they owe to their own fellow citizens, "requires that they should declare the causes which impel them" to adopt so painful, yet so necessary, a measure.

"We hold these truths to be self evident that all men are created equal; that they are endowed by their creator with certain unalienable rights; that among these are life, liberty and the pursuit of happiness; that to secure these rights" against the undue influence of other classes of society, prudence, as well as the claims of self-defense, dictates the necessity of the organization of a party, who shall, by their representatives, prevent dangerous combinations to subvert these indefeasible and fundamental privileges. "All experience hath shown, that mankind" in general, and we as a class in particular, "are more disposed to suffer, while evils are sufferable, than to right themselves," by an opposition which the pride and self-interest of unprincipled political aspirants, with more unprincipled zeal or religious bigotry, will willfully misrepresent. "But when a long train of abuses and usurpations" take place, all invariably tending to the oppression and degradation of one class of society, and to the unnatural and iniquitous exaltation of another by political leaders, "it is their right, it is their duty" to use every constitutional means to reform the abuses of such a government and to provide new guards for their future security. The history of the political parties in this state, is a history of political iniquities, all tending to the enacting and enforcing of oppressive and unequal laws. To prove this, let facts be submitted to the candid and impartial of our fellow citizens of all parties:

1. The laws for levying taxes are all based on erroneous principles, in consequence of their operating most oppressively on one of society, and being scarcely felt by the other.

2. The laws regarding the duties of jurors, witnesses, and militia trainings, are still more unequal and oppressive.

3. The laws for private incorporations are all partial in their operations; favoring one class of society to the expense of the other, who have no equal participation.

4. The laws incorporating religious societies have a pernicious tendency, by promoting the erection of magnificent places of public worship, by the rich, excluding others, and which others cannot imitate; consequently engendering spiritual pride in the clergy and people, and thereby creating odious distinctions in society, destructive to its social peace and happiness.

5. The laws establishing and patronizing seminaries of learning are unequal, favoring the rich, and perpetuating imparity, which natural causes have produced, and which judicious laws ought, and can, remedy.

6. The laws and municipal ordinances and regulations, generally, besides those specially enumerated, have heretofore been ordained on such principles, as have deprived nine-tenths of the members of the body politic, who are not wealthy, of the equal means to enjoy "life, liberty and the pursuit of happiness" which the rich enjoy exclusively; but the federative compact intended to secure to all, indiscriminately. The lien law in favor of landlords against tenants, and all other honest creditors, is one illustration among innumerable others which can be adduced to prove the truth of these allegations.

We have trusted to the influence of the justice and good sense of our political leaders, to prevent the continuance of these abuses, which destroy the natural bands of equality so essential to the attainment of moral happiness, "but they have been deaf to the voice of justice and of consanguinity."

Therefore, we, the working class of society, of the city of New York, "appealing to the supreme judge of the world," and to the reason and consciences of the impartial of all parties, "for the rectitude of our intentions, do, in the spirit, and by the authority of that political liberty which has been promised to us equally with our fellow men, solemnly publish and declare, and invite all under like pecuniary circumstances, together with every liberal mind, to join us in the declaration, "that we are, & of right ought to be," entitled to equal means to obtain equal moral happiness, and social enjoyment, and that all lawful and constitutional measures ought to be adopted to the attainment of those objects. "And for the support of this declaration, we mutually pledge to each other" our faithful aid to the end of our lives.

The Working Men's Party would dissolve quickly, but its influence extended across the next several decades, as Evans turned his attention to forging a land-reform movement that would address the laws, ordinances and regulations that "deprived nine-tenths of the members of the body politic, who are not wealthy, of the equal means to enjoy 'life, liberty, and the pursuit of happiness' which the rich enjoy exclusively ..."

Evans and his allies borrowed boldly from the concepts and ideals of Paine's later writings, becoming known as "Agrarians." They forged a movement that employed Paineite language to promote "Man's Right to the Soil" and that attracted and inspired a generation of young radicals, including Horace Greeley, who would in his one term as a congressman introduce legislation proposing to give land free of charge to the poor; and Abraham Lincoln, who as president signed into law a milder version of Evans's proposal—the Homestead Act of 1862. The Agrarian free soil movements were decried as "Red Republicanism" by northern conservatives and bitterly opposed by southern plantation owners, who feared that freeing up the land of the western states for production of food and agricultural products would undermine the claim that slavery was an economic necessity. As early as 1846, Evans anticipated that the United States would eventually see the development of two opposing parties that would do battle over all the economic and social issues of the nation: "the great Republican Party of Progress and the little Tory Party of Holdbacks."

Predictably, if not always easily, Evans's land reformers and the burgeoning abolitionist movement found common ground, and common
adherents—among them a young organizer in Evans's National Reform
and Industrial Congress project, Alvan Bovay. Active in the populist
"Vote Yourself a Farm" campaign, which urged urban workers and their
rural allies to organize an independent political movement with the
purpose of gaining control of legislatures and Congress and then enacting
radical reforms, Bovay became a prominent player in many of the radical
reform movements of the 1840s and 1850s, delivering speeches and
writing articles that were broadly circulated in Evans's *Working Man's
Advocate* and *Young America* newspapers, as well as Greeley's nationally-
circulated *New York Tribune.*

When he moved to Wisconsin in the early 1850s, Bovay settled in the
village of Ripon, where a utopian socialist community had until recently
existed, on a model outlined by the Paine-influenced French socialist
Fourier. Evans's protégé began to draw together the radicals of the region.
In consultation with Greeley and Evans, he planned a radical new party
comprised of members of various older parties and movements. As congressional debates about whether to allow the expansion of slavery into
western states heated up, early in 1854, Bovay saw his opening. He called a
public meeting at the Congregational church in Ripon, where the crowd
adopted a resolution declaring that if the Whigs and Democrats in
Congress did not block the most controversial legislation, the Kansas-
Nebraska Act, from becoming law, then it would be time to "throw old
party organizations to the winds and organize a new party on the sole
issue of slavery." When Congress passed the act, Bovay and sixteen of the
most committed radicals gathered in a local school and agreed to create a
new party that would be called "Republican," in reflection of George
Evans's advocacy of almost a decade earlier and with hopes that a name
linked to Paine and Jefferson would identify the new party as uniquely
American.

Hailed by Greeley as the launch of a new movement that would change
not just the politics of the nation but the nation itself, by uniting the
struggle to free southern slaves from bondage and northern workers from
"wage slavery," the early Republican Party invariably linked the themes.
Reflecting on Bovay's outsized contribution to the shaping of the Grand

Old Party—he is credited even today in the US Senate Republican Conference's history of the GOP: "Bovay named the party Republican
because it was synonymous with equality." Historian John R. Commons
would write in his classic essay on "the working-class origins of the
Republican Party" that: "Whether (Bovay) was the only father of the
party or not, it is significant that it was these early views on the natural
right to land, derived from Evans and the workingmen, that appeared in
the Republican party wherever that party sprang into being." And it did
indeed spring up across the northern US, winning within months of
its founding key statewide and congressional elections that were fought
with the slogan: "Free Soil, Free Labor, Free Speech, Free Men." By 1856,
when the name of its presidential candidate, John C. Fremont, allowed
for a convenient extension of the slogan—"… and Fremont"—the party
would carry eleven states, setting the stage for the election in 1860 of
Lincoln, who like other radicals of his time had begun reading and mem-
orizing Paine's books as a young man in New Salem, Illinois. Lincoln's
law partner, W. H. Herndon, recalled that "Paine became a part of Mr.
Lincoln from 1834 to the end of his life." The sixteenth president's biographer, Carl Sandburg, would observe with regard to Paine: "In
philosophy, no other writer of the eighteenth century, with the exception
of Jefferson, parallels more closely the temper and gist of Lincoln's later
thought." Even as the *New York Times* was dismissing the author of
Common Sense as the tribune of a dangerous "Red Republicanism,"
Lincoln would declare: "I never tire of reading Paine."

Sixty years later, Eugene Victor Debs, who quoted the first Republican
president at least as frequently as he did Paine, would celebrate (and
perhaps exaggerate) the Illinoisan's radicalism by declaring: "Lincoln was
a revolutionary, now he is defied." As he prepared to launch his last
campaign for the presidency on the Socialist ticket, Debs reflected:
"Lincoln would not belong to the Republican Party of today any more
than Thomas Jefferson would consent to become a member of the Democratic Party now in the saddle." While he dismissed both major parties as
"wings of the same bird of prey," Debs in particular bemoaned the turn
toward economic conservatism by the party of Lincoln. "The Republican
Party was once red," declared Debs, recalling the history of how Evans,
Greeley, Bovay and others had forged a radical Paineite party in the

middle of the previous century. Now, "the many socialist Paineites" of a new century had their own party. And when their popular leader was prosecuted for exercising his freedom of speech in a time of war—and condemned for identifying himself as an internationalist when nationalism was all the rage—Eugene Victor Debs rejected the notion that he was at odds with America.

Yes, Debs acknowledged, without apology or the caution of a man facing a long prison term: he was a critic of the military and economic policies that a ruling class had imposed upon America. Yes, he proposed to change these policies in order to transform America. Yes, he believed that he had much in common with radicals in other lands. But these were not imported ideas, not a "foreign disease" contracted from afar, as Glenn Beck might imagine. These were, Debs explained to his prosecutors, American ideals expressed long ago by the pamphleteer whose words George Washington ordered read at Valley Forge to the soldiers of a revolutionary army. Further,

> It is because I happen to be in this minority that I stand in your presence today, charged with crime. It is because I believe, as the revolutionary fathers believed in their day, that a change was due in the interests of the people, that the time had come for a better form of government, an improved system, a higher social order, a nobler humanity and a grander civilization. This minority that is so much misunderstood and so bitterly maligned, is in alliance with the forces of evolution, and as certain as I stand before you this afternoon, it is but a question of time until this minority will become the conquering majority and inaugurate the greatest change in all of the history of the world. You may hasten the change; you may retard it; you can no more prevent it than you can prevent the coming of the sunrise on the morrow.
>
> My friend, the assistant prosecutor, doesn't like what I had to say in my speech about internationalism. What is there objectionable to internationalism? If we had internationalism there would be no war. I believe in patriotism. I have never uttered a word against the flag. I love the flag as a symbol of freedom. I object only when that flag is prostituted to base purposes, to sordid ends, by those who, in the name of patriotism, would keep the people in subjection.
>
> I believe, however, in a wider patriotism. Thomas Paine said, "My country is the world. To do good is my religion."

CHAPTER THREE

Reading Marx with Abraham Lincoln: Utopian Socialists, German Communists and Other Republicans

These capitalists generally act harmoniously and in concert, to fleece the people …

—Abraham Lincoln, from his first speech
as an Illinois state legislator, 1837

Everyone now is more or less a Socialist.

—Charles Dana, managing editor of *New York Tribune*,
and Lincoln's Assistant Secretary of War, 1848

The workingmen of Europe feel sure that, as the American War of Independence initiated a new era of ascendancy for the middle class, so the American Antislavery War will do for the working classes. They consider it an earnest of the epoch to come that it fell to the lot of Abraham Lincoln, the single-minded son of the working class, to lead his country through the matchless struggle for the rescue of an enchained race and the reconstruction of a social world.

—Karl Marx and the First International Workingmen's
Association to Lincoln, 1864

On December 3, 1861, a former one-term congressman, who had spent most of the past dozen years studying dissident economic theories, mounting challenges to the existing political order and proposing ever more radical responses to the American crisis, delivered his first State of the Union address as the sixteenth president of the United States.

Since assuming office eight months earlier, this new president had struggled, without success, first to restore the severed bonds of the Union and then to avert a wrenching civil war. Now, eleven southern slave states were in open and violent rebellion against the government he led.

His inaugural address of the previous spring had closed with a poignant reflection on the prospect of eventual peace, imagining a day when the Union might again be touched "by the better angels of our nature." But, now, in the last month of what Walt Whitman would recall as America's "sad, distracted year"—"Year that suddenly sang by the mouths of the round-lipp'd cannons"—the better angels seemed to have deserted the continent. Every effort to restore the republic had been thwarted. There was no room for accommodation with the Confederate States of America. Fort Sumter had been fired upon and the flag of southern rebellion now flew above Charleston Harbor. Virginia, the cradle of presidents, the state of Washington, Jefferson and Madison, had joined the revolt and assembled a capital of the Confederacy less than 100 miles from Washington. Hundreds of Union and Confederate soldiers had died, with thousands more wounded at the First Battle of Bull Run. Armies had been reorganized and generals replaced with the recognition that this was no skirmish. This was a protracted war which would eventually force all Americans to "[throw] off the costumes of peace with [an] indifferent hand."

In the presence of the remaining congressmen and senators who filled only a portion of the seats in the Capitol chamber on that December day, the new president knew that he needed to address the circumstance of a nation that was no longer in any sense united. He did so as an agitated, angered American who spoke no more of angels and instead bemoaned "the disloyal citizens of the United States who have offered the ruin of our country ..." He warned, ominously, of how "A nation which endures factious domestic division is exposed to disrespect abroad, and ... is sure sooner or later to invoke foreign intervention." He fretted about a strained federal budget, expressing hope "that the expenditures made necessary by the rebellion are not beyond the resources of the loyal people." He noted that three vacancies would need to be filled on a suddenly abandoned Supreme Court and observed that "one of the unavoidable consequences of the present insurrection is the entire suppression in many places of all the ordinary means of administering civil justice by the officers and in the forms of existing law."

This was a wartime State of the Union address delivered not so much by a president as a commander-in-chief. Its purpose was to rally what remained of the House and Senate—after the exodus of the southern Solons who had joined a mutiny against the elected government—and to portray the struggle as not merely one for the preservation of a system of governance but for democracy itself. "It continues to develop that the insurrection is largely, if not exclusively, a war upon the first principle of popular government—the rights of the people," declared the solemn speaker. "Conclusive evidence of this is found in the most grave and maturely considered public documents, as well as in the general tone of the insurgents. In those documents we find the abridgment of the existing right of suffrage and the denial to the people of all right to participate in the selection of public officers except the legislative boldly advocated, with labored arguments to prove that large control of the people in government is the source of all political evil. Monarchy itself is sometimes hinted at as a possible refuge from the power of the people."

These were the words that might have ended the address, had the president not begged the pardon of his listeners to add: "In my present position, I could scarcely be justified were I to omit raising a warning voice against this approach of returning despotism."

There was something more that Lincoln wanted to say to America. He needed to speak of another division, another struggle. The man who so carefully chose his words did not relinquish the podium before devoting "brief attention" to his fears regarding "the effort to place capital on an equal footing with, if not above, labor in the structure of government."

Amid all the turbulence of a burgeoning Civil War, Abraham Lincoln wanted it to be known that he was unsettled by the rising assumption "that labor is available only in connection with capital; that nobody labors unless somebody else, owning capital, somehow by the use of it induces him to labor. This assumed, it is next considered whether it is best that capital shall hire laborers, and thus induce them to work by their own consent, or buy them and drive them to it without their consent. Having proceeded so far, it is naturally concluded that all laborers are either hired laborers or what we call slaves. And further, it is assumed that whoever is once a hired laborer is fixed in that condition for life."

That false construct could not be allowed to take hold in a free country, argued the president. It must be understood, he concluded: "Labor is prior to and independent of capital. Capital is only the fruit of labor, and could never have existed if labor had not first existed. Labor is the superior of capital, and deserves much the higher consideration."

To be sure, Lincoln related this observation to the wrenching questions posed by the Civil War. "A few men own capital, and that few avoid labor themselves, and with their capital hire or *buy* another few to labor for them. A large majority belong to neither class—neither work for others nor have others working for them. In most of the Southern States a majority of the whole people of all colors are neither slaves nor masters, while in the Northern a large majority are neither hirers nor hired."

But Lincoln was speaking now of a broader concern: his fear that the few who were possessed of capital might, in a time of turbulence, seek to bend the rule of law—diminishing the historic respect for the rights of man outlined by Lincoln's hero Tom Paine in order to favor their interests above those of the great many Americans who toiled for wages, or the fees paid farmers. "No men living are more worthy to be trusted than those who toil up from poverty; none less inclined to take or touch aught which they have not honestly earned," the president warned. "Let them beware of surrendering a political power which they already possess, and which if surrendered will surely be used to close the door of advancement against such as they, and to fix new disabilities and burdens upon them till all of liberty shall be lost."

Lincoln's insistence that labor guard against the surrender of political power to capital—a point he began to outline before his presidency and would repeat throughout his tenure—is rarely afforded the attention paid to his rhetoric regarding the state of "a house divided against itself," "the proposition that all men are created equal" or the faint hope that: "Government of the people, by the people, for the people, shall not perish from the Earth."

Yet, how can we neglect the words that this most instructive of presidents chose to insert in so critical a commentary as his first State of the Union address?

How can we fail to recognize the echoes of a language which scholars of economic, social and political rhetoric might associate less with the sixteenth president than with one of his contemporaries: a Prussian-born son of the Enlightenment, who was causing a stir on both sides of the Atlantic at precisely the moment when Lincoln was casting about for a language to describe the economic forces that were carrying America from its agrarian roots to its industrial future?

Didn't Karl Marx take an interest in the relation of labor and capital? Was it not the co-author of *Das Manifest der Kommunistischen Partei* who observed that: "the essential condition of capital is wage-labor"? And that: "Capitalist production, therefore, develops technology, and the combining together of various processes into a social whole, only by sapping the original sources of all wealth—the soil and the laborer"?

Well, there can surely be no connection, no tangible link between Abraham Lincoln, the log cabin–born, rail-splitting, archetypal nineteenth-century American and founding Republican, and Karl Marx, the bearded, brooding, archetypal "European" and proud socialist plotter.

Unless, of course, we bother to examine the tattered copies of the American outlet for Marx's revolutionary preachments during the period when Lincoln was preparing to leave the political wilderness and make his march to the presidency. That journal, the *New York Tribune*, was the most consistently influential of nineteenth-century American newspapers. Indeed, this was the newspaper that engineered the unexpected and in many ways counter-intuitive delivery of the Republican nomination for president, in that most critical year of 1860, to an Illinoisan who just two years earlier had lost the competition for a home-state US Senate seat. The *Tribune* is remembered, correctly, as the great Republican paper of the day. It argued against slavery in the south. But it argued as well, with words parallel to Lincoln's in that first address to the Congress, that: "Our idea is that Labor needs not to *combat* but to *command* Capital."

Seven years before he and Lincoln served together in the Congress (during each man's sole term in the US House) Horace Greeley—or "Friend Greeley," as Lincoln referred to the editor in their correspondence—began the *Tribune* with a stated purpose: "to serve the republic with an honest and fearless criticism." He succeeded, more wholly than any American editor before or after his transit of the mid-nineteenth century, in creating a newspaper that was not merely a newspaper. Greeley's nationally-circulated *Tribune* was, as Clarence Darrow aptly remembered it, "the political and social Bible" of every reforming, radical and Republican household. The *Tribune* was surely that for Lincoln, whose engagement with the paper would last the better part of a quarter-century and eventually extend to wrangling with Greeley about the proper moment at which to issue the Emancipation Proclamation. Lincoln's involvement was not just with Greeley but with his sub-editors and writers, so much so that the first Republican president appointed one of Greeley's most radical lieutenants—the Fourier- and Proudhon-inspired socialist and longtime editor of Marx's European correspondence, Charles Dana—as his Assistant Secretary of War.

Greeley's newspaper was the *Tribune* of the agitation that spawned the Republican Party and its successful presidential campaign of 1860. Lincoln would say of the editor: "every one of his words seems to weigh about a ton."

This was as Greeley, an epic figure of American journalism, a political and social reformer who reveled in his ability not merely to report upon but to bend the arc of history, intended it.

After learning the printer's trade at the *Northern Star* in tiny Poultney, Vermont, Greeley arrived in New York in 1831, during the period when Fanny Wright and her allies were forging explicitly socialist political parties and movements in the city. Greeley came both to make his fortune—and that he did—and to steer the political progress of a young nation. William Seward, the radical Republican whose presidential ambitions were thwarted when Greeley switched his allegiance to Lincoln, celebrated the young newspaper editor as a Whitman-esque figure: "rather unmindful of social usages, yet singularly clear, original, and decided, in his political views and theories."

Greeley was what the British refer to as a "campaigning editor." He started newspapers as platforms to promote ideas—for example, the *Jeffersonian* was established to advance Seward's successful Whig Party challenge to conservative Democratic Governor William Marcy, a hack of the highest order who preached the patronage gospel of "to the victor belong the spoils." Two years later Greeley would edit a national newspaper, the *Log Cabin*, as the campaign journal of another Whig, William Henry Harrison, who would win and briefly hold the presidency.

With the *Tribune*, however, Greeley would no longer crusade for candidates—although he certainly had his favorites—but for a set of ideals that would come to define the Whig Party, to which he and Lincoln remained in many senses true loyalists. When the Whigs failed to effectively confront issues of slavery, urbanization and economic transition, however, the *Tribune* became the prime proponent of a new and more radical political constellation that took as its name the word used to describe proponents of the "constructive treason" that began with a rejection of "the divine right of kings" and with it of the favored position of the propertied classes: "Republican."

"It has been urged as an objection to *The Tribune* that it proposed to 'give hospitality to every new thought.' To that profession we shall be constant, at whatever sacrifice," Greeley wrote when the paper's radicalism began to shake some political foundations in the mid-1840s. "Full of error and suffering as the world yet is, we cannot afford to reject unexamined any idea which proposes to improve the moral, intellectual, or social condition of mankind."

Greeley practiced an advocacy journalism that was not cautious about taking sides in the great debates of his day. His first editorial duty, he explained, was to keep "an ear open to the plaints of the wronged and suffering, though they can never repay advocacy, and those who mainly support newspapers will be annoyed and often exposed by it; a heart as sensitive to oppression and degradation in the next street as if they were practiced in Brazil or Japan; a pen as ready to expose and reprove the crimes whereby wealth is amassed and luxury enjoyed in our own country as if they had only been committed by Turks or Pagans in Asia some centuries ago."

That final reference to reproving "the crimes whereby wealth is amassed and luxury enjoyed" might not meet with the applause of the trickle-down economists and laissez-faire fabulists who today guide the policies of what has become of Greeley's Republican Party. But Greeley would never have recognized today's so-called "Republicans" as heirs to the party he and his comrades forged.

Greeley welcomed the disapproval of those who championed free markets over the interests of the working class, a class he recognized as including both the oppressed slaves of the south and the degraded industrial laborers of the north. In a memorial column that the *Tribune* published after his death in 1872—at the close of the editor's quixotic "Liberal Republican" presidential campaign—it was recalled of Greeley:

> If there was any special class of whom this plain man was the champion, for whom he used all his skill, and his zeal, and influence, it was the class of the poor and the oppressed and the forsaken, of those who were abused and outraged by their fellow men. ... [The] sober verdict of history will be that no single man did so much for the overthrow of human bondage in this land as the editor of *The New York Tribune*. If he did not lay his ax so unsparingly to the root of the tree as some other of the reformers, he destroyed it quite as effectually by steadily hacking away its limbs and tendrils, and ruining so its inner life. That he wished and longed for its destruction, who ever dared to doubt? That he was the enemy of every form of social wrong and iniquity, who ever doubted?
>
> You cannot imagine this man palliating or tolerating any custom or traffic which degrades or imbrutes or depraves men. Not to one, but to many, moral reforms his time and heart were given. To education, thorough and universal; to sobriety, in eating not less than in drinking; to cleanliness, with him very near to godliness; to humanity, for beasts not less than for men; to free homes for emigrants; to cordial welcome of exiles from other lands, seeking refuge on these shores; to the liberation of all oppressed and struggling peoples. When was his word of cheer and sympathy wanting? With the weak against the strong, with the abandoned ones, his heart went, and he would give to these more than justice. This made him the friend of Hungarians and Poles and Irishmen, and the defender even of the Pagans against Christians. When the weak and the needy called, he did not stop to ask whether these shared his political or his religious creed, or what his race or his party would gain in befriending them. He obeyed the Divine call, and not seldom was made half a martyr in obedience to his instinct of compassion. His fame for wisdom suffered in the promptness of his sympathetic zeal.

Greeley's sympathetic zeal was that of a distinct breed of nineteenth-century social reformer, who was not satisfied merely with the repair of the breach created when the founders of the American experiment failed to keep faith with their initial recognition of the self-evident truth "that all men are created equal, that they are endowed by their Creator with certain unalienable Rights, that among these are Life, Liberty and the pursuit of Happiness." He was profoundly concerned, as was Lincoln, with the question of how to maintain a measure of economic equality in a time of unprecedented and overwhelming accumulation of wealth—not merely by southern planters but by northern bankers and business-men. These concerns led him to embrace the teachings of Charles Fourier, the French utopian socialist who complained: "Once upon a time people talked about the infallibility of the pope; today it is that of the merchant which they wish to establish." In Fourier's view, the promise of equality was an idle one unless it was coupled with economic protections for the great mass of working men and women. The French socialist held:

> Equality of rights is another chimera, praiseworthy when considered in the abstract and ridiculous from the standpoint of the means employed to introduce it in civilization. The first right of men is the right to work and the right to a minimum [income]. This is precisely what has gone unrec-ognized in all the constitutions. Their primary concern is with favored individuals who are not in need of work.

Fourier's writing was popularized in the United States by Albert Brisbane, an American who traveled to France in the 1820s, studied with the philos-opher and then returned to the US to spread the socialist gospel. He found a comrade in Greeley, who referred to Fourier's views in the *Log Cabin* and championed them in the *Tribune*. Greeley made Brisbane a columnist for the paper and, when the new journal was attacked for spreading such radical views, the editor wrote: "Do not stand there quar-reling with those who have devised or adopted a scheme which you consider absurd or impracticable, but take hold and devise something better. For, be assured, friend! that this generation will not, must not pass without the discovery and adoption of some method whereby the Right to Labor and to receive and enjoy the honest reward of such labor, shall be secured to the poorest and least fortunate of our people."

In the mid-1840s, explains historian Roy Marvin Robbins, "Greeley preached a new order of society with Brisbane's socialistic ideas as its basis." Even as the utopian ideals of Fourierism proved difficult to realize in practical form—despite the best efforts of social reformers such as Brisbane and his compatriot Bronson Alcott—Greeley evolved his own advocacy and that of the *Tribune* to champion land reforms that combined elements of Fourier's socialism and the pioneering ideal. Greeley's famous line "Go west, young man" was the practical expression of a broader vision of distributing open and unsettled land to the poor—even if, at the same time, it shamefully disregarded the Native Americans of the western lands, who both the editor and Lincoln failed to ever fully or even adequately respect or protect.

Attacked by a rival newspaperman in James Watson Webb's *Courier and Express*—which journalist and historian Francis Brown describes as "a Wall Street paper" that "catered to mercantile interests, to finance, and to shipping, and editorially … voiced the conservative views of the merchant class"—on grounds that he was a "Fourierist, an Agrarian, and an Infidel," Greeley replied:

> We admit and insist on the legal right of the owner of wild lands to keep them uninhabited forever, but we do not consider it morally right that he should do so when land becomes scarce and subsistence for the landless scanty and precarious … yes … something will be done, in spite of any stupid clamor that can be raised about "Infidelity" and "Agrarianism," to secure future generations against the faithful evils of Monopoly of Land by the few.

The boldness of Greeley's stances won him a good deal of personal popularity among the radical Whigs of New York and the champions of the nascent "Free Soil" movement, which Greeley urged to "secure to each and all … a really Free Soil!—especially free from the hated speculators." In a 1848 special election, he was sent to Congress as a representative from New York. Greeley served for only a few months, but he used his time in the House to propose and promote an early version of the Homestead Act. Challenged by a western conservative to explain why an urban member was so interested in freeing up rural land for settlement, Greeley countered that he "represented more landless men than any other member" of the Congress. A good line, but unlikely to please a chamber that did not share the editor's radicalism. One of his few allies was the young first-term Whig congressman from Illinois, who Greeley recalled as a comrade with whom he "agreed on the slavery issue as one which must be answered permanently in the course of a few years." The two men spoke on a daily basis during their joint tenure in the nation's capital and formed a bond that would last until Lincoln's assassination seventeen years later.

It was not mere personal acquaintance that linked Greeley and Lincoln, however. By 1848, Greeley's *Tribune* was already a journalistic and political phenomenon. "Acknowledged the most influential Whig editor in 1844, [Greeley] had by 1850 become the most influential anti-slavery editor—the spokesman not of Whigs merely but of a great class of Northerners who were thoroughly antagonistic to slavery," recalls Frank W. Scott in his study of nineteenth-century American newspapers. As the slavery issue came to a head, the *Tribune*'s influence grew so that it became not just a popular newspaper in New York City but a widely-circulated national journal of opinion, distinguished by what Scott characterizes as "some of the most vigorous and trenchant editorial writing America has ever known." In the early 1850s, the circulation of the *Tribune*'s weekly national edition nearly tripled to more than 110,000 copies as it became what another historian, James Ford Rhodes, described as "pre-eminently the journal of the rural districts, [where] one copy did service for many readers. To the people in the Adirondack wilderness it was a political bible, and the well-known scarcity of Democrats there was attributed to it. Yet it was as freely read by the intelligent people living on the Western Reserve of Ohio"—not to mention in Abraham Lincoln's Illinois.

By the late 1850s, the weekly *Tribune*'s Illinois circulation was close to 20,000, making the New York-based journal one of the midwestern state's most widely circulated newspapers. There is no debate that Lincoln was among the most avid of the *Tribune*'s Illinois readers. His correspondence with Greeley confirms this passionate relationship with the paper, as does his more extensive correspondence with his third and last law partner, William Herndon, in which Lincoln would sometimes complain that Greeley's newspaper was not being supportive enough of his political ambitions. It was in one of these fretful notes that Lincoln first expressed the view that "every one of [Greeley's] words seems to weigh about a ton."

Lincoln did not merely consume Greeley's words, however. He devoured the whole of his weekly *Tribune*, as he did every other newspaper he could get his hands on. "What Lincoln really liked to read were newspapers, reading them, a friend said, 'more than books,'" writes Lincoln biographer John C. Waugh. "Another friend said he 'never saw a man better pleased' than when Lincoln was appointed postmaster, because he could read [newspapers from around the country] before delivering them to their subscribers."

In his period of deepest inquiry, the five years after his 1848 departure from Congress as a disappointed Whig and before his return to the political hustings as a champion of what would become the Republican Party, Lincoln devoted himself to examining, debating and ruminating on the reports in the national newspapers that were delivered to his Springfield law office—especially Greeley's *Tribune*. Keenly aware of the rising tide of liberal, radical and socialist reform movements in Europe, a tide that would peak—at least for a time—in the "revolutionary wave" of 1848 and its aftermath, the young congressman joined other American Whigs in following the development of that year's "Springtime of the Peoples," which saw uprisings against monarchy and entrenched economic, social and political power in Germany, France, Hungary, Denmark and other European nations. For Lincoln, however, this was not a new interest.

Long before 1848, German radicals had begun to arrive in Illinois, where they quickly entered into the legal and political circles in which Lincoln traveled. One of them, Gustav Korner, was a student revolutionary at the University of Munich who had been imprisoned by German authorities in the early 1830s for organizing illegal demonstrations. After his release, Korner returned to his hometown of Frankfurt am Main where, according to historian Raymond Lohne, "he was one of about fifty conspirators involved in an attack upon the two main city guardhouses and the arsenal at the police facility and jail. This admixture of students and soldiers had planned to seize cannon, muskets, and ammunition; free political prisoners accused of breaking press-censorship laws, and begin ringing the great *Sturmglocke* (storm bell) of the Dom, the signal for the people to come in from the countryside. At that point, the democratic revolution would be announced ... Unfortunately, they were walking into a trap ... Betrayed by both a spy in their midst, and the reluctance of the common people to rise, nine students were killed, twenty-four were seriously wounded, and by August 3, 1833, Gustav Körner found himself riding into downtown Belleville, Illinois."

Within a decade, Korner would pass the Illinois bar, win election to the legislature and be appointed to the state Supreme Court. Korner and Lincoln formed an alliance that would become so close that the student revolutionary from Frankfurt would eventually be one of seven personal delegates-at-large named by Lincoln to serve at the critical Republican State Convention in May 1860, which propelled the Springfield lawyer into that year's presidential race. Through Korner, Lincoln met and befriended many of the German radicals who, after the failure of the 1848 revolution, fled to Illinois and neighboring Wisconsin. Along with Korner on Lincoln's list of personal delegates-at-large to the 1860 convention was Friedrich Karl Franz Hecker, a lawyer from Mannheim who had served as a liberal legislator in the lower chamber of the Baden State Assembly before leading an April 1848 uprising in the region—an uprising cheered on by the newspaper Marx briefly edited during that turbulent period, *Neue Rheinische Zeitung—Organ der Demokratie*.

Thwarted by military forces loyal to the old order, Hecker fled first to Switzerland and then to Illinois, where he would join Lincoln in forging the new Republican Party and become a key speaker on his American ally's behalf in the 1858 Senate race that is remembered for the Lincoln–Douglas debates. With a commission from Lincoln, Hecker served as a brigade commander in the Union Army during the Civil War, as did a number of other '48ers.

The failure of the 1848 revolts, and the brutal crackdowns that followed, led many leading European radicals to take refuge in the United States, and Lincoln's circle of supporters would eventually include some of Karl Marx's closest associates and intellectual sparring partners, including Joseph Weydemeyer and August Willich. Weydemeyer, who maintained a regular correspondence with Marx and Engels, soon formed a national network of Kommunisten Klubs to promote what the *New York Times* decried as "Red Republicanism." Weydemeyer then allied with the new Republican Party and the presidential campaign of Abraham Lincoln, who would at the start of the Civil War appoint the former Prussian military officer as a technical aide on the staff of General John C. Fremont—the 1856 Republican presidential nominee who became the commander of the Army's Department of the West. Later, Lincoln issued Weydemeyer a commission as a colonel of the Forty-first Infantry Missouri Volunteers, charging the German Marxist with the defense of St. Louis. Willich, known as "the Reddest of the Reds," was a leader of the left faction of the German Communist League, which decried Marx's relative caution when it came to revolutionary agitation. As a key commander of the radical Free Corps in the Baden-Palatinate uprising of 1849, Willich chose as his aide-de-camp a young Friedrich Engels. Forced to flee to the United States after the defeat of the uprising, Willich decamped to Cincinnati, where he became editor of the socialist *Republikaner* newspaper and backed the candidacies of Fremont in 1856 and Lincoln in 1860. At the outset of the Civil War, Willich recruited a regiment of German immigrants and became its first lieutenant, quickly rising to the rank of brigadier general and making a name for himself by having military bands play revolutionary songs such as the "Arbiter [Workers'] Marseillaise"—"A reveille for the new revolution! The new revolution!"

Lincoln did not merely invite the '48ers to join his campaigns, he became highly engaged with their causes. As Lohne notes, "Lincoln was paying attention to these revolutionaries." In his hometown of Springfield, the former congressman rallied support for revolutionary movements in Europe, particularly the Hungarian revolt of Lajos Kossuth. Lincoln's name led the list of signatories on calls for public meetings to discuss the Hungarian revolt that appeared in the *Illinois State Register* and the *Illinois Journal* in January 1852. A week later, Lincoln helped to pen a resolution declaring that: "we, the American people, cannot remain silent" about "the right of any people, sufficiently numerous for national independence, to throw off, to revolutionize, their existing form of government, and to establish such other in its stead as they may choose."

Lincoln's resolution argued:

That the sympathies of this country, and the benefits of its position, should be exerted in favor of the people of every nation struggling to be free; and whilst we meet to do honor to Kossuth and Hungary, we should not fail to pour out the tribute of our praise and approbation to the patriotic efforts of the Irish, the Germans and the French, who have unsuccessfully fought to establish in their several governments the supremacy of the people.

The proclamation even took a shot at the British Empire, resolving:

That there is nothing in the past history of the British government, or in its present expressed policy, to encourage the belief that she will aid, in any manner, in the delivery of continental Europe from the yoke of despotism; and that her treatment of Ireland, of O'Brien, Mitchell, and other worthy patriots, forces the conclusion that she will join her efforts to the despots of Europe in suppressing every effort of the people to establish free governments, based upon the principles of true religious and civil liberty.

What set Lincoln and his compatriots off?

There's no mystery.

The Illinois agitators had merely to open their weekly editions of Greeley's *Tribune*, which was declaring at the time that: "of the many popular leaders who were upheaved by the great convulsions of 1848 … the world has already definitely assigned the first rank to Louis Kossuth, advocate, deputy, finance minister, and finally governor of Hungary." The great historian of the *Tribune*'s ideological and political battles, Adam Tuchinsky, notes: "Louis Kossuth and the Central European national liberation movements remained familiar subjects in the pages of the paper"—so much so that conservative critics of the gazette objected to its "Kossuthism, Socialism, Abolitionism and forty other isms."

Greeley believed that 1848's European revolts and their aftermath revealed "boundless vistas" along with the outlines of the "uprising which must come." Predictably, his paper covered the revolutionary ferment of Europe with an intensity that made it virtually a local story for radicals in places like Springfield, Illinois. They pored over their copies of the *Tribune* for the latest from the front in what the paper's editor portrayed as a global struggle for "the larger liberty" of "The Rights and Interests of Labor, the Reorganization of Industry, the Elevation of the Working-Men, the Reconstruction of the Social Fabric."

The *Tribune* did not urge a "to-the-barricades" moment for the United States. Greeley and most of his editors still believed in the prospect of reform, although their frustration with the spread of the evil they referred to as "the slave power" would at times cause the paper's proprietor to ponder whether "revolution is the only resource left." Ultimately, however, what most excited Greeley and his readers about the stirrings of 1848 were the new and radical ideas that had emerged, and the mingling of those ideas with action that might lead to their implementation.

The *Tribune*'s European correspondent in the early stages of the period of uprisings, Henry Bornstein, admitted in his columns that he was "giddy" at the developments in France, Germany and other countries. "Every day comes fresh news, each thing more astonishing than the next," wrote Bornstein, who spiced his correspondence with exclamations such as: "Hurrah! How gaily it burns!" The *Tribune* was not just publishing news, Greeley announced; it wanted analysis, "to increase the aggregate of information afforded by our columns." Bornstein agreed, arguing: "Correspondents now have to talk about other topics besides political events because these topics are outdated. Now they have to provide the 'big picture' about what is going on in Europe. Explain the reason for events to supplement the dry telegraph reports."

Correspondent Bornstein, notes Tuchinsky, was "the paper's link to Karl Marx and a more class-conscious radicalism that would emerge in Europe during the 1848 revolutions and in their aftermath."

But Bornstein's "big picture" reporting style—which he would eventually bring to the United States as an astute observer of the Civil War—was only the start of the *Tribune*'s emergence as the primary source of detailed reporting on international events and ideas that would reshape the way American radicals and reformers thought about their own struggles, against slavery in particular and economic and social injustice in general. No longer satisfied with the pastoral reforms of Fourier and the romantic French communalists, the *Tribune* now considered more radical responses.

"Ultimately, 1848 would unearth an immense variety of French and European radical discourse; as a result, *The Tribune* diversified its coverage of socialist ideas," explains Tuchinsky. "But more than that, socialism itself became not simply a mode of reform but also, significantly, of explanation, a way to interpret events. Fourierism was a sectarian movement, and it failed, but along with the revolution it cleared the way for a new language and a new political mentality through which American progressive intellectuals perceived and critiqued their social and political world."

To understand and interpret that new language, Greeley dispatched a recent hire, Charles Dana, to Paris. An idealistic polymath, Dana had for several years in the mid-1840s been a central player in the Brook Farm Association for Industry and Education in West Roxbury, Massachusetts. A utopian experiment in communal living that sought to implement Fourier's ideals, Brook Farm counted among its residents, investors, supporters and allies Greeley, Nathaniel Hawthorne, the Alcotts and Ralph Waldo Emerson, who wrote of the prospect that residents might be "Fourierized or Christianized or humanized," with the observation that "in a day of small, sour, and fierce schemes, one is admonished and cheered by a project of such friendly aims, and of such bold and generous proportion; there is an intellectual courage and strength in it, which is superior and commanding: it certifies the presence of so much truth in the theory, and in so far is destined to be fact."

Dana sought to spread the "build-heaven-on-earth" gospel in the *Harbinger*, a journal edited by Brook Farm founder (and future *Tribune* literary editor) George Ripley, where the younger man's writing skills came to Greeley's attention. Impressed with the twenty-nine-year-old wordsmith's intellect and style—and also, perhaps, by the fact that the *Harbinger* hailed the "indomitable *Tribune*" as the nation's great newspaper—Greeley began grooming Dana to be the *Tribune*'s managing editor. But the protégé had grander goals. "Dana longed to travel to Europe. More than that, like most members of the *Tribune*'s socialist circle, Dana viewed the European revolutions as a historical turning point and he was anxious to witness them firsthand," observes Tuchinsky. In particular, he was looking for new notions that might propel the socialist discourse beyond the romantic "associationist" thinking of Fourier's followers. Along with Greeley, Dana had just a few years earlier hailed Fourier's ideas as the "last hope of Divine Providence" on earth; now, however, he was anticipating the moment when reformers and radicals would "yield to necessity" and recognize that the "harmonious" agrarian ideal must give way to the barnburner battle cry of "Free soil, free labor, free speech, free men."

Leaving New York in June 1848, Dana arrived in France just in time to race into the thick of the Parisian turmoil. He penned an immediate report that declared he was witnessing "a glorious chance to do something immortal." While the calculus of how the immortal leap might be made remained indefinite, the ideological impulse was, to Dana's view, certain. "Socialism is thus not conquered nor obscured in France by [the turmoil] but strengthened. It is no longer Fourierism, nor Communism, nor this nor that particular system which occupies the public mind of France, but it is the general idea of Social Rights and Social Reorganization. Everyone now is more or less a Socialist."

Dana's small-"c" catholic approach to the ideological divisions on the ground in Europe allowed him to sample freely from the different streams, to consult broadly and to keep American readers abreast of what seemed to the young writer to be a continent-wide struggle to throw off "the royalty of money … the aristocracy of capital." Still clinging to at least some of his Fourierist ideals, Dana inclined toward the libertarian socialist preachments of the French philosopher and parliamentarian Pierre-Joseph Proudhon, who argued for the establishment of workingmen's associations around a "revolutionary program" of "No more governments, no more conquests, no more international police, no more commercial privileges, no more colonial exclusions, no more control of one people by another, one State by another, no more strategic lines, no more fortresses …" In particular, Dana was inspired to turn the *Tribune*, which had traditionally been friendly toward trade unionism, into an even more explicit advocate for organized labor, arguing editorially that: "we see no other mode in which Labor can protect itself against the overwhelming power of Capital than by this very method of Combination." Lincoln, the voracious *Tribune* reader, would frequently express such sympathies, not merely in debates and State of the Union addresses but in direct communications to labor groups. To the New York Workingmen's Association, the sitting president would in 1864 observe: "The strongest bond of human sympathy, outside of the family relation, should be one uniting all working people, of all nations, and tongues, and kindreds."

But even as he was busy popularizing Proudhonist cures for the ailments of capital—especially the project of creating a popular bank ("banque du peuple") with the purpose of freeing up credit for workers and farmers—Dana was searching for new correspondents for Greeley's paper. In particular, he wanted to identify radical thinkers who could interpret for American readers not just the transitory developments in Germany, France, Holland or Hungary but also the social, economic and political currents that might resolve the great challenge that the *Tribune* outlined in an editorial of the era: "[While] no theorist has yet truly solved the great problem of the harmonious and beneficent combination of Labor, Skill and Capital, it is none the less palpable that the problem must be solved, and that Society fearfully suffers while awaiting the solution."

In this search for "alternative strains of socialist thought," Dana made his way to the city of Cologne, where a friend of Henry Wadsworth Longfellow, the poet Ferdinand Freiligrath, was working with a radical paper that intrigued the American visitor. The editor of the paper had recently co-authored a much-circulated German-language pamphlet, *Das Manifest der Kommunistischen Partei*, which argued: "The essential condition for the existence and rule of the bourgeois class is the accumulation of wealth in private hands, the formation and increase of capital; the essential condition of capital is wage-labor. Wage-labor rests entirely on the competition among the workers." To upset that condition, the writers had declared in February of 1848 for a "Communistic revolution" with the words: "The proletarians have nothing to lose but their chains. They have a world to win. Workers of the world, unite!"

The pamphlet would be translated two years later into English as *The Communist Manifesto*. The editor in question was, of course, Karl Marx, with whom Dana spent a midsummer day in the *Neue Rheinische Zeitung—Organ der Demokratie* office. Neither Dana nor Marx recorded the details of the meeting, although we are afforded a sense of the man the American writer encountered from a mutual acquaintance, Carl Schurz, the German editor and revolutionary who would flee to Wisconsin, help to form the Republican Party and return to Europe in 1861 as Abraham

Lincoln's ambassador to Spain. Visiting Marx during the same long, hot summer of 1848, Schurz observed "the recognized head of the advanced socialistic school. The somewhat thickset man, with his broad forehead, his very black hair and beard and his dark sparkling eyes. I have never seen a man whose bearing was so provoking and intolerable. To no opinion which differed from his, he accorded the honor of even a condescending consideration. Everyone who contradicted him he treated with abject contempt; every argument that he did not like he answered either with biting scorn at the unfathomable ignorance that had prompted it, or with opprobrious aspersions upon the motives of him who had advanced it. I remember most distinctly the cutting disdain with which he pronounced the word 'bourgeois' ..." Somehow, Dana and Marx connected. Indeed, they hit it off so famously that Dana would, according to Marx's biographer Francis Wheen, provide the philosopher with "the closest thing he ever had to a steady job."

That job was as one of the most frequently-published correspondents for the *New York Tribune*, with which Dana served a dozen years as managing editor. After Dana returned to New York to take up his new duties, he contacted Marx in London, where he had been forced to flee after German authorities shuttered the *Neue Rheinische Zeitung*, with an invitation to begin writing for the *Tribune*. And write Marx did. As Wheen notes, "*The Tribune* was by far the largest publisher of Marx's (and to a lesser extent, Engels's) work ... *The Tribune* articles take up nearly seven volumes of the fifty-volume collected works of Marx and Engels—more than *Capital*, more than any work published by Marx, alive or posthumously, in book form." The "singular collaboration" between Greeley's paper and Marx continued from the early 1850s until the time of Dana's departure to join Lincoln's White House staff. "During this period," according to historian William Harlan Hale's masterly examination of the relationship, "Europe's extremest radical, proscribed by the Prussian police and watched over by its agents abroad as a potential assassin of kings, sent in well over 500 separate contributions to the great New York family newspaper dedicated to the support of Henry Clay, Daniel Webster, temperance, dietary reform, Going West, and, ultimately, Abraham Lincoln." The official count of articles published by the *Tribune* under Marx's byline was 350, while Engels wrote 125 and the duo produced 12 together. But, as the philosopher himself noted, many more articles ended up running as the official line of the *Tribune*. "Of late, *The Tribune* has again been appropriating all my articles as leaders [unsigned editorials]," Marx complained in 1854.

Even if Marx did not always get the credit he thought he deserved (and what ink-stained wretch does?), Dana was unstinting in his praise. "It may perhaps give you pleasure to know that [the articles] are read with satisfaction by a considerable number of persons and are widely reproduced," the editor wrote Marx, describing the correspondent as "not only one of the most highly valued, but one of the best-paid contributors attached to the newspaper."

Greeley and Dana were so excited about Marx's contributions, in fact, that they showcased the German's first article in the paper's newly expanded Saturday edition on October 25, 1851. An editorial announced that among the "articles from … foreign contributors that are especially worthy of attention [was a rumination] upon Germany by one of the clearest and most vigorous writers that country has produced—no matter what may be the judgment of the critical upon his public opinions in the sphere of political and social philosophy."

The "worthy" article, "Revolution and Counter-Revolution," appeared over the byline "Karl Marx" (even though it was actually a collaboration written largely by Engels). The language was, well, Marxist:

> The first act of the revolutionary drama on the continent of Europe has closed. The "powers that were" before the hurricane of 1848 are again the "powers that be," and the more or less popular rulers of a day, provisional governors, triumvirs, dictators with their tail of representatives, civil commissioners, military commissioners, prefects, judges, generals, officers, and soldiers, are thrown upon foreign shores, and "transported beyond the seas" to England or America, there to form new governments *in partibus infidelium*, European committees, central committees, national committees, and to announce their advent with proclamations quite as solemn as those of any less imaginary potentates.
>
> A more signal defeat than that undergone by the continental revolutionary party—or rather parties—upon all points of the line of battle, cannot be imagined. But what of that? Has not the struggle of the British middle classes for their social and political supremacy embraced forty-

eight, that of the French middle classes forty years of unexampled struggles? And was their triumph ever nearer than at the very moment when restored monarchy thought itself more firmly settled than ever? The times of that superstition which attributed revolutions to the ill-will of a few agitators have long passed away. Everyone knows nowadays that wherever there is a revolutionary convulsion, there must be some social want in the background, which is prevented, by outworn institutions, from satisfying itself. The want may not yet be felt as strongly, as generally, as might ensure immediate success; but every attempt at forcible repression will only bring it forth stronger and stronger, until it bursts its fetters. If, then, we have been beaten, we have nothing else to do but to begin again from the beginning. And, fortunately, the probably very short interval of rest which is allowed us between the close of the first and the beginning of the second act of the movement, gives us time for a very necessary piece of work: the study of the causes that necessitated both the late outbreak and its defeat; causes that are not to be sought for in the accidental efforts, talents, faults, errors, or treacheries of some of the leaders, but in the general social state and conditions of existence of each of the convulsed nations.

It happened that Marx's article appeared at a time of "beginning again from the beginning" for a great many American radicals. The Whig Party, with which Greeley, Lincoln and compatriots of like mind had aligned themselves, was collapsing under the weight of its internal divisions between those who believed in aggressively confronting the spread of the "slave power" and more cautious reformers. Lincoln, who with Greeley had left the Congress in 1849, was practicing law in Springfield and on "the circuit" of county courthouses in Illinois. But he had not left politics behind. William Herndon observed years later that his law partner was in the early years of the 1850s "like a sleeping lion ... waiting for the people to call." Biographer John Waugh writes of a future president who "with this tightly-disciplined, deeply honed mind he read what he really considered important—newspapers. Now, on the circuit, out of politics, he was reading newspapers more than anything else, reading them aloud, carefully following the rise and drift of political sentiment over the divisive issue of slavery—reading them more closely, [fellow lawyer] Henry Whitney thought, than anybody he knew."

Slavery was an omnipresent issue, but surely not the only issue for Lincoln, whose circle of close compatriots now included a number of the radical '48ers who had turned Wisconsin, Illinois and Missouri into new hubs of agitation. Lincoln watched international developments with frustration following the setbacks of the late 1840s and early 1850s, bemoaning in a letter to Herndon his sense that: "The world is dead to hope, deaf to its own death struggle made known by a universal cry. What is to be done? Is anything to be done? Who can do anything and how can it be done? Did you ever think on these things?"

While studies of Lincoln place appropriate focus on his domestic engagements, there has been far too little attention paid to his global interests, especially during the period "in the wilderness" between the end of his congressional term and his return to the political stage. Yet, there can be no doubt that the future president was conscious of and highly engaged with developments in foreign lands—thanks no doubt to his close reading of the *Tribune* and its most prominent European correspondent—or that the future president made connections between what he read of distant divisions and what he thought about developments at home. Eulogizing his political hero Henry Clay in 1852, Lincoln would make frequent reference to Clay's international interests and involvements, declaring: "Mr. Clay's efforts in behalf of the South Americans, and afterwards, in behalf of the Greeks, in the times of their respective struggles for civil liberty are among the finest on record, upon the noblest of all themes; and bear ample corroboration of what I have said was his ruling passion—a love of liberty and right, unselfishly, and for their own sakes." Lincoln invoked the struggles of the European revolutionaries and denounced "oppression of any of its forms ... crowned-kings, money-kings, and land-kings." He dismissed the rhetoric of his arch-rival, Illinois Senator Stephen Douglas, finding it "as bombastic and hollow as Napoleon's bulletins sent back from his campaign in Russia." And when Douglas compromised on the issue of allowing the spread of slavery to new territories, he declared: "Equality in society alike beats inequality, whether the latter be of the British aristocratic sort or of the domestic slavery sort."

Lincoln was arguably at his most radical when he penned those words in 1854. The man whose law partner described him as "always calculating, and always planning" would grow more circumspect as he proceeded from the political backwater of Springfield to the podium at New York's Cooper Union and the prospect of the presidency. In the immediate aftermath of Douglas's betrayal, however, Lincoln's language bore the distinct accent of Greeley's *Tribune* and its most radical writers.

When Lincoln emerged in 1854 from his self-imposed political exile, it was with the intention of doing electoral battle not just with slavery but with those who stood in the way of the free soil and free labor movements the *Tribune* had popularized. "Free labor has the inspiration of hope; pure slavery has no hope," declared the future president in one of his frequent linkages of ideological mantras. As he returned to politics, initially as a campaigner for old Whigs and new Republicans, and then as a contender in his own right for the Senate, Lincoln echoed the ideals and language of the era's fresh and determined radicalism. This is not to say that he embraced all the views of the *Tribune*'s European correspondent; he was never so bold as to argue, in the way that Marx would in *Capital*— a book that borrowed liberally from his writings for the *Tribune*—that: "In the United States of North America, every independent movement of the workers was paralyzed so long as slavery disfigured a part of the Republic. Labor cannot emancipate itself in the white skin where in the black it is branded."

But, now "primed" by what his biographer Waugh describes as "all of his newspaper reading ... all of his study and thinking and analyzing for all those five cheerless politically deprived years," Lincoln recognized that the most radical promise of America's founding—that "all men are created equal"—was being destroyed in a manner that would thwart progress not merely for black slaves, but for white workers and farmers who sought their own freedoms. In his remarkable letter of August 15, 1855, to former Kentucky Congressman George Robertson, a compatriot of Henry Clay and champion of the old-school Whig hope that slavery would gradually be abandoned, the forty-six-year-old Illinoisan would bemoan the dying of the Founders' faith. Recalling an address delivered decades earlier by Robertson, Lincoln wrote:

You are not a friend of slavery in the abstract. In that speech you spoke of "the peaceful extinction of slavery" and used other expressions indicating your belief that the thing was, at some time, to have an end[.] Since then we have had thirty-six years of experience; and this experience has demonstrated, I think, that there is no peaceful extinction of slavery in prospect for us. The signal failure of Henry Clay, and other good and great men, in 1849, to effect any thing in favor of gradual emancipation in Kentucky, together with a thousand other signs, extinguishes that hope utterly. On the question of liberty, as a principle, we are not what we have been. When we were the political slaves of King George, and wanted to be free, we called the maxim that "all men are created equal" a self-evident truth; but now when we have grown fat, and have lost all dread of being slaves ourselves, we have become so greedy to be masters that we call the same maxim "a self-evident lie." The fourth of July has not quite dwindled away; it is still a great day—for burning fire-crackers!!!

That spirit which desired the peaceful extinction of slavery, has itself become extinct, with the occasion, and the men of the Revolution. Under the impulse of that occasion, nearly half the states adopted systems of emancipation at once; and it is a significant fact, that not a single state has done the like since. So far as peaceful, voluntary emancipation is concerned, the condition of the negro slave in America, scarcely less terrible to the contemplation of a free mind, is now as fixed, and hopeless of change for the better, as that of the lost souls of the finally impenitent. The Autocrat of all the Russias will resign his crown, and proclaim his subjects free republicans sooner than will our American masters voluntarily give up their slaves.

The letter to Robertson was composed during a period in which Lincoln was arguing to his law partner, William Herndon, that: "The day of compromise has passed. These two great ideas (slavery and freedom) have been kept apart only by artful means. They are like two wild beasts in sight of each other, but chained and apart. Some day these deadly antagonists will one of the other break their bonds, and then the question will be settled."

What did Lincoln mean when he spoke of freedom as a great idea that stood in conflict with slavery? Was he merely addressing the condition of those physically enslaved by the southern plantation owners—and the political and legal structures that supported them? Or was he speaking of a broader freedom? The answer is found in the records of Lincoln's public addresses from the time.

While much is made of the Lincoln–Douglas debates of 1858, Abraham Lincoln and Stephen Douglas first contended in a series of dialogues prior to the election of 1854, which saw Lincoln return to the campaign trail with an energy and earnestness not seen since he made his House race eight years earlier. In the months after Douglas reopened the slavery question with his advocacy of the hated Kansas-Nebraska Act, the sitting senator and Lincoln, the former congressman who suddenly wanted very much to be a senator, clashed rhetorically in cities up and down Illinois. The speeches that Lincoln delivered that fall—several lasting more than three hours—wrestled mightily with the meaning of words such as "equality," "liberty" and "freedom." At Peoria, he tossed his jacket aside on an uncommonly hot October day and delivered an address that Lincoln historian Lewis Lehrman would describe as "a rhetorical and literary masterpiece" that "dramatically altered the political career of the speaker and, as a result, the history of America.'"

A young journalist who covered the session in Peoria recalled both the words and the remarkable passion with which they were uttered. "Progressing with his theme, his words began to come faster and his face to light up with the rays of genius and his body to move in unison with his thoughts," wrote Horace White, the city editor of the *Chicago Daily Journal.* "His gestures were made with his body and head rather than with his arms. His speaking went to the heart because it came from the heart. I have heard celebrated orators who could start thunders of applause without changing any man's opinion. Mr. Lincoln's eloquence was of the higher type, which produced conviction in others because of the conviction of the speaker himself. His listeners felt that he believed every word he said, and that, like Martin Luther, he would go to the stake rather than abate one jot or title of it. In such transfigured moments as these he was the type of the ancient Hebrew prophet as I learned that character at Sunday-school in my childhood."

While Lincoln on that day may have been of "the type of the ancient Hebrew prophet," the "biblical" text to which he turned was not the Old Testament, nor the New. He was relying instead on Euclid's *Elements*, the philosophical study the former congressman had read and re-read during his wilderness years, honing the logical constructs that would less than a decade later prepare him to deliver his best remembered address on a blood-soaked battlefield where the Army of the Potomac and the Army of Northern Virginia had over the course of three days sacrificed a combined 7,500 soldiers. As he would in those "few appropriate remarks" at Gettysburg about a country "dedicated to the proposition that 'all men are created equal,'" Lincoln at Peoria summoned ancient algorithms—and more contemporary rhetorical flourishes—to identify the greatest common divisor of a young republic. It was in Jefferson's promise of a great equality that the debater of 1854 and the president of 1863 would find his moral grounding.

In particular, Lincoln spoke of how:

Little by little, but steadily as man's march to the grave, we have been giving up the OLD for the NEW faith. Near eighty years ago we began by declaring that all men are created equal; but now from that beginning we have run down to the other declaration, that for SOME men to enslave OTHERS is a "sacred right of self-government." These principles cannot stand together. They are as opposite as God and Mammon; and whoever holds to the one, must despise the other. When Pettit, in connection with his support of the Nebraska bill, called the Declaration of Independence "a self-evident lie" he only did what consistency and candor require all other Nebraska men to do. Of the forty-odd Nebraska Senators who sat present and heard him, no one rebuked him. Nor am I apprized that any Nebraska newspaper, or any Nebraska orator, in the whole nation, has ever yet rebuked him. If this had been said among Marion's men, Southerners though they were, what would have become of the man who said it? If this had been said to the men who captured Andre, the man who said it, would probably have been hung sooner than Andre was. If it had been said in old Independence Hall, seventy-eight years ago, the very doorkeeper would have throttled the man, and thrust him into the street.

Let no one be deceived. The spirit of seventy-six and the spirit of Nebraska, are utter antagonisms; and the former is being rapidly displaced by the latter.

Fellow countrymen—Americans south, as well as north, shall we make no effort to arrest this? Already the liberal party throughout the world, express the apprehension "that the one retrograde institution in America, is undermining the principles of progress, and fatally violating the noblest political system the world ever saw." This is not the taunt of enemies, but the warning of friends. Is it quite safe to disregard it—to despise it? Is there no danger to liberty itself, in discarding the earliest practice, and first precept of our ancient faith? In our greedy chase to make profit of the negro, let us beware, lest we "cancel and tear to pieces" even the white man's charter of freedom.

Our republican robe is soiled, and trailed in the dust. Let us repurify it. Let us turn and wash it white, in the spirit, if not the blood, of the Revolution. Let us turn slavery from its claims of "moral right," back upon its existing legal rights, and its arguments of "necessity." Let us return it to the position our fathers gave it; and there let it rest in peace. Let us re-adopt the Declaration of Independence, and with it, the practices, and policy, which harmonize with it. Let north and south—let all Americans—let all lovers of liberty everywhere—join in the great and good work. If we do this, we shall not only have saved the Union; but we shall have so saved it, as to make, and to keep it, forever worthy of the saving. We shall have so saved it, that the succeeding millions of free happy people, the world over, shall rise up, and call us blessed, to the latest generations.

While Lincoln may have recognized a need to "repurify," he was not himself ideologically or morally pure. The man who as president would stand justifiably accused of mangling civil liberties, disregarding the aspirations and basic humanity of Native Americans and willingly sacrificing principle on the alter of political expediency had learned too well from his fellow Whig Henry Clay, "the great compromiser." Lincoln was an imperfect foe of slavery, as even his most generous biographers now acknowledge. Yet, it is reasonable to suggest that the Lincoln of 1854 was in the process of becoming the president who would—pressured by Greeley—finally sign an Emancipation Proclamation. What he was coming to understand, intellectually and emotionally, was that slavery was an oppression of a kind with other oppressions. And he was not on the side of the oppressors. He was on the side of freedom—not merely as a moral or social construct, but as an economic one.

This was a concept that was hard-wired into the Republican Party from the moment of its founding—by followers of Fourier's utopian socialist vision, by German '48ers and especially by the muscular veteran campaigner for radical land reform Alvan Bovay. It was an idea that

Lincoln emphasized as he campaigned in 1856 for "Free Soil, Free Labor, Free Men and Fremont." Slavery was an issue that year, and Frederick Douglass was surely right when he argued that voting Republican was the best way to strike "the severest, deadliest blow upon Slavery that can be given at this particular time." But slavery was not the only issue, as a southern Illinois newspaper, the *Belleville Weekly Advocate*, noted after Lincoln stumped across the region on behalf of the ticket of General John C. Fremont and former New Jersey Senator William Dayton (who had defeated Lincoln for the new party's vice-presidential nomination in a 253 to 110 vote at the first Republican National Convention that summer in Philadelphia). "He vindicated the cause of free labor, 'that national capital,' in the language of Col. FREMONT, 'which constitutes the real wealth of this great country, and creates that intelligent power in the masses alone to be relied on as the bulwark of free institutions.' He showed the tendency and aim of the Sham Democracy to degrade labor to subvert the true ends of Government and build up Aristocracy, Despotism and Slavery."

Two years later, on October 15, 1858, in the last of the Lincoln–Douglas debates, the Republican candidate would frame the issues in the boldest possible terms, linking physical and economic slavery—"It is the same principle in whatever shape it develops itself"—as he addressed a crowd of 5,000 that had gathered in front of the Alton, Illinois, city hall. "That is the real issue. That is the issue that will continue in this country when these poor tongues of Judge Douglas and myself shall be silent. It is the eternal struggle between these two principles—right and wrong—throughout the world," Lincoln thundered. "They are the two principles that have stood face to face from the beginning of time; and will ever continue to struggle. The one is the common right of humanity and the other the divine right of kings. It is the same principle in whatever shape it develops itself. It is the same spirit that says, 'You work and toil and earn bread, and I'll eat it.' No matter in what shape it comes, whether from the mouth of a king who seeks to bestride the people of his own nation and live by the fruit of their labor, or from one race of men as an apology for enslaving another race, it is the same tyrannical principle."

As he prepared for the 1860 presidential race, Lincoln would align with those who "hold that labor is the superior—greatly the superior—of capital." That line, from one of Lincoln's most striking speeches of the period, his September 30, 1859, address to the Wisconsin State Agricultural Society, was reprised with minor variations throughout the difficult campaign for the Republican nomination. It was a nomination that saw Lincoln prevail with strong support from Greeley, who argued that the Illinoisan's determination to mingle free soil and free labor messages with his condemnations of "the Slave Power" established the right mix for a winning campaign in a country that the editor believed "will only swallow a little Anti-Slavery in a great deal of sweetening." Whether it was Greeley's calculus, the fact of a divided opposition, Lincoln's oratory or Carl Schurz's successful rallying of German-American '48ers and their immigrant communities to fight the "slaveholding capitalists" on behalf of a "society, where by popular education and continual change of condition, the dividing lines between the ranks and classes are almost obliterated"—or, as is always the case in politics, by a proper mingling of all the messages—the Republicans won the opportunity to preside over the conflict.

"The Republicans therefore attacked the rule of the slaveholders at their root," argued Marx in one of his many articles celebrating the rise of the new radical party in the United States—just as he decried "the connivance of the Northern Democrats" (or, as he referred to them, "Slavocrats") with "the Southern Slavocracy." The columnist, often displaying enthusiasms as idealistic as the Republican campaigners of Vermont or Wisconsin, argued that the party's rapid rise offered "many palpable proofs that the North had accumulated sufficient energies to rectify the aberrations which United States history, under the slaveholders' pressure, had undergone for half a century, and to make it return to the true principles of its development." Lincoln's victory was in Marx's view a signal that the workers of the north would not "submit any longer to an oligarchy of 300,000 slaveholders ..." That would not sit well with the south, and Greeley's European correspondent explained to readers of the *Tribune* what they well knew to be the next stage in the history of the United States: "The Republican election victory was accordingly bound to lead to open struggle between North and South."

The Civil War defined Lincoln's tenure in the White House. The nation's first Republican president was more than a mere warrior, however. He sought, sincerely if not always successfully, to strike the difficult balance between the duties of a commander-in-chief and a domestic policymaker, a balance he recognized in that first State of the Union address. Just as there were triumphs on the battlefield, there were triumphs in the economic debates that Lincoln had outlined. Chief among these was the enactment of the Homestead Act of 1862, a soft version of the land reforms proposed by Paine-influenced agrarian socialists and social democrats of varying stripes—led by George Henry Evans, who suggested the movement be dubbed "Republican" as early as the mid-1840s, and Evans's aide, Bovay, who would apply the name a decade later when he called the party into being at Ripon, Wisconsin. The act, which promised "land for the landless," allowed any adult citizen (or anyone who had applied for citizenship) to claim a 160-acre parcel of land in the public domain. Greeley hailed it as "one of the most vital reforms ever attempted" and predicted it would usher in a post-war era of economic equity characterized by "Peace, Prosperity and Progress."

Even as they agreed on homesteading, Greeley and Lincoln wrangled over the timing and scope of an emancipation proclamation. The editor joined Frederick Douglass in demanding that the president take steps to make the Civil War not merely a struggle to preserve the Union, but "an Abolition war." Even as Greeley and Lincoln exchanged sometimes pointed letters, the *Tribune's* longtime managing editor Charles Dana was now working for Lincoln. Officially assigned to the War Department—where he would eventually serve as assistant secretary—Dana's real role was as an aide and adviser to the president on questions of what the former newspaperman described as the "judicious, humane, and wise uses of executive authority." That Lincoln spent much of his presidency reading dispatches from and welcoming the counsel of Marx's longtime editor—like the fact that he awarded military commissions to the numerous comrades of the author of *The Communist Manifesto* who had come to the United States as political refugees following the failed European revolutions of 1848—is a shard of history rarely seen in the hagiographic accounts that produce a sanitized version of the sixteenth president's story. In the years following Lincoln's death, his law partner and political comrade, William Herndon, complained that Lincoln's official biographers were already attempting "to make the story with the classes as against the masses," an approach that he suggested "will result in delineating the real Lincoln about as well as does a wax figure in the museum."

The real Lincoln was more of a Jeffersonian, and especially a Paineite, than an orthodox Marxist. The president rejected the idea of "a law to prevent a man from getting rich" as an impractical plan that would "do more harm than good." He expected that, while labor was "superior" to capital, there "probably always will be a relation between labor and capital." But if he was something less than a Marxist, Lincoln was also something less than a laissez-faire capitalist—indeed, quite a bit less. Even as he accepted a relationship between capital and labor, he expounded on the "error" of "assuming that the whole labor of the world exists within that relation."

To the extent that sides were to be taken, Lincoln was on the side of labor. He urged working men to "combine" and organize labor unions— "uniting all working people, of all nations, and tongues, and kindreds." He wanted "free labor" to be able to make demands on capital, without apology or compromise. He proposed this, not as a young man in a "radical phase," but as the president of the United States. And he said as much when leaders of the New York Workingmen's Democratic-Republican Association arrived at the White House in March of 1864, to inform the president that they had elected him as an honorary member of their organization. Lincoln "gratefully accepted" the membership, read the attending paperwork and then responded appreciatively to his visitors: "You comprehend, as your address shows, that the existing rebellion means more, and tends to more, than the perpetuation of African Slavery—that it is, in fact, a war upon the rights of all working people. Partly to show that this view has not escaped my attention, and partly that I cannot better express myself, I read a passage from the Message to Congress in December 1861 …"

Having recalled his declarations about the superiority of labor, Lincoln spent a good deal more time with the Workingmen, despite a busy schedule that placed on his shoulders all the weight of decisions regarding the war and an impending re-election campaign. The campaign would see Lincoln's supporters distribute handbills in working-class wards of New York and other cities, arguing that the war was a fight not just to free slaves in the south but to free workers in the north from "Slave Wages." The most ardent abolitionists, such as Frederick Douglass, had always reasoned that: "Liberty to the slave is peace, honor, and prosperity to the country." But now this message was becoming central to the appeal of Lincoln's campaign to voters in the swing states that would decide whether the president could see the war through to "an Abolition peace" characterized by "liberty for all, chains for none." Emancipation, argued Lincoln's supporters, would allow African Americans in the south to "demand wages that would allow them to live in a decent manner, and therefore would help the poor white man to put up the price of labor instead of putting it down as [slavery does] now."

"Let the workingman think of this and go to the polls and vote for Abraham Lincoln, who is the true democratic candidate, and not the representative of the English Aristocracy, or their form of government, to be rid of which so many have left their native shores, and which form the leaders of the Rebellion are in favor of, in evidence of which we have the fact that in many of the Southern States no people can hold office but a property holder ..." went one leaflet's class-based appeal, which was critical to building the majority that would allow Lincoln to carry New York and retain the presidency with a decisive national landslide.

From afar, Marx (who corresponded with Dana and other American compatriots during and after the war) cheered on the campaign, writing to Engels in September of 1864 with considerable enthusiasm: "Should Lincoln succeed this time—as is highly probable—it will be on a far more radical platform and in completely changed circumstances."

Marx and Engels had been busy in the fall of 1864 with the work of organizing the International Workingmen's Association—the "First International" of the communist movement and its allies on the left. At the meeting on November 19 of the International's general council in London, Marx presented a letter of congratulation to Lincoln, which the council endorsed. It read:

Sir: We congratulate the American people upon your re-election by a large majority. If resistance to the Slave Power was the reserved watchword of your first election, the triumphant war cry of your re-election is Death to Slavery.

From the commencement of the titanic American strife the working-men of Europe felt instinctively that the star-spangled banner carried the destiny of their class. The contest for the territories which opened the dire epopee, was it not to decide whether the virgin soil of immense tracts should be wedded to the labor of the emigrant or prostituted by the tramp of the slave driver?

When an oligarchy of 300,000 slaveholders dared to inscribe, for the first time in the annals of the world, "slavery" on the banner of Armed Revolt, when on the very spots where hardly a century ago the idea of one great Democratic Republic had first sprung up, whence the first Declaration of the Rights of Man was issued, and the first impulse given to the European revolution of the eighteenth century; when on those very spots counter-revolution, with systematic thoroughness, gloried in rescinding "the ideas entertained at the time of the formation of the old constitution," and maintained slavery to be "a beneficent institution," indeed, the old solution of the great problem of "the relation of capital to labor," and cynically proclaimed property in man "the cornerstone of the new edifice" —then the working classes of Europe understood at once, even before the fanatic partisanship of the upper classes for the Confederate gentry had given its dismal warning, that the slaveholders' rebellion was to sound the tocsin for a general holy crusade of property against labor, and that for the men of labor, with their hopes for the future, even their past conquests were at stake in that tremendous conflict on the other side of the Atlantic. Everywhere they bore therefore patiently the hardships imposed upon them by the cotton crisis, opposed enthusiastically the pro-slavery intervention of their betters—and, from most parts of Europe, contributed their quota of blood to the good cause.

While the workingmen, the true political powers of the North, allowed slavery to defile their own republic, while before the Negro, mastered and sold without his concurrence, they boasted it the highest prerogative of the white-skinned laborer to sell himself and choose his own master, they were unable to attain the true freedom of labor, or to support their European brethren in their struggle for emancipation; but this barrier to progress has been swept off by the red sea of civil war.

The workingmen of Europe feel sure that, as the American War of Independence initiated a new era of ascendancy for the middle class, so the American Antislavery War will do for the working classes. They consider it an earnest of the epoch to come that it fell to the lot of Abraham Lincoln, the single-minded son of the working class, to lead his country through the matchless struggle for the rescue of an enchained race and the reconstruction of a social world.

The letter was duly delivered to Charles Francis Adams, Sr., the grandson of John and son of John Quincy, who had since the beginning of the war served in the delicate capacity of Lincoln's ambassador to the Court of St. James. Adams was well acquainted with Marx. A Greeley man, who would campaign for the vice presidency in 1872 on a "Liberal Republican" ticket led by the editor, he had been the subject of glowing accounts by Marx in the *Tribune* since his arrival in London in 1861. His own son and private secretary, Henry, after attending "a democratic and socialistic meeting" organized by Marx and Engels, had reported approvingly to Washington that the speakers emphasized "that their interests and those of the American Union were one, that the success of free institutions in America was a political question of deep consequence in England and that they would not tolerate any interference unfavorable to the north." Marx, Engels and their comrades, suggested the great-grandson of one American president and the grandson of another, were among the best friends that Lincoln and the Union cause had in London.

The senior Adams dispatched the letter from Marx and the leaders of the First International in a packet of diplomatic correspondence that was delivered to the State Department in Washington. Secretary of State William Seward promptly replied that: "These interesting papers have been submitted to the president." Seward then communicated Lincoln's response, which Adams in turn delivered to Marx and his comrades:

"I am directed to inform you that the address of the Central Council of your Association, which was duly transmitted through this Legation to the President of the United [States], has been received by him," began Adams. He went on:

So far as the sentiments expressed by it are personal, they are accepted by him with a sincere and anxious desire that he may be able to prove himself not unworthy of the confidence which has been recently extended to him by his fellow citizens and by so many of the friends of humanity and progress throughout the world.

The Government of the United States has a clear consciousness that its policy neither is nor could be reactionary, but at the same time it adheres to the course which it adopted at the beginning, of abstaining everywhere from propagandism and unlawful intervention. It strives to do equal and exact justice to all states and to all men and it relies upon the beneficial results of that effort for support at home and for respect and good will throughout the world.

Nations do not exist for themselves alone, but to promote the welfare and happiness of mankind by benevolent intercourse and example. It is in this relation that the United States regard their cause in the present conflict with slavery, maintaining insurgence as the cause of human nature, and they derive new encouragements to persevere from the testimony of the workingmen of Europe that the national attitude is favored with their enlightened approval and earnest sympathies.

Marx was thrilled by "the fact that Lincoln answered us so courteously," as he was with the rejection of "reactionary" policies and the expression of solidarity with "the friends of humanity and progress throughout the world." No fool, the philosopher recognized, as he wrote during the war, that "Lincoln's principal political actions contain much that is aesthetically repulsive, logically inadequate, farcical in form and politically, contradictory ..." He did not imagine the president as a revolutionary, let alone a likely recruit to the International. Yet he was inclined to believe, based on his many years of following and commenting upon the economic and political struggles of the United States, that the American erred to the left, and he was certain that: "Lincoln's place in the history of the United States and of mankind will, nevertheless, be next to that of Washington!" As such, the organizer in him delighted in the broad reporting of the exchange between the International and the Lincoln White House, which was featured news in the *Times of London*, along with other British and American papers. "The difference between Lincoln's answer to us and to the bourgeoisie [anti-slavery groups that had also written the president] has created such a sensation here that the West End 'clubs' are shaking their heads at it," Marx informed Engels. "You can understand how gratifying that has been for our people."

In the decades following Lincoln's assassination, the story of his exchange with the First International was well known and often recounted. Eugene Victor Debs would stop his 1908 presidential campaign train—"The Red Special"—in Springfield to deliver a celebratory address at Lincoln's grave. Years later, in the midst of another presidential campaign, Debs would argue that: "The Republican Party was once red. Lincoln was a revolutionary." It is indisputable that the Republican Party had at its founding a red streak. And it is arguable that the party's first president was a radical; his great struggle, rooted in the ideals of the founding, was for "a new birth of freedom" that would be aptly characterized by the historian Charles Beard as the "Second American Revolution, and in a strict sense, the First." The fight, Lincoln argued at Gettysburg, was waged to give meaning to the founding promise that "all men are created equal." This did not, as some of the more excitable revisionists of the 1930s imagined, make Lincoln a communist. The man who clung so tightly in his Gettysburg Address to the enlightenment visions that birthed the nation kept the faith in "that continual and fearless sifting and winnowing by which alone the truth can be found"—as the plaque on display for more than a century near the great Lincoln statue on the University of Wisconsin campus describes it. Lincoln was not a Marxist, but the first Republican president belonged to a time when men such as he were familiar with the writings of Marx and the deeds of the revolutionary circle that spread from Europe to the United States in the aftermath of the 1848 rebellions. He sifted and winnowed the radical ideas of his day. He found truth in notions about the superiority of labor to capital, just as he found important—at times essential—allies among the radicals who shared the view that a dying southern aristocracy was mounting not merely a last desperate defense of slavery but "in fact, a war upon the rights of all working people."

A century after Lincoln's death, and barely five weeks before his own assassination, the Rev. Martin Luther King, Jr. would recall the connection. King's comment came at a celebration of the life of W. E. B. Du Bois, which had been organized by the journal *Freedomways* at Carnegie Hall. Addressing the issue of Du Bois' radicalism, King used the address to urge a break with the "red scare" thinking that demonized everything and everyone associated with communism:

> We cannot talk of Dr. Du Bois without recognizing that he was a radical all of his life. Some people would like to ignore the fact that he was a Communist in his later years. It is worth noting that Abraham Lincoln

warmly welcomed the support of Karl Marx during the Civil War and cor-responded with him freely. In contemporary life the English-speaking world has no difficulty with the fact that Sean O'Casey was a literary giant of the twentieth century and a Communist, or that Pablo Neruda is gener-ally considered the greatest [living] poet, though he also served in the Chilean Senate as a Communist. It is time to cease muting the fact that Dr. Du Bois was a genius and chose to be a Communist. Our irrational obses-sive anti-communism has led us into too many quagmires to be retained as if it were a mode of scientific thinking.

While King offered a corrective to the casual dismissal of socialists, communists and other radicals, and of those—including American presi-dents—who might have been informed by them, it was Du Bois, a half century earlier, who offered the perspective on Lincoln that remains the most useful for those seeking a sense of what distinguished the most nuanced of American presidents.

As a product of his times and of the great debates that defined them, as a student of ancient ideas and fresh ones, as an American born in the last weeks of Thomas Jefferson's presidency, when it was still perhaps possible to detect the fading glimmers of the Age of Enlightenment, Abraham Lincoln understood that the best answers to societal challenges were found in "regions hitherto unexplored." This is why he read so widely. This is why he followed the freedom struggles that played out in distant lands so closely—and so passionately. This is why he befriended radicals, many of them refugees from the great revolutions of 1848; and this is why he sampled so broadly from their proposals and platforms—even if the man Du Bois recognized as "big enough to be inconsistent" refused to embrace the whole of any one. "He did not always see the right at first," Du Bois said of Lincoln. But, the scholar noted, America's sixteenth presi-dent retained a remarkable "capacity for growth." It was that latter capacity that led Du Bois to suggest that Americans would do well to "take pattern of Lincoln" and emulate his openness to ideas generated in those regions hitherto unexplored—a newspaper office in Cologne, a Spring-field meeting organized in solidarity with a Hungarian revolutionary, a Wisconsin schoolhouse filled with Fourierists and "Vote Yourself a Farm" land reformers, a workingmen's club in New York, a gathering in London of the First International. Presidents who choose to dismiss individuals, ideas and ideologies with which they do not fully agree take too many options off the table; in so doing they ill serve the republic. There are points on every nation's arc of history where radical ideas are more than merely interesting, intriguing or perhaps unsettling; they are the "new enlightenments" that enable and encourage the pursuit of "the welfare and happiness of mankind." Jefferson, at his best, recognized this. Paine as well. And, surely, Lincoln, when he observed in the darkest hours of his presidency: "The dogmas of the quiet past are inadequate to the stormy present. The occasion is piled high with difficulty, and we must rise with the occasion. As our case is new, so we must think anew, and act anew. We must disenthrall our selves, and then we shall save our country."

CHAPTER FOUR

A Legal and Peaceable Revolution of the Mind: The Socialism That *Did* Happen Here

We, the Social Democrats, do not simply "want to make a noise like Socialists." We actually want to do something as Socialists. We want to be constructive and build up, not only destructive and tear down. Our Socialism is not thunder—not simply hot air—it is lightning that strikes, purifies, and enlightens the world …

— Victor Berger, America's first Socialist congressman, 1906

The city campaign was but an episode in the socialist work of public education. We expect to continue the work right along with increased intensity. Socialism will hereafter have to be reckoned with as a potent factor in the public life of the country, and it will be a purifying and a salutary factor in politics and in the social policies of the country.

— New York mayoral candidate Morris Hillquit, 1917

We proved in Milwaukee and Reading that workers can govern a city better than Republicans, Democrats or capitalists governed them. And a city is harder to run than a state because it is more intricate. And if we can run a city, we can run a state and a nation.

— Milwaukee Mayor Daniel Webster Hoan, 1932

I was born in the shadow of socialism. Like many people of my place and time, I knew the word "socialism" before I knew the word "capitalism." And, as I recall it, "socialism" had the better associations in my young mind. After all, the mayor of the great city that served as the commercial, social and political center of the region in which my village was located preached a social gospel that outlined the failures and corruptions of corporate monopolies, and ridiculed the assumption that private businesses could or would ever do a credible job of delivering basic services. He dismissed the notion that free markets were really free and rejected any suggestion that they offered all the answers—or, perhaps, any of them. He hailed public ownership as the humane and responsible alternative to rapacious capitalism. He championed trade unionism, cooperatives and collectives. International solidarity was his faith and, with predictable regularity, he decried the grasping reach of America's military-industrial complex.

The mayor's self-declared purpose was to forge "a brotherhood of workers, the Cooperative Commonwealth."

His predecessor, who governed for a quarter century, was a second-generation socialist who, according to a *Time* magazine cover story written in the twentieth year of his long tenure, "gives Karl Marx the credit for his municipal success." That mayor set up cooperative housing projects, along with a municipal waterworks, sewage plant, stone quarry and harbor facilities. His administration even subsidized the production of food and set up municipal stores to provide bread and other staples to the poor. His was a class-conscious leadership. Invited to welcome King Albert of Belgium's state visit, he demurred. "I stand for the man who works," the mayor declared. "To hell with kings."

That rigid egalitarianism, that recognition of a class divide, that belief that it mattered to be on the right—actually the left—side: these were articles of faith among the socialist rulers with whom I was raised.

Where was this Soviet city? What did we call this gulag?

It was in Wisconsin. We called it "Milwaukee."

From the early 1900s to the 1960s, Milwaukee was not just a "hotbed of socialist activism." What was then one of the largest and most prosperous of American cities was actually governed for decades by Socialists. The first member of the Socialist Party to take charge of a major American city, Emil Seidel, was elected mayor of Milwaukee in 1910 and (perhaps with a rhetorical assist from his chief aide, the poet Carl Sandburg) declared: "Socialists have been given a chance to show their merits."

The *New York Times*, which along with other major newspapers across the country relayed on an almost daily basis the progress of the Milwaukee Socialists, argued after Seidel's election that: "From any standpoint, Mayor Seidel will become one of the most interesting figures in America from this time until the close of his term."

The interest, it turned out, was sufficient to make Seidel—just two years after his election—the vice-presidential nominee on a Socialist ticket headed by labor leader Eugene Victor Debs.

The Debs–Seidel ticket pulled close to one million votes in 1912—six percent of the total cast in an election year that would see Democrat Woodrow Wilson, independent "Bull Moose" Progressive Teddy Roosevelt, and even Republican William Howard Taft show more inclination to borrow ideas from the Socialists than to denounce their influence. Wilson, the winner, certainly got the point. He would appoint prominent Socialists to federal posts and dispatch a key player in the party, the writer and 1913 Socialist nominee for mayor of New York City, Charles Russell, as one of his most trusted international envoys. During his first term, the twenty-eighth president would, as well, keep an open door to active Socialists, meeting in January 1916 with three party leaders —New York Congressman Meyer London, Pennsylvania Federation of Labor President James Maurer, and party co-founder and national executive committee member Morris Hillquit—to discuss the SP's proposal that "the President of the United States convoke a congress of neutral nations, which shall offer mediation to the belligerents and remain in permanent session until the termination of the war." As Hillquit recalled in his autobiography, *Loose Leaves From a Busy Life*, Wilson was initially "inclined to give us a short and perfunctory hearing," but the session quickly "developed into a serious and confidential conversation." (Hillquit recalled that he and the others thought Wilson—who would seek re-election that year with the slogan "He Kept Us Out of War"— seemed genuinely interested in keeping the United States neutral in World War I. They would be proven wrong barely a year later, when Wilson would not only lead the country into the war but preside over a brutal crackdown on dissent that landed Debs in federal prison and put Hillquit to work as the lawyer for Socialist-aligned daily newspapers— including the English-language *New York Call* and *Milwaukee Leader* and the Yiddish-language *Jewish Daily Forward*—that were threatened with loss of mailing privileges after they expressed anti-war views.)

The remarkable level of national support for the 1912 Debs–Seidel ticket was paralleled by victories at the local and state levels. By the end of the year, the Socialist Party had elected thirty-four mayors, along with city councilors, school board members and other officials in 169 cities from Butte, Montana, to New York City. In some of the thirty-three states where Socialists won elections that year, the party displaced the Demo-crats or the Republicans as the second party of politics and government. In my native Wisconsin, for instance, Republicans held the majority of legislative seats during the 1910s and 1920s, but Socialists often formed the opposition caucus; Democrats barely registered a presence.

The first Socialist elected to the US Congress was Seidel's campaign manager, Milwaukeean Victor Luitpold Berger, who took his seat in 1911 and held it, on and off, until 1929. At various points he caucused in the House with a New York Socialist, Meyer London, and briefly, if only semi-officially, with a future mayor of the nation's largest city who was elected in 1924 on the Socialist line, Fiorello LaGuardia. Far from being marginalized, the Socialists aligned with the "insurgent" Republican caucus led by Wisconsin Senator Robert "Fighting Bob" La Follette, whose 1924 presidential bid earned a Socialist Party endorsement and five million votes nationwide. When some of his more doctrinaire comrades questioned the wisdom of endorsing a lifelong Republican, Milwaukee Mayor Dan Hoan, a Socialist who had been elected four years after Seidel finished his single term and who would continue at the city's helm for twenty-four years, shouted: "He says the supreme issue is whether the wealth of the nation shall remain in the hands of the privi-leged few. What is the matter with you Socialists that this does not satisfy you? Is not that the thing we have been ding-donging for forty years?"

So it was that, as Socialists made their most dramatic advances, not just electorally but as the peddlers of ideas and ideals that would eventually shape the rough outlines of the "New Deal," the "Fair Deal" and the "Great Society" reformations of the American experiment, a municipal socialist who was characterized in a magazine account as a party leader who "subscribes to Marxist doctrines because he thinks they are the ideal means to his ends in life" made the practical argument for doing what was necessary to advance the cause.

This is not just a story of Milwaukee and its Socialists, however, nor even of Wisconsin and the progressives who sampled so frequently—if not always definitionally—from the Socialist plate. It is a story of "sewer socialism," the distinct brand of local government that was a staple of urban politics in the United States throughout much of the twentieth century and, in a few communities, remains so to the present day. While it is important to recall the extent to which the Socialist Party was a serious player at the national level, electorally in the period from 1912 to 1932 and as a forger of policies adopted by Democratic presidents and congresses (and even some Republican governors and legislators) in the period from 1932 to 1980, it is even more vital to recognize that Socialists and socialism had their greatest success throughout the twentieth century, and continue to succeed in the twenty-first, at the most human level of our politics. Socialism, so supposedly "scary" in the macro, has proven to be remarkably popular in the micro. And, while the Socialist Party's success was far broader, the Communist Party of the 1930s and 1940s had its own victories on the municipal level, electing and reelecting the pioneering civil rights lawyer Ben Davis and veterans activist Peter Cacchione to the New York City Council but also winning races on the Farmer-Labor and Workers Party lines in places like Sheridan County, Montana, and Crosby, Minnesota—where union activist Karl Emil Nygard took office in 1933 as the self-proclaimed "first Communist mayor in America."

The Communists, working inside New York's American Labor Party during the 1940s, also played a significant role in the election of a pair of ALP Congressman—Vito Marcantonio, who served seven terms representing East Harlem, and Leo Isacson, who briefly represented the Bronx—and a number of legislators and local officials in New York City. Frequently, ALP candidates were elected with cross-endorsements from Republicans who worked openly with Communists and non-Communist ALP members to beat the Tammany machine.

In the overall scheme of things, however, the Socialist Party won far more races across the country. Yet, the history of all these electoral successes by parties of the left tends to be glossed over and forgotten. That's a mistake, as leftists serving at the municipal and state levels generated, implemented and proved the worth of many of the ideas—unemployment insurance, workplace-safety protections, so-called "relief" programs, public housing and public ownership of utilities—that eventually went national with Franklin Roosevelt and the New Deal.

Even historians who are sympathetic to socialism and aware of the electoral history of the left in America tend to focus on the multiple Socialist Party presidential campaigns of Debs, who made five runs from 1900 to 1920, and Norman Thomas, who picked up the mantle and ran with it six times from 1928 to 1948, rather than on the actual Socialist governments that administered major cities and participated in the management of municipalities and counties across the country. This neglect especially pronounced today, as an increasingly homogenized American media and punditocracy tends to obsess about presidential politics while paying scant attention to local affairs. The shorthand of socialism as an ideology and the Socialist Party as a political movement is that both failed in America. After all, Debs lost, and lost and lost again, and then Thomas lost, and lost and lost again. Ergo, socialism and the Socialists were losers.

Yet, to borrow a line from a socialist (and contributor of the "Woody Sez" column to the Communist Party's *Daily Worker* newspaper) named Woody Guthrie, Socialists won elections and governed communities "from California to the New York Island, from the Redwood Forest to the Gulf Stream waters." No less a national figure than Thomas, the party's most generally well-regarded leader and its "face" for the middle passage of the twentieth century, described grass-roots campaigns in communities across the country as the party's "great inclusive crusade for the building of a new society."

Socialist Party members and independent socialists and social democrats have governed hundreds of cities, villages, towns and school districts in the vast majority of American states as "sewer socialists." And not just in the distant past. Seventy years after Emil Seidel assumed the mayoralty of Milwaukee with a declaration that "socialists are prepared to govern,"

Bernie Sanders would take charge of Burlington, Vermont, as his state's most prominent socialist. Sanders now serves as an independent socialist senator, caucusing with Democrats but voting to their left on issues ranging from health-care reform to bank regulation and the forging of an economic democracy. Today, one hundred years after Seidel's election was reported with headlines on the front page of the *New York Times*, socialists and social democrats of varying stripes and degrees are elected—without the headlines—and serve on local school boards, town councils and city commissions, as well as in city halls across the country.

I once asked my friend Charlie Uphoff, a proud democratic socialist who has served on school and village boards in relatively conservative suburban and rural communities, why he thought his neighbors—many of them Republicans, who no doubt nod along with Fox News commentators as they rant and rave about Marxist moles burrowing into the warrens of the Obama administration—voted for him. Did they not know he, Charlie, was a red? Surely they were aware of his socialism. After all, his father Walter had been a frequent Socialist Party nominee for the governorship and the US Senate (one of the first candidates ever to challenge Joe McCarthy in a political debate), and served for a number of years on the party's national executive committee. And Charlie really is his father's son.

"They think it's an eccentricity, maybe, but not a disqualifying one," he explained to me. "A lot of them, I think, figure that someone who is honest enough to admit to being a socialist will be honest enough when they're elected. Socialists actually like government; we want to make sure it works. I guess what I'm saying is that a lot of people trust socialists—if they know them."

Charlie's right, of course. And in his wisdom he unintentionally but ably defines "sewer socialism."

The term gained popularity after a joke told by Morris Hillquit, a frequent Socialist candidate who counted among his enthusiastic supporters Helen Keller and Upton Sinclair and polled hundreds of thousands of votes in his runs for mayor of New York. Chairing the party's 1932 national convention in Milwaukee, Hillquit teased the locals about their boastful pride in the recently-upgraded municipal sewer system. Sewer systems, public health programs, municipal power plants were all public responses to what the city-hall Socialists described as "the dirty and polluted legacy of the Industrial Revolution." The historian John Gurda recalls: "Seidel [mused] about some of the more ideologically pure socialists. They thought that Milwaukeeans were so obsessed with public works that they called them sewer socialists. It may have been meant in a less than flattering sense and Milwaukee Socialists embraced it. They were determined to be efficient, to be effective, and you also have to remember that during a time when public water supplies were very suspect, when you had uncontrolled dumping of sewage in the rivers, these were not polite infrastructure projects. This was a matter of life and death to a lot of citizens of Milwaukee. That was a very important cause of theirs and it goes to the whole notion of public enterprise. You spend public funds for the public good."

Gurda is certainly correct that some "pure socialists" saw locally-based "sewer socialism"—or the "municipal socialism" celebrated by Sidney Webb in the classic Fabian tract *Socialism in England*—as a dialectical disappointment. No less a critic than Vladimir I. Lenin would argue, around the time that Milwaukee Socialists were getting started, that: "The bourgeois intelligentsia of the West, like the English Fabians, elevate municipal socialism to a special 'trend' precisely because it dreams of social peace, of class conciliation, and seeks to divert public attention away from the fundamental question of the economic system as a whole, and of the state structure as a whole, to minor questions of local self-government. In the sphere of questions in the first category, the class antagonisms stand out most sharply; that is the sphere which, as we have shown, affects the very foundations of the class rule of the bourgeoisie. Hence, it is in that sphere that the philistine, reactionary utopia of bringing about socialism piecemeal is particularly hopeless."

While Lenin was dismissive of municipal socialism, he was not arguing for inaction. His was a tactical objection based at least in part on the distinct experiences of different countries, and the American Socialists tended to see it as such. Unperturbed, they read their Marx with an eye toward the sections that recognized the role of incremental progress while tending to reject suggestions that "the rigidity of the class structure prevented the achievement of meaningful reforms for the worker until the demise of capitalism." Many of the most radical Americans, especially those associated with the Industrial Workers of the World's "One Big Union," objected to the whole idea of waiting for a right revolutionary moment, which they ridiculed as a "pie-in-the-sky" promise that had about as much meaning for hard-pressed working families as the preachers' assurance that they would get their just deserts in the next life. Joe Hill paraphrased what he saw as an empty vision with the words:

> You will eat, bye and bye,
> In that glorious land above the sky;
> Work and pray, live on hay,
> You'll get pie in the sky when you die.

The "sewer socialists" were not averse to heavenly rewards, but felt that serving up some dessert in the here and now might be necessary to advance the cause. This incrementalism put them at odds with more radical players, including old allies in the IWW at home and leading Communists abroad, over the question of whether it was ever appropriate to employ violence. To this end, many of the "sewer socialists" took counsel from the pragmatic German socialist Eduard Bernstein, who asserted that, while theory, plotting and preparation for the glorious revolution had appeal, a practical plan for putting food on the table might inspire the masses to mobilize. Among those who most highly regarded Bernstein's view that it was possible to "[dispense] with the need for violence" was Victor Berger, the great proponent of American socialism in the late nineteenth and early twentieth centuries. Berger, the man who drew Debs to the cause, declared that "we do not care a [wit] whether our Socialism is Marxian or otherwise, as long as we change the present system and emancipate all the people."

Berger understood and respected America as a democracy, even if it was imperfect in his time and might remain so. "[It] is foolish," he explained, "to expect results from riots and dynamite, from murderous attacks and conspiracies, in a country where we have the ballot, as long as the ballot has been given a full and fair trial." The point was to achieve "the revolutionizing of the mind"—something Berger sought to do as a newspaper editor, magazine writer and author of four decades' worth of campaign pamphlets. "In the world's history there are no sudden leaps," he preached, arguing that it might take "another century or two" before capitalism was replaced. What were needed along the way, said Berger, were "installments" and "stepping stones," which should be seen as markers on the path rather than endpoints. "We shall never forget for one moment that while the Social Democratic Party fights the battles of the worker—now and here—while it fights the battle for honesty and for all the people alike as far as good government is concerned—the ultimate aim of our party is not reform, it is revolution—a legal and peaceable revolution, but none the less a revolution."

"Socialism is the next phase of civilization" was Berger's catchphrase, whether addressing Congress or a street-corner rally in the German and Jewish immigrant neighborhoods of Milwaukee. To that end, the great theorist, agitator, successful campaign manager and successful candidate announced in 1906:

> We agitate for the organization of the masses. And organization every-where means order. We educate, we enlighten, we reason, we discipline. And, therefore, besides order we bring also law, reason, discipline, and progress.
>
> It is therefore absolutely false to represent our Social Democratic Party as merely destructive, as intending to overthrow and annihilate society, as an appeal to the brute passions of the masses.
>
> Just the opposite is true.
>
> Our Social Democracy wants to maintain our culture and civilization, and bring it to a higher level.
>
> Our party wants to guard the nation from destruction.
>
> We appeal to the best in every man, to the public spirit of the citizen ...

Four years after Berger penned those words, the appeal was received favorably, as the campaign he managed for Seidel and the Milwaukee Socialists swept to power, winning for mayor, city treasurer and city attorney, and taking two thirds of the city's council seats.

The immediate mission of the Socialists in Milwaukee—as it was in many of the other cities where they won control of local government, from Butte to Bridgeport—was to prove that government could operate honorably and as an extension of the people, rather than as a burden to them.

Berger, the great philosopher and tactician of the "sewer socialist" movement, understood that socialists could only make the case for government ownership of power and gas plants, waterworks, transit systems and other services if they established a reputation for absolute honesty and "good burgher" management. While Democrats and Republicans held out the hope of honest governance as an end in itself, Berger said: "With us, this is the first and smallest requirement." His acolyte Frank Zeidler would write that the "sewer socialists" were distinguished by "a passion for orderly government; and by a contempt for graft and boodling."

It was that contempt that opened the way for the first great Socialist Party victories in the United States.

"Before the Socialists took charge, Milwaukee was just as corrupt as Chicago at its worst. Our mayor at the turn of the twentieth century was David Rose, a political prince of darkness who allowed prostitution, gambling dens, all-night saloons and influence-peddling to flourish on his watch. Grand juries returned 276 indictments against public officials of the Rose era. 'All the Time Rosy' escaped prosecution himself, but district attorney (and future governor) Francis McGovern called him 'the self-elected, self-appointed attorney general of crime in this community,'" recalls Gurda. "In 1910, fed-up voters handed Socialists the keys to the city. Emil Seidel, a patternmaker by trade, won the mayor's race in a landslide, and Socialists took a majority of seats on the Common Council."

Seidel explained the point of Socialist rule in human terms:

Some eastern smarties called ours a Sewer Socialism. Yes, we wanted sewers in the workers' homes; but we wanted much, oh, so very much more than sewers.

We wanted our workers to have pure air; we wanted them to have sunshine; we wanted planned homes; we wanted living wages; we wanted recreation for young and old; we wanted vocational education; we wanted a chance for every human being to be strong and live a life of happiness.

And, we wanted everything that was necessary to give them that: playgrounds, parks, lakes, beaches, clean creeks and rivers, swimming and wading pools, social centers, reading rooms, clean fun, music, dance, song and joy for all.

> That was our Milwaukee Social Democratic movement. There was but
> one way to get all of that—GO AFTER IT AND GET IT.

The Milwaukee Socialists did just that, by forging close alliances with organized labor and groups of small-business owners, by developing their own media (including a widely-circulated daily, *The Milwaukee Leader*, edited by Berger) and an elaborate organization of "bundle brigades"— ward-level groups of party activists who were at the ready to distribute campaign pamphlets in English, German, Polish, Yiddish, Italian and other languages to every household in the city within forty-eight hours after they were printed on the party's presses. Seidel himself only served for two years. And that is an important part of this story. Milwaukee's "sewer socialism" was not the work of one man or one moment; it extended across decades, as many municipal socialist experiments have in US cities. Indeed, some with roots in the past century continue to this day.

There are historians who would have us believe that the heyday of American socialism was a brief period on the eve of World War I, when the party's opposition to aligning American soldiers with the cause of an English king made it the target of a "red scare" so intense that Debs would be jailed, Berger would be arrested and thousands of their followers would be hounded from the political sphere, harassed and deported. My friend Jimmy Weinstein even wrote a book titled *The Decline of Socialism in America: 1912–1925*. Now, I loved Jimmy, wrote for the magazine he founded (*In These Times*) and was honored to contribute laudatory words to the cover of the last of his many fine books, *The Long Detour: The History and Future of the American Left*. But Jimmy's downbeat assessment of socialism's fortunes—electorally and otherwise—was, I think, a product of that old tendency to dismiss the serious work and serious successes of the "sewer socialists."

To be sure, the epic campaign that Debs waged for the presidency in 1912 established a national electoral milestone for the party. Though Debs would win a slightly higher actual vote total eight years later, when he campaigned from the Atlanta Federal Penitentiary as "Prisoner 9653"—jailed for the "crime" of delivering an anti-war speech in which he noted that it had become "extremely dangerous to exercise our constitutional right of freedom of speech in a country fighting to make democracy safe in the world"—the percentage of the vote he earned in 1912 was the highest ever accorded a Socialist presidential nominee running solely on the party line. (The explanation for the higher vote but lower percentage in 1920 was the expansion of the electorate with the enfranchisement of women.)

Accepting the 1912 vote totals at face value—a compromise, as it is well understood that urban machines aligned with the Democratic and Republican parties deliberately undercounted votes for the Socialists in big cities, while some rural states kept the party off the ballot altogether— the 6 percent of the vote that Debs and Seidel received that year was the same as that attained at the time by the British Labour Party, which would eventually govern the United Kingdom. Domestically, the Debs–Seidel ticket earned a vote percentage comparable to that obtained by Congressman John Anderson and billionaire Ross Perot in their highly publicized independent presidential campaigns of 1980 and 1996, and more than twice the percentages accorded the Green candidacy of Ralph Nader in 2000, the Progressive Party run of former Vice President Henry Wallace in 1948, or that year's States Rights Party run by South Carolina Governor Strom Thurmond.

Particularly noteworthy were the percentages of the 1912 vote attained by Debs and Seidel in states where the Socialists had built strong political organizations—and, in many cases, networks of Socialist clubs and Sunday schools, labor affiliations and party-aligned weekly newspapers. In seven western states—Nevada (16.47), Oklahoma (16.42), Montana (13.64), Arizona (13.33), Washington (12.43), California (11.68) and Idaho (11.31)—Debs and Seidel broke into double digits.

But to close the book on Socialist electioneering in 1912 is to miss the most significant chapters.

Twelve years after Debs hit the Socialist Party's solo high-water mark, La Follette would attach the Socialist banner to his own progressive Republican movement—which imagined the possibility of renewing the radicalism of the Grand Old Party's founding—and win fully 16.6 percent of the national vote for a campaign to "break the combined power of the private monopoly system over the political and economic life of the American people ..." Sounding themes that echoed Debs to a far greater extent than cautious "progressives" such as Theodore Roosevelt or Woodrow Wilson, La Follette declared: "Free men of every generation must combat the renewed efforts of organized force and greed to destroy liberty," and he and his supporters outlined their strategy for doing so in a platform that called for the government takeover of the railroads, elimination of private utilities, easier credit for farmers, the outlawing of child labor, the right of workers to organize unions, increased protection of civil liberties, an end to US imperialism in Latin America, and a national referendum vote before any president could again lead the nation into offensive war.

Running in some states on his own independent Progressive ballot line and in other states on the Socialist line, La Follette won double the national vote percentage achieved by the Populists in 1892, gained a substantially higher percentage than that of Alabama Governor George Wallace's 1968 American Independent Party campaign, and finished almost as well as Perot in 1992. Indeed, of all third-party campaigns of the twentieth century, La Follette's 1924 run as an endorsed candidate of the Socialists was more successful than any but Perot's 1992 race and former president Teddy Roosevelt's 1912 "Bull Moose" bid. In Wisconsin, La Follette won 54 percent of the ballots and all the state's electoral votes; in North Dakota, he won 45 percent of the vote; in Minnesota, 41 percent; in Montana, 38 percent. Across the country, twenty-six states would accord double-digit percentages of their votes to the candidate who proudly carried the Socialist endorsement and was hailed by Eugene Victor Debs as the tribune of "the gathering forces of liberation."

The Socialist Party would never again play as big a role in presidential politics as it did in 1924, a transformational year when Progressives and Socialists laid the groundwork for the New Deal that, in the words of historian Bernard Weisberger, "completed the elder La Follette's work."

Even after 1924, however, the Socialist Party did not disappear as an electoral force. In 1932, Debs's successor as the party's semi-official "spokesman for American socialism" mounted what was arguably the most thoroughly-reported Socialist presidential campaign in American history. Norman Thomas, a Princeton-educated Presbyterian minister who preached the "social gospel" with a passion comparable to Debs's union organizer oratory, mounted a campaign that year that gave voice not just to frustration with the economic turmoil caused by a global depression, but also to a prescient wariness about the unsettling political responses to the downturn already on display in Germany, Italy and a number of other European states. "The choice now confronting the world is between Socialism and catastrophe!" announced Thomas, who warned that "capitalism needs nationalism as the opium to keep the workers exploited." The presidential candidate portrayed the 1932 election as a tipping-point moment, not just for the economic battle between capitalism and socialism but for the broader question of whether fascism or democracy would prevail. The *New York Times*, which regularly reported Thomas's campaign pronouncements, described this part of his message in a breathless September 20, 1932, account headlined: "Fascist Trend Here Feared By Thomas: Holds Marxism Only Hope":

> Capitalism, Mr. Thomas concluded, is dying before our eyes. Fascism may be the Indian Summer of capitalism, but it will only serve to stave off the catastrophe that is facing the country unless socialism triumphs, and fascism will make the catastrophe even "more dire" and terrible, he said.

That internationally-savvy appeal was dismissed by some commentators of the time as wrongheaded or politically paranoid—in much the same way that the American communists, socialists and anarchists who would join the Abraham Lincoln Brigade to fight from 1936 to 1939 with Spanish republicans against Franco would be labeled "premature anti-fascists." Over time, however, it would help to forge Thomas's global reputation as a visionary and consistent foe of totalitarianism, whose willingness to call out dictators of the right and left made him the genuine political embodiment of a "card-carrying member of the ACLU." But the real strength of the 1932 socialist campaign was the specificity of its platform, which even Democrats would eventually acknowledge picked up where La Follette had left off to set the rough parameters for the New Deal. While New York governor Franklin Roosevelt ran a cautiously liberal Democratic campaign that, much like Barack Obama's in 2008, promised nothing so much as a break with the failed policies of a rigid Republican stalwart, Thomas and the Socialists pledged to spend ten billion dollars on federal unemployment relief and public works programs, to place a two-year moratorium on foreclosures and tax sales of homes and farms, and to pay for these initiatives by hiking inheritance taxes for the rich and income taxes for corporations.

The Socialists also promised long-term structural changes that would establish a compulsory system of unemployment compensation with adequate benefits, based upon contributions by the government and by employers; old-age pensions for men and women sixty years of age and over; comprehensive labor-law reform with an eye toward making it dramatically easier for workers to organize unions, and support for credit unions, cooperatives and other alternative economic arrangements. "Only in Socialist planning is there practical hope for the unemployed, for exploited workers and the whole class of farmers," Thomas explained during a thirty-eight-state campaign tour that attracted hundreds of thousands of cheering supporters to mass rallies.

What did the presidential candidate and his supporters call this agenda for "Socialist planning"? Before a wildly enthusiastic crowd of 20,000, which packed Madison Square Garden for a rally five days before the November 8, 1932, election, the Socialists described their platform. According to the *New York Times* report of the following day: "Mr. Thomas and other speakers pronounced their indictment of the prevailing social order and called for a '*new deal*' along Socialist lines." To be sure, Democrats had used the phrase, as well, during the course of an election year that would see the radical alteration of American politics. But while the Democrats were vague, the Socialists were specific. "We Socialists are building for the future. We are creating a new political force in the country. We are offering a new deal to the people," Morris Hillquit told a pre-election rally. "We propose to recreate society from the bottom up, to make it fairer, saner, more humane." That message appealed to a great many Americans who knew it was time for a radical renewal of the American promise—as the crowds Thomas attracted in the fall, and the votes he gained on Election Day, well illustrated.

The fact did not go unnoted by Franklin Roosevelt.

On November 8, 1932, when the American people rejected not just a president—Herbert Hoover—but a royalist vision of federal policymaking that had allowed tens of millions of citizens to suffer as the Great

Depression swept across the land, Roosevelt found himself with an unprecedented mandate. Like Obama seventy-six years later, he had been elected after promising "hope" and "change" but not a lot in the way of specifics; the University of Chicago economics professor Paul Douglas, a Thomas backer, dismissed the Roosevelt platform as "extremely incomplete." If the rhetorical and policy parallels of the Democratic campaigns of 1932 and 2008 are striking, however, even more notable is the extent to which the winners of those elections diverged upon taking office. While Roosevelt was bold, challenging, confrontational, Obama was soft, compromising and conciliatory.

What distinguished the two? Obama's victory was politically isolated; a man and his party prevailed. In contrast, Roosevelt's victory came in the context of broader political turbulence, and the thirty-second president was influenced by much more than his own result.

The election of 1932 is now generally accepted as a realigning moment in US politics, the point at which the country took the great leap forward from a past that favored limited federal and state involvement in economic affairs—except where it came to securing the interests of the wealthy—and embraced a more humane and democratic approach to governing.

To be sure, that approach has been much battered of late. Yet, Social Security remains, as does the Federal Deposit Insurance Corporation, the Fair Labor Standards Act and the minimum wage. Those of us with roots in small-town America still enjoy the benefits of Rural Electrification. And Americans of every region, race and religion retain at least a few of the liberties that were defined and protected by Roosevelt-nominated Supreme Court Justices William O. Douglas, Hugo Black and Felix Frankfurter. There's still a Securities and Exchange Commission, which sometimes does its job, and a Federal Communications Commission, which has the power (if not always the inclination) to make our communications democratic rather than monopolistic.

The agent of these reforms—and of the fundamental shift in the American experience they embodied—was Roosevelt, the Democratic governor of New York who displaced Republican President Hoover. But it is important to remember that Roosevelt, the most patrician of our nation's many patrician politicians, did not compete in the 1932 election as the radical reformer that he became. The Democratic platform of that year was a compromise document, dictated by fear rather than the courage that would later be associated with Roosevelt.

What made Roosevelt so remarkable, and so radical?

The results that were tabulated in November 1932 influenced FDR to evolve his policies in a direction that was more egalitarian and democratic. His critics still use the term "socialistic" to describe the program Roosevelt implemented, and they are not entirely wrong. It is certainly fair to say that the thirty-second president's evolution redefined not just American politics but America.

Roosevelt won a stunning victory in 1932. He secured 57.4 percent of the popular vote, as compared with just 39.7 percent for Hoover. The Democrat carried forty-two states, most by wide margins, while the Republican won just six.

But these numbers do not begin to tell the whole story of what happened on that distant November 8. Roosevelt's popular vote total of 22,821,277 was 52 percent higher than that received by Al Smith, the Democratic nominee in the election of four years earlier. The Roosevelt landslide was sufficient to create a coat-tail effect that dramatically increased a narrow Democratic majority in the House of Representatives, and gave the party control of the Senate.

A total of ninety-seven new Democrats were elected to the House, most of them young and left-leaning, a number of them veterans of past campaigns by the Socialists and of La Follette's 1924 presidential run. Their numbers were augmented by five members of the Minnesota Farmer-Labor Party, who made no apologies for their radicalism—to such an extent that the *New York Times* would describe the party as "officially red." Thus, 73 percent of the seats in the House (313 out of 435) were held by members who had been elected on pledges to alter the economic equation to favor Main Street over Wall Street. Even some Republicans, especially from New York and the upper midwest, espoused a progressive vision that was well to the left of what Roosevelt had advocated while campaigning in 1932.

Nine Republican senators were defeated that year by the Democrats, who also won three open seats. This shifted control of the chamber from 48–47 Republican to 59–36 Democratic, with one Farmer-Laborite. A half dozen "insurgent" Republican senators stood with Roosevelt or to his left on economic issues. Referred to as the "sons of the wild jackass," these renegade Republicans had in many cases followed the lead of Nebraska Senator George Norris—one of La Follette's closest allies—and actually endorsed Roosevelt. Others, such as Idaho Senator William Borah, simply refused to back Hoover while arguing that the GOP should reposition itself as a more liberal party than the Democrats.

These congressional majorities would free Roosevelt to move steadily to the left, knowing that if he did not make the shift Congress would force his hand on a host of relief measures and related economic initiatives: Norris and others had already begun the process, forging coalitions of liberal Democrats, Republicans and third-party leftists to enact reform legislation in the last days of Hoover's presidency. For his part, Roosevelt was inclined to move. It was not just the size of the Democratic landslide that influenced him. It was the clear evidence that many American voters were looking to the left of the new president and his party for responses to the economic crisis.

On November 8, 1932, more than a million Americans—almost 3 percent of the electorate—cast ballots for presidential candidates who proposed radical changes that really did amount to "a new deal." Socialist Thomas won 884,885 votes, for a 230 percent improvement in his party's total. Communist William Z. Foster won 103,307 votes, for a 112 percent increase in his party's total—and its best finish ever in a presidential race. And southern populist William Hope Harvey, who had helped manage Democratic populist William Jennings Bryan's 1896 presidential campaign, secured another 53,425 votes—most of them in Washington state, where the politics were taking a dramatic turn to the left.

Roosevelt was conscious of the fact that, in a number of states outside the south, Thomas and the Socialists were a genuine political presence. They had won almost 5 percent of the vote in the reform-inclined states of Wisconsin and Oregon. In New York state, the Thomas–Maurer ticket took 177,000 votes (displacing the Republicans as the second party in many New York City precincts), and in Pennsylvania it won almost 100,000.

Roosevelt, a political junkie who was known to pore over election statistics for hours, got the picture.

Shortly after the poll, the president-elect met with Thomas and Henry Rosner, a frequent contributor to the *Nation* magazine who had authored the Socialist Party's 1932 platform, and who would go on to be a key aide of New York Mayor Fiorello LaGuardia. With veteran Socialists Pauline Newman, an International Ladies' Garment Workers Union leader who served as vice president of the National Women's Trade Union League (WTUL), and Theresa Wiley, a Schenectady activist and frequent SP candidate for statewide office in New York, they had developed plans to have New York implement "a system of immediate unemployment relief, the establishment of unemployment insurance … a five-day week and a six-hour day," that they hoped to see implemented in late 1932, before the finish of Roosevelt's term as governor. As Roosevelt prepared to relinquish the governorship and move to the White House, however, he was thinking bigger—and listening more intently to the Socialists.

The new president did not adopt the whole of the Socialist platform. But he packed his administration with old Bob La Follette allies such as Harold Ickes, and Norman Thomas backers such as Paul Douglas, who brought Socialist and social-democratic ideas into the White House. And, as historian Paul Berman has observed, "Roosevelt lifted ideas from the likes of Norman Thomas and proclaimed liberal democratic goals for everyone around the world …" FDR's borrowing of ideas about Social Security, unemployment compensation, jobs programs and agricultural assistance from the Socialists was sufficient to pull voters who had rejected the Democrats in 1932 into the New Deal coalition that would sweep the congressional elections of 1934, and re-elect the president with 61 percent of the popular vote and 523 of 531 electoral votes in 1936—the largest Electoral College win in the history of two-party politics.

As for Norman Thomas, he ran again in 1936, conducting what *Time* magazine would refer to as "a more civilized and enlightened campaign than any other candidate." But he amassed only 187,910 votes, for 0.4 percent of the total.

Thomas would joke during the 1930s that "Roosevelt did not carry out the Socialist platform, unless he carried it out on a stretcher." It was an uncharacteristically bitter acknowledgement that FDR had read the results of the 1932 election as a signal to turn left, for, as *Time* noted, "When Franklin Roosevelt's New Deal made those ideas (old-age pensions and public works, unemployment insurance) law, socialism's appeal to the US working class began to diminish."

Thomas experienced that diminishment personally, as his presidential campaigns of 1936, 1940, 1944 and 1948 struggled to attain nationally the number of votes his 1932 campaign had won in New York City alone. In 1946, the Socialists endorsed the development of a new third party that would be "consistent ... with democratic socialism" while operating under another name. But President Harry Truman short-circuited the initiative, at least to some extent, by proposing a national health-care plan and generally moving to the left—so that, while Thomas would insist "Mr. Truman is not a Socialist," he would acknowledge in 1950 that the president had "cut completely loose from the old moorings of genuine free enterprise" and begun to implement programs along the lines of "the old 'immediate demands' that we Socialists pioneered." Thomas mocked Republican plans to mount a "socialism versus liberty" campaign against the Democrats that year. Yet it was true that many backers of Thomas's presidential campaigns had migrated to the Democratic camp, not just as voters and activists but as elected officials. George Rhodes, a veteran labor leader and Socialist Party campaigner who had been a delegate to the 1932 convention that nominated Thomas for his most successful presidential run, was in 1948 elected to Congress as a Democrat representing the old Socialist hotbed of Reading, Pennsylvania; Rhodes would serve in the House until 1968, maintaining a left-wing voting record that earned praise from his former comrades. Paul Douglas, the former Chicago professor who in 1928 had dismissed the Democratic Party as "sterile and corrupt" and organized educators across the country to vote Socialist, and who in 1932 had chaired the "Thomas and Maurer Committee of 100,000" campaign, became a Democrat in 1942 and six years later was elected to the US Senate, where he would serve for eighteen years as one of its most liberal members. Attacked as a "Socialist" during his 1954 re-election campaign, which took place during the darkest days of the McCarthy era, Douglas retorted that the "S" word was an honorable one, and secured re-election by more than 200,000 votes.

Many other Socialists poured their energies into the building of the trade union movement with which the party remained closely aligned, as did the Communists who had early on made a deeper commitment to work within the unions than electoral politics. A. Philip Randolph, a former Socialist editor, organizer and statewide candidate in New York, founded the Brotherhood of Sleeping Car Porters and became the most prominent African-American member of the American Federation of Labor's executive board. At the urging of Norman Thomas, Arkansas Socialist H. L. Mitchell organized the Southern Tenant Farmers Union, a pioneering multiracial union that evolved into the National Farm Labor Union and spawned a new generation of organizers. Among these was United Farm Workers union president Cesar Chavez, who worked closely with Michael Harrington's Democratic Socialists of America, and longtime farmworkers union vice president Dolores Huerta, who continues to serve as DSA's honorary chair. Walter Reuther, a long-standing party member and former Socialist candidate for the Detroit City Council, built the United Auto Workers union into perhaps the most powerful labor organization in the country—along with his brother Victor, who until his death in 2004 (at age ninety-two) was one of the foremost backers of DSA. Sidney Hillman, who cut his political teeth with the socialist Bund movement in his native Lithuania and burst onto the US political landscape as a key union backer of La Follette's 1924 campaign, built up the Amalgamated Clothing Workers of America and became such a powerful player in the Congress of Industrial Organizations—which was home to most but not all of the unions that aligned with the Socialist and Communist parties—that Franklin Roosevelt would defer decisions on labor and political issues until he could "clear it with Sidney." By the late 1930s, the independent political dreams of 1924 and 1932 had given way to a sense that, on the national level at least, the fight was between the increasingly reactionary Republicans—who in the 1944 primaries rejected the liberal internationalism of Wendell Willkie—and the Democratic Party of Roosevelt and Harry Truman. Though Hillman and his allies in New York City poured their energies at the national level into backing Democrats—for the most part—they were actively engaged in forming local political groupings with distinctly social-democratic tendencies, such as the American Labor Party (ALP) and the Liberal Party. In 1948, many of the most radical unions, some of which were closely allied with the Communists, others of which were simply furious at what they saw as Democratic drift toward Cold War sentiment, gave their backing to the Progressive Party of former Vice President Henry Wallace, whose campaign challenged segregationism at home and militarism abroad and won more than half a million votes in New York State on the ALP line.

For the most part, however, the unions were steering toward the Democratic fold.

This frustrated Thomas, who, despite the decline of Socialist electoral fortunes, was not about to partner with the Democratic Party, which he dismissed as a warren of big-city machine pols and southern segregationists, distinguished by a "proportion of hard-shelled reactionaries" that was competitive with the Republican Party. (Only in the 1960s, after his protégé Michael Harrington had begun advising Democratic Presidents John Kennedy and Lyndon Johnson on fighting poverty—and after the Republicans had nominated arch-conservative Barry Goldwater for the presidency—would the old Socialist suggest that there was anything to be gained by casting a Democratic vote, and then only reluctantly.) In the late 1940s, however, Thomas had begun to feel that the Socialist Party had lost the capacity to mount meaningful campaigns at the national level. So it was that, when Socialists gathered for their party's 1950 convention, Thomas battled with his old comrades over whether to continue playing for the presidency and other federal posts. His final presidential run, in 1948, had earned the sort of acclaim accorded to old warhorses on their last lap. But Thomas, who had willingly been arrested, beaten and run out of town for the socialist cause was not satisfied with the elder-statesman role. He fretted that the Socialist Party—and, more importantly, the democratic socialist ideology—that continued to exercise significant influence in the labor and civil rights movements, and in policymaking at both the federal and state levels, would be measured only by the vote totals it received in quadrennial presidential runs. Thomas wanted to "concentrate what funds we have on educational and promotional activities," while continuing to mount electoral campaigns only at the local level.

In effect, he had thrown in with the "sewer socialists." To some extent, he had been there all along. In between presidential runs, Thomas had campaigned for local posts in New York, winning endorsements even from conservatives for a 1931 bid for Manhattan Borough President that promised to break the corrupt grip of the "Tammany Hall" Democratic machine, and that came close to displacing the Republicans as the No. 2 party in the heart of the nation's largest city.

Even as Roosevelt's New Deal stole the thunder of the Socialists at the national level, millions of Americans continued to vote in the 1930s and 1940s for state-based parties that aligned with the Socialists, as in the case of the Wisconsin Progressives, or that proposed social-democratic agendas, as did the Farmer-Labor Party of Minnesota, the Non-Partisan League of North Dakota and the American Labor and Liberal Parties of New York. Left-wing third parties controlled statehouses, sent members of the US House and US Senate to Washington and became definitional players in city halls across the country. In New York, for instance, Mayor LaGuardia was elected and re-elected as the "fusion" candidate of liberal Republicans and the social-democratic left. (Thomas was nominated to oppose him in 1937, but dropped the bid.) Upon his initial election in 1933, LaGuardia brought in Henry Rosner, the veteran economic theorist for the Socialist Party who had led the fight "to abolish the seven-day work week among New York transit employees, hotel and cafeteria workers, and elevator operators in apartment houses," to help develop workplace rules and to establish city-run social welfare programs—something Rosner would eventually do for other cities, states such as Vermont, and the nation of Israel. LaGuardia appointed one of the city's most prominent Socialists, Jacob Panken, to a municipal judgeship, which Panken used as a platform for advocacy on behalf of child welfare not just in New York but nationally. Though he had once been elected to Congress on the Socialist line, LaGuardia was not a Socialist. Other mayors were, however, and they continued to get elected even as the party faded as a force in presidential politics. The mayor of Bridgeport, Connecticut, Jasper McLevy, first elected in 1933, would keep serving through the presidencies of Roosevelt, Truman and Eisenhower, through the Depression, World War II and the "red scare." Up the road in Norwalk, Mayor Irving Freese and a Socialist-dominated city council would run the city from 1947 to 1951. In Reading, Pennsylvania, cigar union activist and veteran Socialist J. Henry Stump was repeatedly elected mayor, finishing his last term in 1947. But nowhere was the Socialist Party more consistently represented in the corridors of power than in Milwaukee.

Daniel Webster Hoan, whose career in the government of Wisconsin's largest city began when he served as city attorney in the administration of the first "sewer socialist" mayor, Emil Seidel, would complete the last of his six terms as mayor in 1940. Arguably the most combative and class-conscious of the Socialist mayors, Hoan dismissed Democrats and Republicans as two sides of the same coin, suggesting that they would ultimately "fuse [so that] there will be only one capitalist party." To counter that party of the powerful, and the corruption that he saw extending from it, Hoan declared, workers needed to organize the Social-ist Party in city after city. "There is no one man anywhere who can clean up a city. If I had been alone in Milwaukee, they would have had me in the canal in ten days," he told a crowd of 15,000 that gathered for a Socialist picnic in Reading, Pennsylvania, in the fall of 1932. "Unless the workers band together into an army, nominate and elect their own candidates, there is no hope against corruption. No day goes by in Milwaukee when some grafting contractor or an emissary does not appear in City Hall wanting to take some privilege away from the people. The workers need their own close-knit political party."

During the early years of the Great Depression, when substantial numbers of workers looked to the Socialist and Communist parties for leadership, Hoan argued that the most important work of the Socialists was at the municipal level, where services were delivered. The party swept to its strongest position in years following the 1932 municipal elections that saw the reelection of Hoan, the election of Socialist City Attorney Max Raskin and the seating of a number of young comrades on the city council. The "sewer socialists," declared Mayor Hoan, were ready to act. "Down at Washington, the only way they could think of giving relief was to give the railroads, the banks and the insurance companies money," roared Hoan. "The men in Washington don't have a plan." So it fell to the Socialists in the cities. "Twenty-five thousand families must be fed this winter in Milwaukee and we propose to feed them, if it's the last thing we do," the mayor announced in October 1932. "People are entitled to eat and families are entitled to a roof over their heads." And Hoan was as good as his word, developing a pioneering municipal program that pur-chased food in bulk and then made it available at low cost to Milwaukee families via a network of pristine public markets. He also developed a municipally-funded public housing program to provide "a roof over their heads."

While Hoan's rhetoric was revolutionary—he declared that Milwaukee's private streetcar company operated "under the black flag of monopolistic piracy"—his governance was practical and efficient. He got things done, so ably that in 1936, after two decades with Hoan at the helm, *Time* magazine would describe Milwaukee as "perhaps the best-governed city in the US." The Milwaukee Police Department got the highest marks in the country for honesty and public service, with the national Wickersham Commission (headed by a former Republican Attorney General) hailing it as the only municipal force deserving of "unqualified endorsement." The city was garlanded with awards for municipal programs to promote traffic safety, fire prevention and, above all, public health. As historian John Gurda notes, "The health prize came home so often that Milwaukee had to be retired from competition to give other municipalities a chance."

It was in the area of public health policy that the Milwaukee Socialists most influenced national affairs. The ideas developed in Milwaukee influenced state and national leaders as they began to develop models for everything from food safety to mass immunization to neighborhood and school clinics. Harry Hopkins, one of the architects of the New Deal, had studied Milwaukee's public health innovations while overseeing programs of the New York Association for Improving the Condition of the Poor; Hopkins brought that background to the White House, where he would eventually supervise the Federal Emergency Relief Administration (FERA), the Civil Works Administration (CWA), and the Works Progress Administration (WPA). The influence of the Milwaukee Socialists on debates about public health programs would extend well into the 1960s when, after he finished serving three terms as the city's Socialist mayor, Frank Zeidler worked for many years as a consultant to the Ford Foundation. Similarly, after Milwaukee became the first city to enact comprehensive zoning rules, Hoan became one of the leading spokesmen in the US on issues relating to city planning, with his ideas influencing debates in cities across the country.

Amusingly, the Socialists were also recognized for practicing what might today be referred to as "fiscal conservatism." Because they feared "bondage to the banks," Hoan and his fellow "sewer socialists" operated on a pay-as-you-go basis that eventually made Milwaukee the only major city in the United States that was debt free.

Urban affairs writer Melvin Holli and a group of experts on local government would in 1999 hail Hoan as one of the finest mayors in the nation's history, with Holli observing: "Perhaps Hoan's most important legacy was cleaning up the free-and-easy corruption that prevailed before he took office. Hoan's quarter century in office made the change stick, and it seems to have elevated Milwaukee's politics above that of other cities in honesty, efficiency and delivery of public services."

Though his was the longest Socialist administration in American history, lasting twenty-four years, Hoan left office at the relatively young age of fifty-nine. He was not finished with politics. Like Pennsylvania's George Rhodes and Illinois' Paul Douglas, among many others, Hoan made his way into the Democratic Party and became its nominee for governor of Wisconsin in 1944 and 1946. While the transition was somewhat ironic, considering the ferocity with which he had condemned Democratic corruption in the early 1930s, the fact that Hoan found a home within the Democratic Party—as a determined social democrat who still quoted Marx—was not a sign of political hypocrisy. The Roosevelt years changed the character and focus of the Democratic Party in states such as Wisconsin, such that when the old Progressive Party (which at its peak had aligned with the Socialists) ceased to stand candidates for office in 1946, many of its younger members (such as future US Senator Gaylord Nelson) became Democrats.

Hoan was not elected to the governorship in those campaigns of the mid-1940s. But a Milwaukee Socialist who had chosen to stay within the party's fold was about to again raise the red flag over the city.

After Hoan left office in 1940, non-Socialists governed the city for eight years. But Socialists continued to serve in municipal and school posts, with one of the most ardent of their number, Frank Zeidler, winning election to the school board. In 1948, two years after the election of Joe McCarthy as Wisconsin's US Senator, at a time when the Cold War was dawning and McCarthy and Richard Nixon were plotting a "red scare" that would make absurd associations of even the mildest reformers (especially the supporters of civil rights) with the sins of the Soviet Union's Joe Stalin, Zeidler would be elected to the first of three terms as mayor of Milwaukee.

From a historical standpoint, the most remarkable thing about Zeidler's tenure as a socialist mayor was the fact that it coincided with the McCarthy era, a brutal time when the junior senator from Wisconsin along with California Congressman, Senator and then Vice President Nixon and their acolytes in both political parties used the new medium of the moment—television—to create a Cold War at home. The McCarthyites engaged in guilt-by-association assaults not just on the handful of Americans who remained enthusiastic about Stalin after the US partnered with the Soviet leader during World War II but on the thousands of activists and artists whose only "crime" had been a willingness to support broad campaigns on behalf of peace and economic and social justice. Blacklists were developed, not just in Hollywood, where many of the country's most talented actors, writers and directors were hounded out of the entertainment industry, but in virtually every corner of the country. Universities, public school systems, radio and television networks, newspapers and government agencies, trade unions and private businesses purged able employees who had mistakenly presumed that the First Amendment to the Constitution protected their right to freedom of speech, assembly and association.

The House Committee on Un-American Activities, the Senate Internal Security Subcommittee, and the Senate Permanent Subcommittee on Investigations (led by McCarthy) conducted 109 high-profile hearings between 1949 and 1954, at which members of the Communist Party, prominent entertainers, trade unionists and community organizers were forced to testify about their past activities, their personal lives and, above all, their political views. The process was repeated a thousand times over, as state and local Un-American Activities committees and police agencies conducted their own, often more irresponsible hearings and investigations. Government agencies and schools required employees to swear arcane "loyalty oaths" and to undergo investigations into whether their affirmations had been true. By the late 1950s, it was estimated that roughly one out of every five US workers had been required to undergo some sort of loyalty review. And to stand accused was, in any case, to be devastated. The head of the federal Loyalty Review Board explained what happened to those who were subjected to inquiries and did not satisfy their interrogators: "A man is ruined everywhere and forever. No responsible employer would be likely to take a chance in giving him a job." More than 3,000 members of longshore and seafaring unions were blacklisted and lost their jobs, in just one example of how entire industries purged idealistic, mostly young workers who had dared to join trade unions, campaign for civil rights or oppose militarism.

Much more than employment was lost. Freedom was sacrificed as well. Despite the fact that the American Communist Party's constitution explicitly rejected revolutionary violence, 140 party leaders and activists were during the late 1940s and 1950s charged with violating the Alien Registration Act (Smith Act) that made it a criminal offense to "knowingly or willfully advocate, abet, advise or teach the duty, necessity, desirability or propriety of overthrowing the Government of the United States or of any State by force or violence, or for anyone to organize any association which teaches, advises or encourages such an overthrow, or for anyone to become a member of or to affiliate with any such association." Almost 100 CP members were jailed for the "crime" of joining a political party that had fallen out of favor. Immigrant activists were hounded and often forced to flee the country, as were many of America's best and brightest artists, including screenwriters Dalton Trumbo and Hugo Butler. Charlie Chaplin, who was denied re-entry to the United States after traveling to Britain for a film premiere, would eventually observe: "Since the end of the last world war, I have been the object of lies and propaganda by powerful reactionary groups who, by their influence and by the aid of America's yellow press, have created an unhealthy atmosphere in which liberal-minded individuals can be singled out and persecuted. Under these conditions I find it virtually impossible to continue my motion-picture work, and I have therefore given up my residence in the United States." After being acquitted in a trial brought under the Smith Act, W. E. B. Du Bois, one of the greatest of the nation's scholars and public intellectuals, was at the age of ninety-five denied the US passport that would have allowed him to return to the country of his birth in 1963. Du Bois died in Ghana a few months later, on the day before the Rev. Martin Luther King, Jr. delivered the "I Have a Dream" speech to the March on Washington for Jobs and Justice.

Many of those who were accused of disloyalty suffered from breakdowns, and suicides were common as a result of the fearmongering and frequently false accusations. It was such a dark passage that playwright Arthur Miller suggested the whole of the nation had been overtaken by a madness akin to that seen during the Salem Witch Trials. "In this country," historian Ellen Schrecker explains, "McCarthyism did more damage to the constitution than the American Communist Party ever did." Social movements, especially those that championed civil rights, were targeted for investigation and harassment. Militant labor unions and organizations that had accepted FDR's charge to the left—"go out and make me do it"—were among the primary targets. The point was to soften their messages, blunt their activism and ultimately limit the ability of mass movements to influence presidents and political parties to serve masters who did not maintain addresses on Wall Street. And it worked; even liberal Democrats, such as Hubert Humphrey, took leadership roles in authoring draconian legislation, such as the Communist Control Act of 1954.

Political parties that pressured and challenged the Democrats and Republicans from the left took some of the hardest hits. Just as the first "red scare" of the late 1910s and early 1920s targeted leaders of a political party, Socialists such as Eugene Victor Debs and Victor Berger, the second "red scare" targeted leaders of another political party, the Communists. While the Communist Control Act of 1954 was specifically used to bar Communists only from the ballot in New Jersey, the practical reality of all the laws, hearings and oaths was to suppress and weaken the party and its allies in unions and social movements. Thousands of Communists quit the party and in many cases withdrew from political activism. But McCarthy and his minions were engaged in a broader project, which extended far beyond the boundaries of the CP. The Progressive Party, which in 1948 had nominated former Vice President Henry Wallace for president and attracted more than one million votes (2.4 percent of the national total), was subjected to steady official harassment because of the role Communists (along with FDR New Dealers,

Minnesota Farmer-Laborites, liberals and socialists of varying stripes) had played in its formation. It dissolved in 1955. New York State's American Labor Party, which had elected members of Congress and been embraced by Franklin Roosevelt, who accepted its 1940 and 1944 presidential nominations, lost its ballot line in 1954 and was formally folded by its state committee in 1956. (Intriguingly, some of the last officials holding office in New York State with ALP ties—thanks to New York's fusion-voting system, which allowed candidates to run on multiple party lines—were Republican legislators from the Bronx and Brooklyn. That should come as no great surprise, as the ALP's most prominent player, Congressman Vito Marcantonio, got his start as a Republican and frequently ran with joint Republican-ALP support.)

The Socialist Party shrank to a mere shadow of its former self, with the national vote for its presidential candidates declining from just under 140,000 in 1948 to barely 2,000 in 1956. By the end of the 1950s, the Socialists had—like the Communists—decided to stop nominating presidential tickets. Yet, in Milwaukee, Zeidler remained as a proud Socialist mayor; in addition to leading the city and battling McCarthy, he even found time to work with Thomas on the frustrating project of uniting socialist factions—including the Social Democratic Federation and the Independent Socialist League led by Max Shachtman—under the Socialist banner.

It might seem amazing today, when Glenn Beck describes modest social spending in *Darkness at Noon* terms and when even supposedly moderate commentators conflate social democracy and Stalinism, that the good burghers of Milwaukee would elect and re-elect a Socialist mayor throughout the McCarthy era—and in McCarthy's home state, no less. But there is simply no question that the quality of debate, the range of ideological diversity and the level of social and political awareness were far higher for most Americans in the 1940s and 1950s—and dramatically higher for media commentators. Americans in general, and Milwaukeeans in particular, understood the distinction between municipal socialists who believed in public enterprise and totalitarian dictators who wanted to rule the world. Norman Thomas, at the national level, and the "sewer socialists" in cities across the country, were plenty capable of explaining the difference between democratic socialism and Stalinism.

To be sure, Zeidler experienced his share of red-baiting. He was attacked by opponents who highlighted his socialist views. Henry Reuss, a liberal (and future chairman of the House Banking Committee) whom Zeidler beat in the election of 1948, ranted and raved during the campaign about "Socialist dogma" and announced in a debate two weeks before the election: "My opponent's Socialism is of the authentic Karl Marx variety. He thinks the city ought to be running the corner grocery store." As it happened, Zeidler's socialism was not of "the authentic Karl Marx variety." "I did not, nor do I now, subscribe to the theory of the inevitability of Socialism as described by Marx, nor to his kind of Socialism," Zeidler explained, as he recalled the attacks by Reuss. "I am and was a democratic Socialist who believed that freedom and liberty are important to all individuals and public ownership and socialist controls are necessary to achieve the greatest freedom and greatest liberty for people." In other words, Frank Zeidler wasn't Joe Stalin. He did not want to municipalize grocery stores. He despised monopolies and faceless corporations but he respected—and, more importantly, knew—the neighborhood grocers of the city as working-class men and women who were scared about getting rolled over by the burgeoning grocery-store chains of the post-war era. They didn't mind if Zeidler used some "socialist controls" to assure that locally-owned stores could compete on an even playing field. Indeed, a few days after the debate, the conservative *Milwaukee Sentinel* noted that "Al Hoffman and Joseph Weiss, president and secretary of the Independent Neighborhood Grocers Association here, said they were endorsing Zeidler." As the candidate noted, "There was no better answer to the charge that I would socialize the corner grocery store."

Milwaukeeans got it. They recognized, as historian Gurda would explain years later, that:

> The key to understanding Milwaukee's Socialists is the idea of public enterprise. They didn't just manage, and they didn't just enforce laws and regulations. They pushed a program of public necessities that had a tangible impact on the average citizen's quality of life: public parks, public libraries, public schools, public health, public works (including sewers), public port facilities, public housing, public vocational education and even public natatoria.

Underlying their notion of public enterprise was an abiding faith— curiously antique by today's standards—in the goodness of government, especially local government. The Socialists believed that government was the locus of our common wealth—the resources that belong to all of us and each of us—and they worked to build a community of interest around a deeply shared belief in the common good.

When all was said and done, however, it was not Zeidler's dream of a cooperative commonwealth nor his Socialist Party membership card that generated the most severe abuse. The mayor took harder hits for his ardent advocacy on behalf of desegregation. So brutal were the attacks on his championing of civil rights in the 1950s that *Time* magazine, in an article headlined "The Shame of Milwaukee," would detail how the mayor's re-election campaign of 1956 had been placed in jeopardy by a vicious smear campaign that suggested he was doing too much to make the city hospitable to African Americans. Among other things, it was claimed that Zeidler had erected billboards across the south urging the sharecroppers of Mississippi and Alabama to come north and take the jobs of Milwaukee's ethnic German and Polish workers. Zeidler objected to the attempt by his opponents to sow "racial tension where none existed before," and preached the old Socialist line that elites would always try to divide workers along lines of race and ethnicity—since "the workers united could never be defeated."

Zeidler's backers announced: "We rightly condemn the mistreatment of Negroes in the South. Let no one in Milwaukee condone the mistreatment of Negroes in the North."

A decade before "backlash" campaigns divided cities across the country, Zeidler and his Socialist supporters faced one down, and defeated it. With strong votes from African-American and white ethnic neighborhoods, Zeidler was re-elected to a third and final term.

Twelve years after he beat the red-baiting of Henry Reuss, and four years after he beat the race-baiting of his 1956 opponents, Zeidler would leave office not as a defeated ideologue but as a satisfied man: one who had established a pioneering human rights commission to promote racial tolerance, expanded public housing, developed parks rather than high-rise apartment houses along Milwaukee's Lake Michigan lakefront, gotten a public television station on air and kept local government free of graft and corruption, maintained one of the lowest bonded debts among the country's twenty largest cities, refused pay raises, and rode a city bus home after finishing his tenure as one of the nation's highest-profile urban leaders.

Remarkably, Zeidler would live forty-six years as Milwaukee's former mayor.

We did not get to know one another until the better part of two decades after he left office, at a point when he was seeking the presidency as the nominee of the Socialist Party that had urged the election of Debs in 1912 and La Follette in 1924. For Frank Zeidler there would be no five-million vote result, nor even a one-million result. But his candidacy generated several slightly bemused articles in the *New York Times* and other newspapers around the country. And the two of us began a conversation about democratic socialism that would last the better part of three decades.

One of my favorite political artifacts is a "Zeidler for President" campaign pin that Frank gave me years ago. He was proud of the pin—with its orderly assemblage of anti-militarist and pro-industrial policy symbols—and of the campaign, which, like so many of the great civic gestures he engaged in over nearly eight decades of public life, was as much about "keeping the red flag flying" than actually winning.

In 1976, when the Socialist Party was struggling to get its bearings after a series of internal struggles, splits and resignations, Frank presented himself as its standard-bearer. Campaigning on a platform that promised a shift of national priorities from bloated defense spending to fighting poverty, rebuilding cities and creating a national health-care program, Frank won only a portion of the respect that was due this kind and decent man and the values to which he has devoted a lifetime.

Had Frank been born in another land—perhaps Germany, where the roots of his family tree were firmly planted—his national campaign at the head of the ticket of the Socialist Party would have been a much bigger deal. Indeed, he might well have been elected. His long and well-regarded service as the mayor of a major city and the national attention he earned during the 1960s as an advocate for urban America were certainly qualifiers; after all, his old friend Willy Brandt had risen from the mayoralty of Berlin to the position of foreign minister in the German "grand coalition" of the late 1960s before becoming the first Social Democratic chancellor of what was then known as West Germany.

In 1976 Brandt became president of the Socialist International, in an era when the social-democratic values Frank had advanced throughout his long life were proving to be so popular that a *Time* magazine cover story of the day would open with an observation that:

> It began as an outcry against "the dark satanic mills" of early capitalism, a shuddering reaction against the profound upheavals caused by the Industrial Revolution, a reassertion of the Utopian dream of the heavenly kingdom on earth. It sprang from obscure clubs, from workers' associations, from garrets, libraries, bourgeois parlors and, occasionally, aristocratic salons. It was hounded, reviled, extolled. It became the most pervasive political ideology—or slogan—of the twentieth century. Socialism.
>
> Today it seems to have reached new heights of influence.

Latin America and the Caribbean were experiencing a revival of socialist fervor in the 1970s, as were southern Asia and Africa. Australia elected a socialist government, and so did New Zealand. Virtually every European country took a social-democratic turn during the course of the decade that saw the Socialist International—in which Germany's Social Democrats, Britain's Labourites and France's soon to be dominant Socialists allied with parties of the left from around the world—emerge as one of the great forums for shaping new thinking about civil society, development and peacemaking.

The Socialist Party of the United States was a member in good standing of the Socialist International, but not exactly an electoral powerhouse. Frank collected only 6,038 votes in 1976—4,298 of them from Wisconsin. So my "Zeidler for President" pin is more a rare artifact than a record of consequential electioneering.

Like the man whose name it features, the pin is a reminder of a politics of principle that was once a muscular force in our presidential politics, influential enough to get its adherents invited to the White House and to see its platforms reworked as national policy. Long after Eugene Victor Debs and Norman Thomas stopped bidding for the presidency, Socialists continued to win elections and govern at the grass roots—where

Americans live. In that sense, socialism did happen here. Not at the head-line-grabbing national level, but in the communities where we reside.

"Sewer socialism" remains a political reality, even if it goes by other names in places ranging from Burlington, Vermont, where independent socialists, social democrats and radicals of varying stripes have governed for the better part of thirty years, to San Francisco, where members of Democratic Socialists of America, Greens and local radicals—running with the support of the vibrantly independent San Francisco *Bay Guardian* newspaper—have kept alive the faith in public enterprise and social democracy. The contribution made by "sewer socialism" and its modern manifestations to the quality of our lives, to our national discourse and to a global understanding of socialism in practice remains far greater than tends to be recognized by a distracted media and a disoriented political class.

In the last years of his life, however, Frank Zeidler's contribution—a humane, duty-driven, economically responsible version of socialism grounded in principles of public enterprise and public service—gained a measure of the recognition it deserved. Unfortunately, that recognition came more frequently from foreigners than from Americans.

Frank was the repository of a Milwaukee Socialist tradition with German radical roots and a record of accomplishment—grand parks along that city's lakefront, nationally recognized public health programs, pioneering open housing initiatives, and an unrivaled reputation for clean government—that filled the circumspect former mayor with an uncharacteristic pride for the rest of his life.

Frank always argued that "sewer socialism" was about much more than infrastructure and service delivery. The Milwaukee Socialists engaged in a remarkably successful experiment in human nature, rooted in their faith that cooperation could deliver more than competition.

"Socialism as we attempted to practice it here believes that people working together for a common good can produce a greater benefit, both for society and for the individual, than can a society in which everyone is shrewdly seeking their own self-interest," Zeidler told me one weekday afternoon, as we sat in the tiny office on the edge of Milwaukee's down-town that served as the party headquarters. "And I think our record remains one of many more successes than failures."

Frank and I had gotten together on the eve of an 1999 event at which the contribution he had made to Milwaukee and to the world was honored by people who well understood the significance of what this American Socialist did, and what he continued to do, as someone whose activism flagged only slightly as he passed through his eighties and into his nineties.

At a gathering in the main branch of the Milwaukee Public Library, a favorite haunt of the man who as mayor battled to expand it, the Friedrich Ebert Foundation recognized Zeidler for his many years of public service and his unique contributions to the socialist cause.

Based in Bonn, Germany, the foundation was established in 1925 as a political legacy of Friedrich Ebert, Germany's first democratically elected president. A socialist, Ebert became president of a devastated Germany in the years after World War I, when he struggled to rebuild it as a free and responsible nation.

Banned by the Nazis in 1933, the Friedrich Ebert Foundation began its work anew in 1947 and today operates educational programs and other activities in more than 100 countries. It awards thousands of scholarships in Germany and around the world, and maintains an internationally recognized library on the history of labor.

Dieter Dettke, executive director of the foundation's Washington office, came to Milwaukee to present Frank Zeidler with a bound volume of German constitutions—a text that the former mayor, whose facility with languages was one of his many political assets, could read without the assistance of a translator.

American politics being what they are, Frank was never in his lifetime accorded the full measure of honor due him in his own land. But the rest of the planet took inspiration from the white-haired Milwaukee Socialist whose faith in the possibility of a better world withstood the batterings of economic depression, war, McCarthyism, the Cold War, and the Nixon, Reagan and Bush eras. And Americans who believe this country needs to push beyond the narrow boundaries—and frequently false choices—dictated by status quo politics would do well to recognize the distinct brand of very democratic, very efficient and very popular socialism that Zeidler and his comrades nurtured in cities large and small across the United States.

We don't have to look elsewhere for models. They are here, just below the surface in our great cities, just a few pages further back in the history books. Some years after Frank's death, when the 100th anniversary of the first great Socialist victories arrived on April 6, 2010, a young Milwaukee alderman, who had interviewed Zeidler and used a picture of the former mayor on his campaign literature when he was elected to the common council in 2008, hailed the date. "One hundred years ago today, the citizens of Milwaukee woke up to election results that surprised the rest of the country at the time, and would surprise most Milwaukeeans today," Alderman Nik Kovac began. "On April 5, 1910, we elected a Socialist mayor, former patternmaker Emil Seidel, as well as Socialist majorities to the Common Council and the County Board." Kovac continued:

> The rest of the country—and some of Milwaukee—was unsettled by this boldness at the polls, openly wondering if it meant sedition or perhaps even revolution. In fact, the citizens of Milwaukee and their newly elected leaders had no such plans. All we wanted then, as now, was honest, efficient, transparent, frugal, and socially just government. For thirty-eight of the next fifty years, that is exactly what this city received from Mayors Seidel (1910–12), Daniel Hoan (1916–40) and Frank Zeidler (1948–60).
>
> The Socialists' most immediate and noteworthy accomplishment, 100 years ago, was to root out municipal corruption, much of which came from the brothels in City Hall's shadow and from the privately-owned streetcar which stopped at its front door. With that task complete, Hoan and Zeidler then set about building public institutions which continue to improve our lives today.
>
> Mayor Hoan will forever be remembered not just for his bridge, but also for expanding and improving one of the world's great park systems. Mayor Zeidler was a consistent source of integrity and justice during his three terms and beyond, and his main physical legacy is the human-scale and geographically diverse public housing throughout this city. Both the park system and the housing authority are still winning national awards and setting examples for other cities to follow.
>
> A century ago, the word "Socialism" raised eyebrows and suspicion. And if the rhetoric surrounding the health-care debate in 2010 is any indication, that word still has the power to enrage and divide our chattering classes and voting blocs. But words often confuse, and labels can distort the substance of policy.

> When I hear the word Socialism, my first thought is not of revolutions, wars, or bread lines. We in Milwaukee have our own history, and our own meaning of that word. To us it means a half-century of good government. It means honest politicians and informed voters. It means beautiful parks, dignified housing for all, and well-run utilities free of corruption.

This is how Frank wanted to be remembered: as a Socialist who won elections and accomplished great things—not for personal glory but for a cause that was always bigger than one man, one election or one city.

"The concept that motivates us is a community good as opposed to the concept of an individual pursuing their own self-interest and that somehow the public good comes out of that," Zeidler told me. "Our concept is that a pursuit of the good of the whole produces the best condition for the good of the individual."

The "sewer socialist" credo always recognized the individualism of Americans, but refused to accept that Americans were merely individuals. Socialists like Frank Zeidler believed that this country's rugged individuals were also citizens, and that together they could forge a whole that was greater than the sum of its parts. That whole would, Frank believed, be a cooperative commonwealth, operating first in a municipality, then in a state and finally on a national scale.

Frank Zeidler spent a lifetime pursing this cooperative commonwealth. Even when he was very old, he still believed in the possibility of its arrival. Indeed, he was certain it would come to America, if not in his lifetime, then surely in the lifetime of the children and grandchildren he so cherished. That certainty was grounded not in idealism but in the experience of life spent toiling in the trenches of municipal politics; an experience that told him that patriotic Americans, of different races, ethnicities and backgrounds, could and would cast their ballots for Socialists and for socialism.

"There is always a charge that socialism does not fit human nature. We've encountered that for a long time," Frank told me in one of our last conversations. "Maybe that's true. But can't people be educated? Can't people learn to cooperate with each other? Surely that must be our goal, because the alternative is redolent with war and poverty and all the ills of the world."

CHAPTER FIVE

"Simply a Stupid Piece of Despotism": How Socialists Saved the First Amendment

Today we are confronting a turning point in the history of our country. If the capitalist class can succeed in silencing the radical and Socialist press, all our liberties are doomed. Shall we permit this?

> —Victor Berger, after the federal government restricted his
> newspaper's access to the mails during World War I, 1917

Socialists are the one class of citizens who believe in a lawful, orderly change through education and political action. They are presumptuous enough to believe that the policy of the Government in war or out, the attitude of the President in war or out, are subject to criticism. Socialists the world over have opposed war and the system that makes war inevitable. We do not consider opposition to a condition or policy an equivalent to breaking or violating the laws of the country.

> —Seymour Stedman, attorney for Berger and other Socialists
> indicted for exercising their First Amendment rights, 1918

[His] attempt to enter Congress with such a record savors of impudence.

> —*New York Times*, which supported efforts to prosecute
> Berger, endorsing the decision of the US House to bar
> the Socialist even after he was duly elected, 1919

Has it come to the point that a man who believes certain things cannot be heard?

> —James Mann, Republican congressman for Illinois, 1920

Victor Berger's name will stand in the future as that of a martyr to a great cause—the rights of free speech, free press, and representative government.
—Edward Voigt, Republican congressman for Wisconsin, 1920

On a November afternoon in 1917, Victor Berger, one of America's most prominent newspaper editors, wrote to his wife Meta from the nation's capital. Berger's message was a chilling one: "There is no Constitution in Washington, DC, just now ..."

Over the next five years, Berger would endeavor at daunting personal and political cost to rescue the Constitution in general, and in particular its First Amendment. His struggle would ultimately succeed in renewing freedom of the press protections, as well as other basic liberties, and in so doing establish a framework for robust dissent that remains to this day.

It was Berger, arguably to a greater extent than any journalist of the twentieth century, whose battles enshrined the principle that reporters, editors and commentators have a right to challenge presidents and policies to which they object, even in wartime and even when those objections are to the authority of a commander-in-chief to dictate the nation's direction at home or abroad. When a Rush Limbaugh, a Glenn Beck or a *New York Post* editorial writer vents against a President Obama—just as when a Rachel Maddow or a Keith Olbermann or a *New York Times* editorial writer challenged a President Bush—they do so with the security of knowing that their speech is protected. It does not matter whether a president is enjoying high approval ratings; it does not matter that times are turbulent.

This certainty of protection for dissenting speech was defined as we know it in the modern age by the battles Berger fought, as a patriotic American who believed in the full promise of the Constitution, and as one of the era's leading Socialists.

These facts of our American history should not come as a surprise. Basic liberties are invariably defended and defined by radicals of the left and right who challenge the existing order. After all, a champion of the status quo is unlikely to attract much antipathy from the authorities. But the outlier, the speaker of truths as yet unrecognized as true, the rabble-rouser seeking to rally a dissident movement, the radical who stirs sufficient controversy to inspire an official response—these are speakers and writers who threaten the existing order and hold out the promise of a new age. And it has ever been true that only in the defense of the outlier are the rules of rhetorical engagement meaningfully established.

For journalists working on newspapers—and for the broadcast and digital practitioners of the craft that shapes what we refer to as the free press—it was the courage of Victor Berger and his fellow Socialist editors during the period from 1917 to 1922 that defined our contemporary freedom of inquiry and comment. No one expects Ann Coulter to thank a Socialist for the license she enjoys. No one expects Glenn Beck to dedicate a program to the Socialists who preserved and extended his freedom. But thinking Americans would do well to recognize that, once upon a time in their country, freedom of the press protections hung in the balance. And Socialists tipped that balance toward liberty.

It was not an easy struggle.

Victory was never assured, and often deferred by the authorities, the courts and the Congress.

For not just weeks or months, but years, there was every reason to fear the threat posed by what Berger described in a 1917 letter as "the dangerous autocracy we are establishing here at home."

To all intents and purposes, Berger was correct when he suggested in the fall of that tumultuous year that "there is no Constitution." Of course, the document still existed. It was archived and even taught, if gingerly, in the schools. Members of the US House and Senate still swore to "support and defend the Constitution of the United States against all enemies, foreign and domestic" and to "bear true faith and allegiance to the same; that I take this obligation freely, without any mental reservation or purpose of evasion; and that I will well and faithfully discharge the duties of the office on which I am about to enter: So help me God." But the guarantee of liberty—especially for dissenting journalists and political activists—was disappearing.

From the spring of 1917, when Woodrow Wilson broke his promise to keep the United States out of World War I, the president and his administration, along with its congressional allies and the nation's leading newspapers, waged an often brutal campaign to suppress domestic dissent. There was mass opposition to the war, not just among Socialists and anarchists on the left, but among more conservative German and

Irish immigrants who objected to the rush by Wilson, an Anglophile, to align the United States with the cause of the British monarchy. When the president sought congressional approval for his declaration of war in April 1917, Senator George Norris, a progressive Republican from Nebraska, demanded to know why Wilson and Wall Street were agitating for the sacrifice of American lives in "the useless and senseless war now being waged in Europe." Montana Representative Jeannette Rankin, the first woman elected to Congress (as a progressive Republican, who secured significant support from Socialist precincts in a state that was a hotbed of union organizing), announced her opposition with a declaration that: "the first time the first woman has a chance to say no against war she should say it." In so doing, she joined fifty members of the House and a half dozen senators in an opposition bloc led by Wisconsin Republican Robert M. La Follette, Sr., who charged the president with seeking to "inflame the mind of our people into the frenzy of war."

La Follette, a friend and frequent ally of Berger's, outlined on the Senate floor an argument for why it was appropriate, in fact necessary, to object to what he identified as an ill-conceived and unnecessary militarism:

> I had supposed until recently that it was the duty of senators and representatives in Congress to vote and act according to their convictions on all public matters that came before them for consideration and decision. Quite another doctrine has recently been promulgated by certain newspapers, which unfortunately seems to have found considerable support elsewhere, and that is the doctrine of "standing back of the President" without inquiring whether the President is right or wrong.
>
> For myself, I have never subscribed to that doctrine and never shall. I shall support the President in the measures he proposes when I believe them to be right. I shall oppose measures proposed by the President when I believe them to be wrong. The fact that the matter which the President submits for consideration is of the greatest importance is only an additional reason why we should be sure that we are right, and not to be swerved from that conviction or intimidated in its expression by any influence of power whatsoever.
>
> If it is important for us to speak and vote our convictions in matters of internal policy, though we may unfortunately be in disagreement with the

President, it is infinitely more important for us to speak and vote our convictions when the question is one of peace or war, certain to involve the lives and fortunes of many of our people and, it may be, the destiny of all of them and of the civilized world as well. If, unhappily, on such momentous questions the most patient research and conscientious consideration we could give to them leave us in disagreement with the President, I know of no course to take except to oppose, regretfully but not the less firmly, the demands of the Executive ...

Those words might not seem particularly radical today, and they certainly would not have unsettled the founders of the republic, who crafted a Constitution that included strict checks and balances on the executive branch with the purpose, as George Mason explained, of "clogging rather than facilitating war." In the early years of the American experiment, it would have been thought absurd and anti-American to limit dissent before or during a time of war. During the Anglo-American War of 1812, no less an authority than Daniel Webster, then a young congressman from New Hampshire, would argue against "forcing the free men of the country into the ranks of an army, for the general purposes of war," while the New York Post would dismiss the conflict as "humbugging on a large scale," and warn readers against "the folly of joining the army."

But Wilson, who had just been re-elected as the "He Kept Us Out of War" candidate and was highly conscious of the conflict's unpopularity among key voting blocs, sought to repress dissent with some of the most draconian measures ever enacted by a wartime president. After an initial show of grumbling, most members of Congress became, if anything, even more disregarding of the Bill of Rights than the commander-in-chief. Two months after the war began, Wilson and Attorney General Thomas Gregory developed and secured passage of the National Defense Law, which came to be known in popular parlance as the Espionage Act of 1917. The act made it a crime to express views or to convey information that could be construed by the government as any sort of threat to the war effort.

Vague in its definitions of insubordination and disloyalty, yet specific and extreme in its prescriptions for those charged with violations of the law—punishable in some cases by death and in others by incarceration for up to twenty years—the Espionage Act was immediately implemented, with the intent of scuttling even mild opposition to the war. On the day of its passage, June 15, 1917, US marshals raided the Manhattan office where the No Conscription League of New York published the magazines *Mother Earth* and the *Blast*, in which Emma Goldman and Alexander Berkman spread an anti-draft message that declared: "We oppose conscription because we are internationalists, anti-militarists, and opposed to all wars waged by capitalistic governments."

The crackdown on freedom of the press had begun, albeit in "Keystone Kops" fashion, as Goldman recalled in her address to the jury that would eventually convict her under the Espionage Act:

> On the day after our arrest it was given out by the US Marshal and the District Attorney's office that the "big fish" of the No Conscription activities had been caught, and that there would be no more troublemakers and disturbers to interfere with the highly democratic effort of the Government to conscript its young manhood for the European slaughter. What a pity that the faithful servants of the Government, personified in the US Marshal and the District Attorney, should have used such a weak and flimsy net for their big catch. The moment the anglers pulled their heavily laden net ashore, it broke, and all the labor was so much wasted energy.
>
> The methods employed by [US] Marshal McCarthy and his hosts of heroic warriors were sensational enough to satisfy the famous circus men, Barnum & Bailey. A dozen or more heroes dashing up two flights of stairs, prepared to stake their lives for their country, only to discover the two dangerous disturbers and troublemakers, Alexander Berkman and Emma Goldman, in their separate offices, quietly at work at their desks, wielding not a sword, nor a gun or a bomb, but merely their pens!

It soon became clear that those who wielded the pens—and ran the presses—were primary targets of the "dangerous autocracy" that was being established.

The authorities celebrated the fact that the raid that snatched Goldman and Berkman also yielded "a wagonload of anarchist records and propaganda." Included in that wagonload, according to the marshals, were the subscription lists of the two publications edited by Goldman and Berkman. Those lists contained 10,000 names and served as the basis upon which "red scare" raids were carried out in communities across the country.

Charged under the Espionage Act with conspiracy to "induce persons not to register [for the draft]," Goldman refused at trial to deny or deconstruct her anti-war stance. She proudly defended her position, and suggested that those who would deny her rights to freedom of speech and freedom of the press were making a mockery of what was presented as a war "to make the world safe for democracy":

> We say that if America has entered the war to make the world safe for democracy, she must first make democracy safe in America. How else is the world to take America seriously, when democracy at home is daily being outraged, free speech suppressed, peaceable assemblies broken up by overbearing and brutal gangsters in uniform; when free press is curtailed and every independent opinion gagged? Verily, poor as we are in democracy, how can we give of it to the world?

Goldman had little expectation of receiving justice from a judge, Julius Marshuetz Mayer, who she saw as an extension of the state. But she hoped that a jury of her peers might rise to the constitutional call. Unfortunately, under instructions from Judge Mayer to reject Goldman's description of the First Amendment's intent, the jury convicted the anarchists. Judge Mayer then imposed the maximum sentence for both Goldman and Berkman: two years' behind bars, a $10,000 fine each, and the prospect of deportation upon their release from prison.

Goldman was unrepentant and unbowed: "Two years' imprisonment for having made an uncompromising stand for one's ideal," she declared. "Why, that is a small price." She would pay a greater price ultimately, in the form of deportation. And she was not alone.

With the precedent set, Wilson and his aides began moving aggressively to dismantle the infrastructure of anti-war dissent. The nation's most prominent Socialists, including presidential candidate Eugene Victor Debs, were arrested, tried and convicted for delivering anti-war speeches. Feminist Rose Pastor Stokes was indicted in Kansas City for raising the issue of war profiteering, with the line: "No government which is for the profiteers can also be for the people, and I am for the people, while the government is for the profiteers." Socialist organizer Kate Richards O'Hare was arrested, tried and jailed for allegedly declaring at a rally in North Dakota that: "the women of the United States were nothing more or less than brood sows, to raise children to get into the Army and be made into fertilizer." Immigrant anti-war and labor organizers were rounded up and deported. Socialist, anarchist and union offices were raided and wrecked. Historian Howard Zinn aptly recalled the period as one of

> enormous crimes against the constitutional principle of free speech, in a country that prides itself on its freedom and declares itself a model for democracy all over the world. The result of these crimes, for thousands of Americans, was persecution, imprisonment, sometimes torture and death. For many more, the result was to create an atmosphere of fear, the fear of expressing one's honest opinions, the kind of fear we usually attribute to totalitarian states.

The *Christian Science Monitor* put it another way, observing in 1920: "What appeared to be an excess of radicalism … was certainly met with … an excess of suppression."

Central to that "excess of suppression" was the concerted effort of the Wilson administration to stifle the Socialist press, which circulated widely not just in cities such as New York and Chicago, but via the postal service to every corner of the country. Post offices in North Dakota, Montana and Oklahoma, where the Socialist movement was especially strong, delivered copies of Victor Berger's *Leader* newspaper, Max Eastman's *Masses* magazine and dozens of other publications to rural readers who were every bit as familiar with, and enthusiastic about, the arguments for stopping the war as the objectors who gathered in the beerhalls of Milwaukee or the cafés of Manhattan's Greenwich Village. That is what unsettled the war's proponents. Socialists in the heartland voted and their votes elected some of the loudest and most effective dissenters: Norris of Nebraska, La Follette of Wisconsin, Thomas Pryor Gore of Oklahoma and Charles August Lindbergh of Minnesota, the last of whom preached: "A radical is one who speaks the truth." They organized rallies and welcomed anti-war speakers. They countered the arguments of the administration for expansion of the draft and military spending with questions about war profiteers and the colonial abuses of Wilson's British allies. What to do? Shut down the flow of critical information to the dissenters. How to do it? Crack down on Socialist newspapers and magazines. Charge their editors with crimes, prosecute and jail them where possible, and, above all, prevent their publications from reaching Butte and Fargo and Okemah.

To that end, Wilson's Postmaster General Albert Burleson—a Texan who spent much of his tenure promoting segregation within the postal service and removing African-American postal workers from their positions in the south—joined with Wilson administration insiders who were engaged in crafting the Espionage Act and related laws, such as the Trading with the Enemy Act of 1917 and the Sedition Act of 1918. Even before the war, Burleson and his conservative allies had sought the power to prohibit the use of the mail by any publisher who, in the opinion of the Postmaster General, "is engaged or represents himself as engaged in the business of publishing any books or pamphlets of an indecent, immoral, scurrilous or libelous character." But a 1915 US House proposal along those lines was defeated, after members objected that the legislation

> would invest one man ... with the power to destroy the business of a publisher without affording any opportunity for trial by jury, according to regular court practice. The punishment which may be inflicted upon a publisher by the Postmaster General under the provisions of this bill is most severe, absolutely depriving him of the privilege of using the United States mails, even for legitimate purposes. ... Furthermore, this bill makes it possible for the Postmaster General to inflict what is practically a confiscatory penalty for an offense not clearly defined. ... Under such circumstances as these it is not safe to leave to the decision of one man, after an *ex parte* investigation, a decision which will involve the freedom of the press.

This reasonable standard was abandoned once World War I began, however. Working with Attorney General Gregory, Burleson secured from the Congress an exceptionally broad mandate to go after any editor or publisher he deemed to be conveying information or ideas that might "cause insubordination, disloyalty, mutiny, refusal of duty, in the military or naval forces of the United States, or shall willfully obstruct the recruiting or enlistment service of the United States, to the injury of the service or of the United States."

Title XII of the Espionage Act specifically empowered the Postmaster General to bar distribution through the mails of newspapers, magazines, pamphlets and books "advocating or urging treason, insurrection, or forcible resistance to any law of the United States." The definition of what constituted such advocacy was left to Burleson and his extensive network of postal investigators, who would eventually interfere with the distribution of more than 100 publications.

There was never much doubt that Burleson was going to go after Berger, a brilliant communicator whom Debs hailed as "a providential instrument" when it came to delivering "the first impassioned message of socialism," and whom the conservative *American Magazine* described before the war as "the sanest and most influential Socialist in this country." A Jewish immigrant from the old Austro-Hungarian Empire, Berger was no anarchist; he identified as an "evolutionary socialist" whose faith in the power of education and organizing—as opposed to violent revolution—made him one of the more ideologically cautious members of the Socialist Party's national leadership. He was a determined anti-militarist, however. And he supported the Socialist Party's "St. Louis Manifesto," a document he had helped to craft at an "emergency convention" of the party just days after Wilson secured his declaration of war.

The manifesto opened with a declaration:

The Socialist Party of the United States in the present grave crisis solemnly reaffirms its allegiance to the principle of internationalism and working-class solidarity the world over, and proclaims its unalterable opposition to the war just declared by the Government of the United States.

Modern wars as a rule have been caused by the commercial and financial rivalry and intrigues of the capitalist interests in the different countries. Whether they have been frankly waged as wars of aggression or have been hypocritically represented as wars of "defense," they have always been made by the [ruling] classes and fought by *The Masses*. Wars bring wealth and power to the ruling classes, and suffering, death, and demoralization to the workers.

They breed a sinister spirit of passion, unreason, race hatred, and false patriotism. They obscure the struggles of the workers for life, liberty, and social justice. They tend to sever the vital bonds of solidarity between them and their brothers in other countries, to destroy their organizations and to curtail their civic and political rights and liberties.

The Socialist Party of the United States is unalterably opposed to the system of exploitation and class rule which is upheld and strengthened by military power and sham national patriotism. We therefore call upon the workers of all countries to refuse support to their governments in their wars. The wars of the contending national groups of capitalists are not the concern of the workers. The only struggle which would justify the workers in taking up arms is the great struggle of the working class of the world to free itself from economic exploitation and political oppression, and we particularly warn the workers against the snare and delusion of so-called defensive warfare. As against the false doctrine of national patriotism, we uphold the ideal of international working-class solidarity. In support of capitalism we will not willingly give a single life or a single dollar; in support of the struggle of the workers for freedom we pledge our all.

Arguing that "in all modern history there has been no war more unjustifiable than the war which we are about to engage," Berger and his fellow Socialists outlined an activist agenda in response to Wilson's militarism:

In harmony with these principles, the Socialist Party emphatically rejects the proposal that in time of war the workers should suspend their struggle for better conditions. On the contrary, the acute situation created by war calls for an even more vigorous prosecution of the class struggle, and we recommend to the workers and pledge ourselves to the following course of action:

1. Continuous, active, and public opposition to the war through demonstrations, mass petitions, and other means within our power.

2. Unyielding opposition to all proposed legislation for military or industrial conscription. Should such conscription be forced upon the people we pledge ourselves to continuous efforts for the repeal of such laws and to the support of all mass movements in opposition to conscription. We pledge ourselves to oppose with all our strength any

attempt to raise money for payment of war expense by taxing the necessaries of life or issuing bonds which will put the burden upon future generations. We demand that the capitalist class, which is responsible for the war, pay its cost. Let those who kindled the fire, furnish the fuel.

3. Vigorous resistance to all reactionary measures such as censorship of press and mails, restriction of the rights of free speech, assemblage, and organization, or compulsory arbitration and limitation of the right to strike.

4. Consistent propaganda against military training and militaristic teaching in the public schools.

5. Extension of the campaign of education among the workers to organize them into strong, class-conscious, and closely unified political and industrial organizations to enable them by concerted and harmonious mass action to shorten this war and to establish lasting peace.

6. Widespread educational propaganda to enlighten *The Masses* as to the true relation between capitalism and war, and to rouse and organize them for action, not only against present war evils, but for the prevention of future wars and for the destruction of the causes of war.

7. To protect *The Masses* of the American people from the pressing danger of starvation which the war in Europe has brought upon them, and which the entry of the United States has already accentuated, we demand—

(a) The restriction of food exports so long as the present shortage continues, the fixing of maximum prices and whatever measures may be necessary to prevent the food speculators from holding back the supplies now in their hands;

(b) The socialization and democratic management of the great industries concerned with the production, transportation, storage, and marketing of food and other necessaries of life;

(c) The socialization and democratic management of all land and other natural resources now held out of use for monopolistic or speculative profit.

"These measures," the manifesto concluded, "are presented as means of protecting the workers against the evil results of the present war. The danger of recurrence of war will exist as long as the capitalist system of industry remains in existence. The end of wars will come with the establishment of socialized industry and industrial democracy the world over.

The Socialist Party calls upon all the workers to join it in its struggle to reach this goal, and thus bring into the world a new society in which peace, fraternity, and human brotherhood will be the dominant ideals."

The St. Louis Manifesto, with its rough mix of anti-war idealism and organizer's language, might have been dismissed by the Wilson administration, save for the fact that the Socialist Party remained politically potent in many parts of the country and counted within its ranks some of the country's ablest editors and writers—including many of the muckraking journalists who had inspired the era of progressive reforms that played out prior to the war, and that in some senses paved the way for Wilson's election in 1912. Berger's *Milwaukee Leader*, a daily newspaper published in a city with a Socialist mayor, was with the *New York Call* one of the most influential of the party-aligned journals.

The *Leader* was a popular paper that devoted its news columns to a full range of international, national, state and local issues, at a time when print publications remained the primary source of information in communities across the country and, via the mails, well beyond their hometowns. But there was never any doubt that Berger and his paper opposed the war. Even allowing for the measure of hyperbole that is the wont of prosecutors and jurists seeking to justify censorship, it was generally true, as the Supreme Court suggested in one of its harsher rulings with regard to Berger's many trials, that the *Leader* considered the conflict to be "unjustifiable and dishonorable on our part, a capitalistic war, which had been forced upon the people by a class, to serve its selfish ends." It was true, as the court contended, that in the paper's pages "Our government was denounced as a 'plutocratic republic,' a financial and political autocracy"; that articles "denounced the draft law as unconstitutional, arbitrary, and oppressive," and that "the President was denounced as an autocrat, and the war legislation as having been passed by a 'rubber-stamp Congress.'"

It was, as well, more or less the case that the *Leader* "sought to convince the [readers] that soldiers could not legally be sent outside the country, and that our government was waging a war of conquest"; that the US was "fighting for commercial supremacy and world domination only, and that when the 'financial kings' concluded that further fighting might endanger their loans to the Allies they would move for peace, which would quickly come." And it was certainly true that US allies in the war—especially Britain, with its monarchy and colonies—"were repeatedly condemned."

Berger and his lawyers might quibble about specifics, and they certainly did challenge the notion that it was possible for the Postmaster General or the courts to determine that the paper's articles contained any "implied counsel" to disobey the laws of the land. But it was surely true that the *Leader* opposed the war, challenged its legitimacy and supported the election of candidates who would seek to end it and to prosecute war profiteers. Berger told the court that: "I am a Socialist and an opponent of war and profiteering." He said he was proud that his paper had asked: "Why should we permit our boys to be killed and maimed by the hundreds of thousands to protect the British commercial interest, or because British profiteers make money out of this war?"

The point, as any schoolchild could explain today (even if some neoconservative commentators still struggle with the concept), is that the First Amendment to the Constitution protects precisely this sort of journalistic dissent. Indeed, it has been practiced with great regularity in the United States: during the Vietnam War, at the time of the invasion of Grenada and of the Reagan administration's meddling in Central America; during George Herbert Walker Bush's first Gulf War and George Walker Bush's invasion and occupation of Iraq, and right up to the present moment with regard to Barack Obama's continuation of the occupations of Iraq and Afghanistan. Publications as diverse as the *Nation* on the left and the *American Conservative* on the right regularly feature criticisms of wars and war-making that are at least as blunt—if not always so colorful—as those published by the *Leader*. And popular Internet sites host dissent of a far more dramatic and uncompromising character, as even the most casual web-surfer will attest.

But the space that now exists for honest and impassioned dissent by journalists and commentators from across the partisan and ideological spectrums, especially during times of war and instability, did not merely open with the passage of time. It was cleared by Socialists, actual and alleged Bolshevists, anarchists and other radicals who fought to protect the nation's freedom of the press at a time when that constitutional commitment was most threatened.

Berger saw the threat coming. "I have already made my plans for the future—if *The Leader* should be suppressed entirely during the war," he wrote to his wife Meta on September 23, 1917, three months after the Espionage Act was passed and Emma Goldman was arrested. Ever the organizer and optimist, the Milwaukee editor predicted that an official move to silence him "will give the paper such an immense prestige that it will be three or four times as big the moment the war is over and war Legislation vanishes." Unfortunately for Berger, his struggles would continue long after the war ended.

The *Leader*'s mailing privileges were formally revoked on October 3, 1917, by Burleson, on the grounds that the paper was "disloyal." The Postmaster General and his aides had, without any formal procedure that might have allowed the editor to defend his newspaper or the basic premises of a free press, effectively censored Berger and the *Leader*—since revoking the second-class mail privileges that allowed newspapers to freely and inexpensively circulate made the freedom to publish a paper a hollow right. The Supreme Court had said as much in 1877, when it determined: "Liberty of circulating is as essential to that freedom as liberty of publishing; indeed, without the circulation, the publication would be of little value."

The ability to use the second-class mail was, by any reasonable measure, the heart of the matter when it came to circulation issues for papers such as the *Leader*. The court acknowledged in its 1921 ruling in a case invoving the *Leader* that: "The extremely low rate charged for second-class mail to carry [newspapers] is justified as a part of 'the historic policy of encouraging by low postal rates the dissemination of current intelligence.' It is a frank extension of special favors to publishers because of the special contribution to the public welfare which Congress believes is derived from the newspaper and other periodical press." To the suggestion that "although a newspaper is barred from the second-class mail, liberty of circulation is not denied, because the first and third-class mail and also other means of transportation are left open to a publisher," one of the court's most distinguished jurists, Justice Louis Brandeis, replied in a dissent from the court's 1921 ruling: "Constitutional rights should not be frittered away by arguments so technical and unsubstantial."

But they were so frittered. In addition to the *Leader*, many of the nation's most prominent Socialist and radical publications—including the widely-circulated *New York Call* newspaper, the *Masses* magazine and foreign-language publications such as New Jersey's *Freie Zeitung*—were targeted by the Postmaster General. In most cases, as the *Call*'s editors noted: "No specific charge of any misuse of the mails is made in the document served upon us. No quotations from any articles which in any manner violated any statute of law of the United States as set forth was given. No charges of any character whatsoever are made against the paper. We are asked to show cause why we should not be penalized, and are not told what we have done to merit punishment."

The "catch-22" circumstance was summed up by an exchange between Berger and Burleson. After he was notified that the *Leader*'s second-class mail privileges were to be denied, Berger sought some sense of the standard to which he and his newspaper were being held. "The instant you print anything calculated to dishearten the boys in the army or to make them think this is not a just or righteous war—that instant you will be suppressed," replied the Postmaster General, who advised that Berger's only real option for restoring the paper's ability to circulate was to avoid any mention of the war.

As that was an entirely unreasonable demand of a newspaper with a readership more keenly interested in the war than any other issue, Burleson's action effectively "destroyed *The Leader*'s ability to reach readers outside Milwaukee," in the words of legal analyst Joseph Ranney, who notes that "one scholar has called Berger's case the low point of freedom of the press in American history and 'utterly foreign to the tradition of English-speaking freedom.'"

The *Leader* lost 85 percent of its out-of-town subscriptions within weeks of the order. It survived thanks to popular support in Milwaukee. But many other anti-war publications collapsed. So it fell to Berger, arguably the most well-established, politically-connected and determined Socialist editor in the country at the time, to mount the defense not just of his newspaper in particular and the anti-war press in general, but of the First Amendment's guarantee of a free press—and of the democratic promise that can only be realized if the people have access to information and ideas that allow and indeed encourage them to question the pronouncements of those in power. Berger undertook the fight with relish, touring the country to sound the alarm that the Constitution was under assault and that a "chain of oppression" was being forged for America.

Burleson's machinations did not merely limit Berger's ability to circulate the *Leader*. "Furthermore," notes historian Michael Stevens, "the post office opened Berger's personal mail throughout the summer of 1918 and refused to deliver any mail to *The Leader* starting in August of that year." Of additional concern to the editor was the fact that Burleson's determination that Berger's newspaper was no longer "mailable" was grounded in an argument that the paper was in violation of the Espionage Act. Burleson, who was described accurately enough by Berger's lawyer as "an oily, slippery Southern politician," had set the editor up for indictment by federal authorities.

In short order, the indictment came.

If Berger had simply abandoned the *Leader*'s mission—either by shutting the paper down, or by following Burleson's advice and avoiding any mention of the war—he might have avoided federal charges. But, as Stevens notes, "because he kept *The Leader* operating despite the loss of its postal permit with the help of donations from party members in Wisconsin, Berger soon found himself subject to prosecution. Federal officials indicted him in Wisconsin and Illinois, charging him with conspiracy to violate the Espionage Act of 1917, which prohibited publications that hindered the war effort."

That the indictments were politically motivated was never seriously in question. "Apparently," Seymour Stedman, Berger's attorney and the Socialist Party candidate for vice president in 1920, told the *New York Times*, "it is considered necessary to place the American Socialist Party on trial. If the truth comes forth as a result of this case, I believe the public will realize that the war profiteers and monster capitalists are the most interested in this prosecution."

Stedman might have added mention of the Democratic and Republican parties, in Wisconsin and nationally, which feared that Berger was on the verge of proving the point. The first indictment against Berger was unsealed on March 10, 1918, three weeks before a closely-watched special election for the vacant US Senate seat of a Wisconsin senator who had died in a hunting accident. La Follette had insisted that an election be held, at least in part as a test of sentiments regarding Wilson's international ambitions, and Berger had entered the contest as an unapologetic and unabashed anti-war candidate, plastering the state with posters that declared: "For a Speedy, General and Lasting Peace—Tax the Profiteers." Beside the candidate's picture on either side of the poster were the words "Free Speech" and "Free Press." Another poster decried attempts to divide working-class voters with the cry: "Against Race Hatred." Reports about the large crowds that Berger drew for rallies not just in Milwaukee but across the state stirred fears in Washington that the Socialist might win the race. There was a general presumption at the time that it was with this threat in mind that a federal grand jury in Chicago hastily indicted Berger—along with the national secretary of the party and two other leading Socialists—on charges of "obstructing recruiting, encouraging disloyalty, and interfering with the prosecution of the war."

The initial indictment cited "twenty-six overt acts" of delivering public speeches or publishing newspaper articles that detailed elements of the St. Louis Manifesto and promoted the withdrawal of US troops from Europe and a negotiated peace. Though Berger privately wrote to his daughter that: "I do not believe in playing martyr, if martyrdom can be avoided without doing greater injury to one's better self or to the movement which a man represents," his public response was filled with bravado. "It is a political move, pure and simple," he said of his indictment. "They were afraid of my candidacy for United States Senator in Washington and took this step to see that I was not elected. But instead of injuring my chances they have made my election certain."

Not quite certain.

Berger fell short of the total he needed to win the seat on April 2, 1918. But his finish was hardly a defeat for the man whose favorite expression was "We lose but we win."

Berger quadrupled the Socialist vote over that cast in the previous election, beating the Republican and Democratic candidates to carry eleven of Wisconsin's seventy-two counties, while winning 26 percent of the vote statewide. Those numbers made the Wilson administration and its allies all the more fearful of Berger, as he immediately began campaigning for a US House seat representing Milwaukee, where rather than martyrdom he had achieved heroic status among the German, Irish, Polish and Jewish voters of the city.

Determined to silence Berger, Wilson's Department of Justice secured an additional indictment from a federal grand jury in Milwaukee one week before the fall election for the US House seat. Along with Berger, three other Socialist congressional candidates from Wisconsin were indicted, along with a Socialist state senator and Elizabeth Thomas, the president of the *Leader*'s Social Democratic Publishing Company.

Berger kept campaigning, and this time he prevailed. On November 7, 1918, a befuddled *New York Times* reported the Socialist's victory by more than 5,000 ballots with the observation: "Berger's vote was a general surprise in the face of two Federal indictments hanging over him." Two days later, the political and media establishment had recovered sufficiently from their surprise to report that preparations were being made for "barring Berger." "Several members of Congress are fortifying themselves with precedents in expectation of the contest which will be made against Victor Berger of Wisconsin when he attempts to take his seat in the House."

Before the fight for the seat to which he had been elected, however, Berger would have to defend himself on charges related to the initial indictment. Barely a month after the voters of Milwaukee chose him as the man they wanted representing them when Congress weighed matters of war and peace, Berger went on trial on December 9 in Chicago. The fix was in from the start. Federal Judge Kenesaw Mountain Landis—who had several months earlier imposed severe sentences on eighty-three members of the Industrial Workers of the World union who had been convicted of Espionage Act violations—declared that "one must have a very judicial mind, indeed, not to be prejudiced against German Americans in this country. Their hearts are reeking with disloyalty." Berger and his co-defendants were not the first Americans to learn that the exercise of First Amendment rights by members of ethnic and racial minorities— especially when they are immigrants—tends to be the least respected and protected practice of freedom. But this lesson would be a particularly bitter one for Berger, a student of the Constitution who could quote at length from the deliberations of the 1787 convention that forged the document. Before one of his many battles with the political and judicial establishment, Berger recalled, "I told [the lawyers] to put it on a high plane—to talk about the right of free speech, free press and the Bill of Rights—the amendments—in the US Constitution ... [The charges] will never be set aside on a legal technicality, or on a dozen of them."

Berger's attorney, Stedman, made the argument, holding that: "Socialists are the one class of citizens who believe in a lawful, orderly change through education and political action. They are presumptuous enough to believe that the policy of the Government in war or out, the attitude of the President in war or out, are subject to criticism. Socialists the world over have opposed war and the system that makes war inevitable. We do not consider opposition to a condition or policy an equivalent to breaking or violating the laws of the country."

The editor and his lawyer were, of course, correct. Yet, standing at the bar of justice as the first great American "red scare" was spreading, and facing a reactionary judge such as Landis, Berger had little hope of getting a fair trial. Nor did the editor help his cause by responding to questions about whether he had penned particular lines—such as a reference to the country having been "plunged into war by the trickery and treachery of the national administration and Congress," or an editorial that decried "the national shame of selecting men to be butchered in the interests of the capitalist classes"—with vigorous assertions that: "I would say that today" and "I still hold that view."

Landis disregarded charges of bias on his part and, after the jury convicted Berger and his co-defendants, sentenced each of them to twenty years in federal prison. A few months later, Landis would tell an American Legion gathering: "It was my great displeasure to give Berger twenty years in Fort Leavenworth. I regretted it exceedingly because I believe the laws of this country should have enabled me to have Berger lined up against a wall and shot." As for the Milwaukee voters who had elected Berger to Congress, Landis said they "ought to get out of this democracy."

The Solons of the Congress came to much the same conclusion. When Berger, out on bail of $145,000 pending appeal of his conviction, presented himself to be seated in the House on May 19, 1919, Speaker Frederick H. Gillett, a staid Republican from Massachusetts, refused to administer the oath of office. Instead, Gillett appointed a committee to assess Berger's eligibility to serve. As the committee took month after month to deliberate, Berger toured the nation, telling a crowd of 5,000 gathered at Madison Square Garden that Congress was "a Soviet of bankers and lawyers" and that "Capitalism not only owns Congress, the courts, the President and the Administration but, above all, it owns all means of public expression and communications—the daily papers, the weeklies (with a few exceptions), the movies, the theaters and the billboards."

Berger was not exactly engaging in hyperbole, as his own struggle for freedom of the press seemed to be going nowhere in the face of insurmountable odds. The Court of Appeals of the District of Columbia had refused earlier in the spring of 1919 to order Postmaster General Burleson to restore the *Leader*'s second-class mail privileges, on the grounds that the newspaper was "a hostile or enemy publication" that no one could read "without becoming convinced that [the editorials] were printed in a spirit of disloyalty to our government."

So labeled, Berger got no slack from the congressional committee, which—cheered on by *New York Times* editorial writers who argued that the House "has a perfect right to exclude him" for having expressed dissident views—determined that the elected representative from Milwaukee ought not be seated, because he had given aid and comfort to the enemy in wartime. Never mind that the war was over, or that his writings had not, in fact, been demonstrated to have undermined Wilson's project. Berger was determined by the committee to have, at the very least, sought to "embarrass the Government of the United States."

When the matter came to the full House for consideration in November 1919, opprobrium was heaped upon Berger, with Massachusetts Republican Frederick Dallinger telling his colleagues that the Department of Justice considered Berger to be "one of the most dangerous men in the United States." Joe Henry Eagle, a Texas Democrat, denounced the editor as "treacherously disloyal."

Berger countered with a remarkable speech from the well of the House, in which he questioned how he could be excluded for having in many instances made statements of fact. He defended all of his wartime writings not just as protected but also as appropriate speech, arguing that "under the same circumstances I would say and write it all over again, only I would make it a great deal stronger, because I have been justified by the events since the armistice was concluded and the war was practically ended." He castigated the "red scare" mentality of the moment, warning congressmen with whom he had once served (from 1911 to 1913) as a warmly-regarded colleague that "this fear has America in its grip now. And fear is always evil." Above all, he expressed his certainty that it was dangerous to democracy and to the republican experiment to exclude the holders of dissident political views from the House, telling the chamber that: "it would be foolish and criminal to deprive the Socialist Party—a party casting over a million votes—of its sole representative in Congress."

"Remember, gentlemen, you may exclude me once. You may exclude me twice. But the fifth district of Wisconsin cannot permit you to dictate what kind of a man is to represent it," Berger concluded. "If representative government shall survive, you will see me or a man of my kind, let us hope many men of my kind—in the Nation's legislature. Therefore, whatever decision you may make, I will just say 'Au revoir.'"

The House was not amused. By a vote of 311 to 1 (that of progressive Republican Edward Voigt from Berger's state of Wisconsin), the Socialist was denied his seat. The great newspapers of the day cheered the exclusion of an editor who dared believe that the First Amendment offered any real guarantee of a free press. The *Washington Post* hailed the House vote as an "impressive demonstration of Americanism"; the *Baltimore Sun* asked why it was that even one vote had been cast in favor of seating the Socialist; the *Toledo Blade* celebrated those members who had barred Berger as patriots who had "preserved their self-respect." The American Legion joined the chorus with a call for declaring Berger a non-citizen and deporting him.

But, as has so often been the case along the arc of American history, the people proved to be more familiar than their governors or their major media with the true purposes of the Constitution.

Following the House's action, Berger's seat was declared vacant. A special election was set for December 19, 1919. The Socialists nominated Berger, even as he was said to have no chance after the Democrats and Republicans united in coalition to ensure that, in the words of the *Milwaukee Journal*, "the spirit of Americanism" would prevail in Milwaukee. The short campaign concluded with full-page advertisements in every local daily newspaper except the *Leader*, asking: "Is Milwaukee Red or

Red, White and Blue?" Berger and his backers countered with images of the editor pointing to a copy of the Constitution and the words: "Congress shall make no law respecting an establishment of religion, or prohibiting the free exercise thereof; or abridging the freedom of speech, or of the press ..."

"Why are they hounding Berger?" asked the *Leader*, before answering its own question with: "Because he shows them up!"

The turnout on Election Day was huge. With the whole of the national press corps, members of Congress and the Wilson administration watching, the voters re-elected Berger by a landslide—giving him 55 percent of the vote and tallying wins for the Socialist in every precinct save one across the city. The Socialist vote total spiked by more than 40 percent from the previous election and, in the words of historian Edward Muzik, "The Fifth District of Wisconsin thus replied to Congress and the nation. The issue of Bolshevism was recognized by many as fraudulent, and Berger, known and respected throughout the district, achieved a momentous personal victory, receiving 40 percent more votes than in 1918, most of which came from non-Socialists."

Berger seized on the result as "the first sign of the reawakening of genuine democracy in this country since the days of the struggle for the emancipation of the black race." While the elected-but-not-seated congressman saw the vote in Milwaukee as having "vindicated one of the basic principles of modern democracy—representative government," the House majority did not share his view. When Berger requested that his oath of office be administered on January 10, 1920, the House refused even to allow the Socialist to speak. It fell to the intrepid Edward Voigt, Berger's sole defender in the previous session, to make the case for the Constitution and democracy, and he did so with words as resounding as any ever uttered in the chamber.

> You may laugh and scoff, gentlemen, but I know Victor Berger. No man can devote his whole life and fortune to the great cause of endeavoring to better the conditions of the toiling millions, stand by his principles like a rock of Gibraltar, regardless of personal consequence, without being morally great ... Victor Berger's name will stand in the future as that of a martyr to a great cause—the rights of free speech, free press, and representative government.

Voigt did not imagine his words would change the sentiments of most members; he confided privately that serious discussions of the Constitution and the intent of the founders were "never referred to around here as it is not considered stylish to do so." But the mood seemed to be shifting, ever so subtly. One of the House's senior Republicans, James Robert Mann, told fellow members: "Mr. Berger has been elected anew to the House by a majority of those who vote in his district, and to me the question is whether we shall maintain inviolate the representative form of government where people who desire changes in the fundamental or other laws of the land shall have the right to be represented on the floor of this House, when they control a majority of votes in a congressional district ..."

Mann went on: "Has it come to the point that a man who believes certain things cannot be heard? His people, his constituents, desire him to represent them. It is not our duty to select a representative from this congressional district. That is the duty of the people back at home. We cannot take the attitude of refusing to permit the voice of the people of a district to be heard by their own selection, with safety to the future of the country."

Challenged by another Illinois Republican to say whether "we ought to admit to this House a disloyal man," Mann replied: "After all, the question of what is a disloyal man is not to be determined by the gentleman from Illinois or myself. You may have the power to do it, but you will not be wise in exercising that power. The Constitution under its amendment gives authority to exclude a person for giving aid or comfort to the enemy. I do not think that the provision contemplated anything which Mr. Berger has done or sought to do ... I do not share the views of Mr. Berger. But I am willing to meet his views in an argument before the people, rather than to say that we shall deny him the opportunity to be heard when selected by this people in the legal form, and invoke them, in effect to resort to violence."

While Mann's words did little to shift the mood of the House—which voted to continue the exclusion of Berger by 330 to 6—they outlined a broader and sounder reading of the Constitution than had been common under Wilson, whose presidency was soon to end. A liberal interpretation of the First Amendment as the genuine guardian of freedom of speech and freedom of the press was again being advanced, even by some in positions of power. Mann and a few of the others who rallied to Berger's defense—including Ohio Democrat Isaac Sherwood, a brigadier general in the Civil War who at age eighty-five was one of the last veterans of the great conflict sitting in the Congress—dared to reiterate the enlightenment view that dissent was better met and countered than isolated and punished; that democracy did not just allow for but in fact demanded a rich and wide-ranging discourse; that faith in government and the rule of law was grounded in a sense that challenging arguments and fresh ideas enriched the debate—and the nation itself. This was not a new construction; it was, in fact, as old as the republic. Indeed, it was a renewed statement of the fundamental faith of the founders. Its expression, defended by Berger and his compatriots in a time of official censorship, prosecutions, incarcerations, fines and deportations, would over time come to be accepted and finally embraced by an American consensus that has held with reasonable consistency to this day.

Of course, Berger was not seated during the term to which he was twice elected. The *Leader* was still denied the same freedom to circulate that was afforded other newspapers of far lower quality and character. And the threat of twenty years in jail still hung over the head of the paper's sixty-year-old editor. But Berger was more than ever certain that in the dirt of defeat were planted the seeds of victory: "We lose but we win." The Milwaukee Socialists renominated him for the House within hours of the decision to refuse him his seat, raising the cry: "The people of the Fifth District want him in Congress and they will not be disregarded by a crowd in Washington."

"We will keep on renominating Berger until Hades freezes over if that un-American aggregation called Congress continues to exclude him," the Socialists vowed. "Berger is our congressman, and the action of Congress in unseating him a second time only starts the real fight ..."

That fight proceeded quickly as Wilson's presidency wound down, the "red scare" waned and a measure of sanity returned to the republic. Berger and his fellow Socialists used the 1920 election season to mount a presidential campaign on behalf of the imprisoned Debs. That campaign garnered almost a million votes for "Convict No. 9653," serving as one of the greatest political education initiatives in the nation's history. "To begin to placate our enemies is to invite decay," declared the incarcerated candidate.

Even as he campaigned for Debs—and for his twice-denied seat in the House—Berger remained primarily focused on the struggles to overturn his own conviction and to restore the *Leader*'s full access to the mails. It was still hard going; he was banned from appearing in Providence, denied an auditorium in Buffalo and run out of Jersey City by the local gendarmes. At home in Wisconsin, he was expelled from the Milwaukee Press Club, while major daily newspapers around the country continued to celebrate the denial of his First Amendment rights. Slowly but surely, however, Berger was building a constituency for a broad reading of the freedom of the press, freedom of speech and freedom of assembly provisions enshrined in the nation's essential document. "If the capitalist class can succeed in silencing the radical and Socialist press, all our liberties are doomed," the editor told the audiences, often numbering in the thousands, that gathered to hear him speak in parks and union halls. "Shall we permit this?"

The Supreme Court had taken both an appeal by Berger of his conviction and an appeal by the *Leader* for its restoration to the mails. On January 31, 1921, the court overturned Berger's Espionage Act conviction. A 6–3 majority held that, after expressing extreme bias against Berger and his co-defendants, Judge Kenesaw Mountain Landis had a responsibility to respect the request from the defense that a new judge oversee the trial. "Judge Landis had no lawful right or power to preside as judge on the trial of the defendants on the indictments," declared Justice Joseph McKenna, who had served as Attorney General of the United States before being appointed to the high court by President William McKinley.

"I hail this decision as the first real sign of returning sanity in our ruling class," declared Berger, who dismissed his trial and conviction as "simply a conspiracy of the 'patrioteers' and the profiteers against the Socialist Party."

Berger still faced the threat of a new trial, however. At best, the court's ruling was only the editor's faint "first sign" of returning sanity. On March 7, the same court upheld Postmaster General Burleson's exclusion of the *Leader* and another Socialist paper, the *New York Call*, from the second-class mails. A 7–2 majority held that imposing mail restrictions that made it difficult for certain newspapers to circulate was not a violation of the First Amendment:

The [Postmaster General's] order simply withdrew from the [publisher] the second-class privilege, but did not exclude its paper from other classes, as it might have done, and there was nothing in it to prevent reinstatement at any time. It was open to the [paper] to mend its ways, to publish a paper conforming to the law, and then to apply anew for the second-class mailing privilege. This it did not do, but, for reasons not difficult to imagine, it preferred this futile litigation, undertaken upon the theory that a Government competent to wage war against its foreign enemies was powerless against its insidious foes at home. Whatever injury the relator suffered was the result of its own choice and the judgment of the Court of Appeals is *Affirmed*.

But even the *New York Times*, for so long unsympathetic to Berger's plight, seemed to recognize that the tide was turning; its front-page headlines highlighted dissents by two of the most widely-respected members not only of this particular high court but of the American judiciary, Justices Oliver Wendell Holmes and Louis Brandeis. "Brandeis Sees Danger to Freedom of the Press in the Majority Decision," announced the *Times*.

Justice Brandeis outlined an understanding of the freedom of the press protection that exposed the fallacy of the arguments made by the Postmaster General, Berger's prosecutors and the court majority—and in so doing he began to foster a recognition that constraints on equal access to the mails and other routes of circulation were forms of censorship entirely at odds with the intents and purposes of the First Amendment. "It is argued that, although a newspaper is barred from the second-class mail, liberty of circulation is not denied, because the first and third-class mail and also other means of transportation are left open to a publisher. Constitutional rights should not be frittered away by arguments so technical and unsubstantial," wrote Brandeis in his most famous statement on the matter, which continued: "The government might, of course, decline altogether to distribute newspapers, or it might decline to carry any at less than the cost of the service, and it would not thereby abridge the freedom of the press, since to all papers other means of transportation would be left open. But to carry newspapers generally at a sixth of the cost of the service, and to deny that service to one paper of the same general character, because to the Postmaster General views therein expressed in the past seem illegal, would prove an effective censorship and abridge seriously freedom of expression."

"How dangerous to liberty of the press would be the holding that the second-class mail service is merely a privilege, which Congress may deny to those whose views it deems to be against public policy," observed Brandeis. He concluded his dissent with these words:

> [It] cannot be stressed too strongly that the power here claimed is not a war power. There is no question of its necessity to protect the country from insidious domestic foes. To that end Congress conferred upon the Postmaster General the enormous power contained in the Espionage Act of entirely excluding from the mails any letter, picture or publication which contained matter violating the broad terms of that act. But it did not confer—and the Postmaster General concedes that it did not confer—the vague and absolute authority practically to deny circulation to any publication which in his opinion is likely to violate in the future any postal law. The grant of that power is construed into a postal rate statute passed 40 years ago which has never before been suspected of containing such implications. I cannot believe that in establishing postal classifications in 1879 Congress intended to confer upon the Postmaster General authority to issue the order here complained of. If, under the Constitution, administrative officers may, as a mere incident of the peacetime administration of their departments, be vested with the power to issue such orders as this, there is little of substance in our Bill of Rights, and in every extension of governmental functions lurks a new danger to civil liberty.

Justice Holmes was, if anything, even more forceful in his expression of concern that "what we decide may determine in large measure whether in times of peace our press shall be free." "To refuse the second-class rate to a newspaper is to make its circulation impossible and has all the effect of [a censorship order]," wrote Justice Holmes in a dissent that explained:

> When I observe that the only powers expressly given to the Postmaster General to prevent the carriage of unlawful matter of the present kind are

to stop and to return papers already existing and posted, when I notice that the conditions expressly attached to the second-class rate look only to wholly different matters, and when I consider the ease with which the power claimed by the Postmaster could be used to interfere with very sacred rights, I am of opinion that the refusal to allow the relator the rate to which it was entitled whenever its newspaper was carried, on the ground that the paper ought not to be carried at all, was unjustified by statute and was a serious attack upon liberties that not even the war induced Congress to infringe.

These principles, framed initially in the dissents of Justices Brandeis and Holmes in the case of Victor Berger and the *Leader* would come over time to be accepted as basic standards regarding press freedom in the United States.

Barely two months after the dissents of Justices Brandeis and Holmes were published, they effectively became the law of the land—as Burleson's replacement as Postmaster General, Republican Will Hays, lifted the postal prohibitions against the *Leader*, the *New York Call* and other Socialist and radical publications. Hays was no liberal; in fact, in his next role as head of the Motion Picture Producers and Distributors of America, he would implement the restrictive production codes that encouraged self-censorship by Hollywood directors, producers and studios. But in 1921 he was part of a new administration, led by President Warren Harding, that recognized Wilson and Burleson had gone too far in restricting liberties.

In the case of some publications, including the *Liberator*, a successor to the *Masses* magazine, Hays ordered the Post Office Department to refund the excess charges that were paid to continue circulating at more expensive rates following Burleson's order. Even these repayments were insufficient to save several publications, which had been ruined by the postal prohibitions of the Wilson years. But Berger's *Leader*, which had survived the assault without missing an issue, surged during 1921 and 1922 to a national circulation of more than 50,000.

The Harding administration did not merely ease restrictions on the press. President Harding—who as a senator had allowed that "from the very beginning it was a lie to say that this was a war to make the world safe for democracy"—commuted Eugene Victor Debs's prison sentence to time served and ordered the old Socialist's release by Christmas Day, 1921. On his way home to Terre Haute, Indiana, where he would be greeted by a cheering crowd of more than 50,000 supporters, Debs would stop at the White House, where Harding greeted his 1920 election foe with a hearty handshake. "Well," Harding announced, "I've heard so damned much about you, Mr. Debs, that I am now glad to meet you personally."

A year later, after tireless lobbying by Berger of Republicans in Congress and the White House, Harding's Department of Justice abandoned the pursuit of a new trial for the editor on charges of violating the Espionage Act, with Attorney General Harry M. Daugherty personally asking that the 1918 indictment of Berger and his four fellow Socialists be dismissed.

Daugherty's move came just weeks after Berger had been re-elected to Congress. With the postal prohibition on the *Leader* lifted and the charges against him dropped, Berger was finally seated, having battled longer and harder than any American in history to assume a seat to which he had been repeatedly elected. As the only Socialist in the chamber, Berger joked that: "when I want to have a caucus I could have one in a telephone booth." But he was not marginalized. Working with La Follette and other insurgents—some Republicans, some Democrats and some new allies from the radical Minnesota Farmer-Labor Party—Berger became the most ardent advocate in the Congress for First Amendment rights. With support from the new American Civil Liberties Union, founded as a response to the repressions of World War I and the "red scare" that followed it, and the editors of the *Nation* magazine—one of the few prominent publications that had recognized the import of the First Amendment struggles in which he had engaged—Berger introduced legislation to repeal the Espionage Act. "The impression prevails that the act making it a crime, punishable by 20 years' imprisonment, to criticize the war policies of the Wilson administration has been repealed," the Socialist congressman told the House. "[But] it is still on the statute books, ready to be revived the moment war is declared. The purpose was not to punish espionage, but to stifle the voices of those ... who dared to exercise their constitutional rights of free speech and free press."

Berger went further. In perhaps the boldest defense of those free speech and free press protections ever mounted in the House, he proposed in 1928 that Congress "put teeth into the First Amendment."

Noting that those who violated the eighteenth amendment to the Constitution (which banned the sale of alcohol) faced criminal sanctions, Berger asked why there could not also be prosecutions of those who undermined and affronted the amendment that Thomas Jefferson, James Madison and Tom Paine most valued. " 'Putting teeth into the Eighteenth Amendment' has become a favorite phrase with the Anti-Saloon League and its servants in public office ever since the amendment has been adopted. The Volstead Act was passed with that object in view. It has never been suggested, however, by any group of 'reformers' and least of all by the Anti-Saloon League that teeth ought to be put into the First Amendment to the Constitution," announced Berger.

Recalling the founders, the Congressman declared, "I also regard the First Amendment as most essential to the preservation of fundamental rights of Americans. It is one of the provisions which extend the freedom of the citizen. Moreover, I believe that the First Amendment can be enforced without trouble if a law is passed, because it is to practice liberty, while the Eighteenth Amendment cannot be enforced, as experience has shown."

Provocative as ever, Berger was out to make a point about just how seriously Americans took their liberties.

"Of course I realize that many Americans today are different from those of the eighteenth and nineteenth centuries. American businessmen today worship Mussolini, who has boasted that he wipes his feet on liberty, and who just last week wiped out the last vestige of democracy in Italy," said Berger. It worried him that amid all the talk of "Americanism" and "patriotism" in 1920s America, there was very little recognition of the threat posed by unequal distribution of basic freedoms across all lines of race, ethnicity, class, gender, partisanship and ideology:

> Our Constitution is an eighteenth-century document. The right of the people to speak freely, write freely and assemble nevertheless lies at the basis of all other rights. Yet, this amendment, like several other amendments, is [increasingly] a dead letter. At this very moment, we find

conditions in the strike regions of Pennsylvania and Colorado unparal-
leled even in Russia under the rule of the Czar. People are thrown into the
dungeon because they dare to exercise their right to free speech. Citizens
are forbidden to sing certain hymns in the churches. Free speech has
become a privilege of the ruling class ... The most important rights in
the Constitution have been suspended. Unless re-established, they will
remain dead.

Berger would die a year later, without having succeeded in "putting teeth
into the First Amendment." But the coming of the New Deal and the
appointment to the Supreme Court of justices like Felix Frankfurter, a co-
founder of the American Civil Liberties Union who during the "red scare"
era had warned that the United States was becoming "the most reactionary country in the world," did much to renew and extend the values for
which Berger campaigned in the period of his own suppression and
prosecution.

Even after he had won most of those battles, Berger was still fighting on
behalf of the Constitution. He defended the civil liberties of Socialists but
also of ideologues of other stripes—including leftists who had abandoned
the Socialist fold to form a Communist Party, anarchists and even radicals on the right. Berger recognized that First Amendment rights were not
the prerogative of one class or one party. And he preached, always, that
the speech that needed most to be protected was that which unsettled,
offended and threatened the economic and political elites.

It was easier to make those arguments in his last years, as the respected
editor of a widely-circulated newspaper and a sitting member of
Congress. But Berger made them with all the fervor he had mustered
in the midst of the struggle during and immediately after World War I, as
he surely would today. The formerly embattled editor understood that
the fight to realize the promise of the First Amendment will never be over.
As well, he recognized that in the forefront of this struggle would ever be
found the truest sons and daughters of liberty.

"I have proven my love for America, my faith in America's justice," he
asserted late in life, "by risking my liberty in defense of the constitutional
rights of American citizens to discuss freely and fully the official acts and
policies of their public servants."

This is the freedom of speech, the freedom of the press, the freedom to petition government for the redress of grievances and the freedom, above all, to dissent, as we know it today. It is freedom bequeathed to us by the founders but made real by their heir and champion in the twentieth century: a Socialist editor named Victor Berger.

For Jobs and Freedom: The "Militant Radical" Socialist Who Dared to Dream of a March on Washington

The reconstruction program for the Negro must involve the introduction of the new social order—a democratic order in which human rights are recognized above property rights.

—A. Philip Randolph, 1919

You can't talk about solving the economic problem of the Negro without talking about billions of dollars. You can't talk about ending the slums without first saying profit must be taken out of slums. You're really tampering and getting on dangerous ground because you are messing with folk then. You are messing with captains of industry ... Now this means that we are treading in difficult water, because it really means that we are saying that something is wrong ... with capitalism ... There must be a better distribution of wealth and maybe America must move toward a democratic socialism.

—Rev. Martin Luther King, Jr., 1966

In the last year of Dwight Eisenhower's presidency, as memories of Joe McCarthy and his "red scare" were fading, an aging socialist stepped to the podium on a New York stage, as he had a hundred, make that a thousand, times before. The speaker, whose street-corner stumping in the Harlem of his youth had earned him labeling as "the most dangerous black man in America," came, once more, to deliver the call to radical action that he had been issuing the better part of fifty years. "We shall not be quiet, polite or content until justice is firmly in our hands," he declared, in an audacious address that would imagine a series of marches on state capitals and then the nation's capital itself. It was time, he said, to march for the purpose of achieving not just an end to segregation in the states of the deep south, not just an abandonment of the false promise of "separate-but-equal" facilities, not just the achievement of voting rights for the millions of African Americans who were still denied the franchise they were supposed to have gained in the aftermath of the Civil War—but for a vision of economic justice that would free workers of all colors from the chains of a crude and exploitive economic system. It was time, he said on this winter night early in 1960, to "march for jobs and freedom."

The campaign would begin the following summer, when the two great political parties of the United States were scheduled to gather for their quadrennial nominating and platform-writing sessions. "I intend to call for marches on the political conventions of both major parties," the old man thundered. "The Negro people must stand up before these conventions and say to the nation and the world: 'We want to be free.'" The man who spoke on that January night in Manhattan admitted that he was not a Republican, as he believed "the party of Lincoln" had abandoned its founding promise. Nor could he vote for a Democratic Party that gave the most powerful committee assignments in the US House and Senate to Dixiecrat southerners, whose purpose it was to maintain the "Jim Crow" laws and patterns of rural and now urban poverty that had made a mockery of the Emancipation Proclamation. His protégé, freshly returned from an Indian sojourn where he had studied Mohandas Gandhi's philosophy of non-violence, took the stage that night and echoed the condemnation of both parties, which the younger man declared had betrayed the civil rights struggle not merely by giving power to their southern wings but by practicing what he decried as "blatant northern hypocrisy." The old man cheered that line with all the enthusiasm of a proudly declared "militant radical" who kept the faith that had made him the target of FBI investigations and the occupant of a jail cell. He had never backed either of the major parties, he explained. He had voted for, and indeed run for office on, the ticket of the Socialist Party.

In the crowd, the candidate the old Socialist had frequently endorsed for the presidency, Norman Thomas, cheered what he hoped would be the opening of a new chapter in the long American struggle to give meaning to the promise that "all men are created equal"—a meaning that recognized equality would only be achieved when deep divisions along lines of race, ethnicity, gender and, above all, class were eased so that every American could enjoy a chance at "life, liberty and the pursuit of happiness."

Thomas was not the only important figure in the audience that night. Sitting a few seats away from the nation's most prominent Socialist was his friend Eleanor Roosevelt, the former First Lady of the United States, who had once suggested that were her husband not a candidate on the Democratic ticket of 1932, she would have voted for Thomas. Nearby sat Minnesota Senator Hubert Humphrey, who in just five years would assume the vice presidency of the United States. New York's senior senator, Republican Jacob Javits, sat with Humphrey. President Eisenhower could not be present, but he sent greetings to mark the radical's seventieth birthday, which was celebrated that night. So, too, did Indian Prime Minister Jawaharlal Nehru and other world leaders. For while it was true that A. Philip Randolph remained not just a socialist but a "radically militant" one, it was also true that he was the man who his protégé, the Rev. Martin Luther King, Jr., referred to as "the chief"—an epic figure who had organized the first major union of African-American railroad workers with the cry "Fight or Be Slaves," who had agitated so aggressively and unapologetically against capitalism and imperialism during Woodrow Wilson's presidency that he ended up behind bars; who had stared down Franklin Delano Roosevelt on the eve of World War II and forced the president to sign an executive order that prohibited discrimination in federally-funded defense industries and established the first Fair Employment Practices Committee; who after World War II organized a national campaign to end "Jim Crow military service," and used the threat of mass civil disobedience against the peacetime draft to force President Harry Truman to sign Executive Order 9981, declaring it "to be the policy of the President that there shall be equality of treatment and opportunity for all persons in the armed services without regard to race, color, religion or national origin." After securing the first charter from the American Federation of Labor for an African-American-led union, Randolph had for many years been a singular African-American presence on the executive boards of the nation's major labor federations; he had, as

well, formed the National Association for the Promotion of Labor Unionism Among Negroes, organized the Negro American Labor Council,
served as the first president of the National Negro Congress and founded
the Leadership Conference on Civil Rights (LCCR).

When the American Federation of Labor and the Congress of Industrial Organizations merged in 1955, Randolph was at the forefront, taking
his place as an executive vice president of the largest and most powerful
labor organization in the country's history—only to be censured several
years later for demanding that the federation address the fact that many
of its union affiliates still forced African-American workers into separate
locals and in some cases actively excluded them from membership. "I am
willing to go through the fires in order to abolish second-class status for
black people in this country," Randolph fired back. "It must be done, and
it must be done now—not tomorrow. We cannot wait for tomorrow. In a
nuclear age, tomorrow may never come." Suitably shamed, the federation's next convention—for the first time since Randolph joined the
AFL in 1929—voted unanimously for a resolution committing the labor
movement "to make fully secure equal rights for all Americans in every
field of life and to assure for all workers, without regard to race, color,
creed, national origin or ancestry the full benefits of union membership."

Randolph was a groundbreaking figure in the history of labor and the
fight to end segregation—it would be said that "if Martin Luther King, Jr.
was the father of the civil rights movement, then A. Philip Randolph was
the grandfather"—but he was also the champion of a tradition that
extended back to the first days of the republic.

Socialists, communists, anarchists and the militant reformers who
preceded them had been aligning with and leading the American labor
movement not just as an economic force, but as a vehicle for achieving
fundamental changes in the political and social order since the years
immediately following the revolution, when the Mechanics Society of
New York denounced "all tyrants, plunderers and funding speculators"
and entered the political fray with their radical cry: "May the light of
freedom which was kindled in America and reflected to France in a blaze
illuminate the world and lay despotism in ashes." By the late 1820s, labor
organizations in New York, Philadelphia, Baltimore and other urban
centers were linking Paineite promises of liberty for all with explicit

economic demands and an organizing agenda that recognized the necessity of uniting "the cultivators of the soil, and the mechanics and every
class of laborers [to overthow] the oppression of the idle, the avaricious
and the aristocratic." Some, like Fanny Wright, counseled that unions
would never succeed unless they embraced the struggles for emancipation of slaves, indentured servants, new immigrants and women to
unite the whole of the working class in a mass movement for economic
equality.

"Fanny Wrightism" did not come to define the first trade unions as
thoroughly as she and her comrades hoped, and the story of the labor
movement in the nineteenth and early twentieth centuries is filled with
dark chapters of cruelty and compromise that saw the dream of the
Knights of Labor spoiled when its leaders refused to organize African-
American and Asian-American workers, that saw American Federation
of Labor President Samuel Gompers accept and encourage "all-white"
unions and union locals, and that accepted the overt racism of the southern states rather than challenge it. Yet, if many union leaders did not "get"
the concept of solidarity, radical labor organizers and activists in the
Fanny Wright tradition gave expression to her faith across the next
century—first on the fringes of the labor movement, then in its most militant organizations and finally in the charters of the House of Labor.
There is nothing new, nothing "modern," about this understanding of
the need to cross lines of race, creed, ethnicity and gender in order to
make a fundamental change. Joseph Weydemeyer, the follower of Marx
and Engels who advocated "true socialism," organized the American
Workers League in 1853 with the stated purpose of uniting workers
"without respect to occupation, language, color or sex." Weydemeyer
would steer the network of radical labor organizations and "communist
clubs" into a political activism that denounced the Kansas-Nebraska Act
of 1854 not merely for "authorizing the future extension of slavery," but
for promoting "capitalist land speculation." In so doing, he would
become a campaigner for the nomination of Abraham Lincoln as the
second Republican candidate for president. In the Civil War that followed Lincoln's election, Weydemeyer rose to the rank of colonel in the
Union Army. (Ever the organizer, he distributed copies of the Marxist
inaugural address of the International Workingmen's Association and

labor literature to soldiers and citizens while commanding the defense of St. Louis.)

Weydemeyer's drive to form national unions uniting all workers and a labor party to go with it never came to fruition in his lifetime—unless we count the Republicans. But the most radical elements of the Knights of Labor would begin to advance the cause in the late nineteenth century and by the tumultuous early years of the twentieth century, the Industrial Workers of the World were uniting hundreds of thousands of workers into "one big union" that declared "an injury to one is an injury to all." The IWW took these preachments seriously enough not merely to organize multiracial locals but to develop African-American leaders such as D. B. Gordon of the Louisiana-based Brotherhood of Timber Workers; Ben Fletcher, the leader of the IWW's Marine Transport Workers Union on the docks of Philadelphia; and Hubert Harrison, the Harlem Renaissance radical known as "Black Socrates." It even earned an endorsement from a young A. Philip Randolph, then a socialist editor, who argued:

> The IWW is the only labor organization in the United States which draws no race or color line. There is another reason why Negroes should join the IWW. The Negro must engage in direct action. He is forced to do this by the Government. When the whites speak of direct action, they are told to use their political power. But with the Negro it is different. He has no political power. Therefore the only recourse the Negro has is industrial action, and since he must combine with those forces which draw no line against him, it is simply logical for him to draw his lot with the Industrial Workers of the World.

The IWW vision would linger long after World War I–era raids, arrests and deportations by government agencies diminished its membership and power. A generation of young radicals spun out from the one big union. William Z. Foster, an IWW militant on the west coast, became the longtime leader of the American Communist Party, while James P. Cannon, an IWW organizer in the midwest, would play a critical role in forging the Trotskyist Communist League of America and then the Socialist Workers Party. Both groupings poured their energies into the organization and expansion of labor unions during the 1920s and 1930s, and they did so as passionate backers of racial equality within organized labor and the broader society. The influence of unions that worked closely with the Communist Party, in particular, led the Congress of Industrial Organizations to embrace a program of industrial organizing that—even if the goal was not always realized—sought to unite all workers and end segregation. CIO unions that worked with the Communists and in some instances elected Communist leadership, such as the International Longshore and Warehouse Union, the United Electrical, Radio and Machine Workers, the United Farm Equipment Workers and the National Maritime Union attracted substantial African-American membership nationally—just as the International Union of Mine, Mill, and Smelter Workers built strong union locals among Mexican-American workers in the southwest, as immortalized in the 1954 film *Salt of the Earth*. West-coast Communists were a particularly potent force in the remarkable United Cannery, Agricultural, Packing, and Allied Workers of America (later the Food, Tobacco, Agricultural, and Allied Workers), which would organize African-American, Asian-American (especially Filipino) and Latino workers nationwide by hiring some of the most radical organizers of the era. These included the Guatemalan immigrant Luisa Moreno, a convener in the 1939 Congreso de Pueblos de Habla Española, which historian Vicki Ruiz has described as the "first national Latino civil rights assembly."

There were certainly American Communists who romanticized the Soviet Union, made absurd apologies for its totalitarian excesses and aligned their positions in domestic debates to parallel "the Moscow line." But there were many other Communists and non-Communist lefties, like Longshore union head and west-coast CIO director Harry Bridges, who were less interested in what was happening in Leningrad than in the intensity of the commitment of CP activists to organize workers in Seattle and Pittsburgh and Birmingham. They tended to share the view expressed by the Australian-born Bridges when the government attempted to deport him on charges that he was a "secret Communist." Bridges denied the affiliation, expressed robust small-"d" democratic views and derided the notion that working with groups that supported strong unions and public ownership of utilities and major industries made him un-American. Radical trade unionists weren't taking orders from abroad, Bridges explained, they were responding to reality on the ground in a United States that had been ravaged by the Great Depression. Asked at a deportation hearing whether he believed in "a capitalistic form of government," the labor leader replied: "If you mean the capitalistic form of society, which, to me, means the exploitation of a lot of people for a profit, and the complete disregard of their interests for that profit, I haven't much use for it."

Nor did Bridges have much use for racism or divisions along lines of ethnicity. When he and Noriko Sawada, the child of Japanese-American immigrants who had been forced to reside in an internment camp during World War II, decided to marry in 1958, they chose to do so in Reno, Nevada, in order to challenge a state law that barred the marriage of white men or women to "any person of the Ethiopian or black race, Malay or brown race, Mongolian or yellow race, or American Indian or red race." A clerk at the local courthouse denied the couple a marriage license because Nikki Sawada was "yellow." Bridges and Sawada sued, got a federal judge to order the issuance of the license and took their vows. Four months later, the Nevada legislature repealed the state's racist anti-miscegenation laws.

The character of the times in which they lived and the challenges they faced led many radicals to align with the Communist Party, whether as members, "fellow travelers" or wary allies in specific fights. The appeal among African Americans in the labor movement was especially strong, for reasons explained by Jack O'Dell, who would go on to become one of Dr. King's closest aides during the most critical struggles of the civil rights movement:

> A good buddy of mine, Jesse Gray, he went into the Merchant Marines. He came back. So I went out to see him and he says, "Man, I found a Union where there's no segregation." He'd shipped out in the SIO where they had—you know—black and white jobs because all blacks were confined to the Steward Department and whites had all the other jobs. He said, "But I found a Union that you could just throw in your card and you could ship deck, you could ship engineer room, absolutely no segregation. It's called National Maritime Union. And guess what? They've got a black who's Secretary General, named Ferdinand Smith." I said, "Oh, you're kidding! So, that inspired the idea that I would go into the

Merchant Marines because I wasn't going to have to put up with a lot of Jim Crow.

Like many young trade unionists of the era, O'Dell joined the Communist Party. In a 1993 oral history, he explained that he did not do so out of misplaced affection for the Soviet Union or any naivety with regard to foreign affairs:

It wasn't just an NMU thing. It wasn't just a CIO thing. There were lynchings going on in the south of veterans returning from World War II. Segregation was still up. What had begun to emerge in the country was an assault on racism coming out of World War II by the NAACP and Unions. And the segregationists defended segregation by saying they weren't against blacks—they weren't against equal rights for blacks—they were against communism. But their interpretation of communist was anybody who supported the right of blacks to have civil rights. While most blacks didn't join the Communist Party, they understood that the communists were the fighters. And they knew individual communists who were fighters, and they were black and white and Latino, and so forth. And with this anti-communism that now was becoming the state religion and with the persecution of the communists, I just said, well to show where I'm at I'll join the communists. I'll join the Communist Party. And I did, and I remained an active member of the Party for about seven years.

I was first and foremost a person with the African-American experience. I knew living in the north and I knew living in the south and I knew the contradiction that this country was living with great hypocrisy. Secondly, I was viewing this as a trade unionist because militancy of the trade union movement appealed to me. I knew you had to fight and you had to fight in an organized way and you had to fight with a weapon. And for me the weapon was the Union. So the fight to keep the Union true to the course that it had set for itself was of great priority. Thirdly, I found within the Union a left called Communists and other variations of that which I respected. I was not, shall we say, inexorably attracted to them for any particular reason except that I saw the role they played in the Union and that there would not have been a good NMU without their participation, from what I could see.

At the same time, the NMU stood as a bulwark against the kind of institutional racism that I had experienced. I knew that people had different views with respect to, say, the Soviet Union. I've never taken a census, but I never met a black person who was in the Communist Party because of the Soviet Union. We joined the Communist Party because they fought against racism and they were dependable in that fight. And they were Union builders. They were mass-movement, organized build-ers. And I knew that as an individual you were strengthened by the fact of unity with other people. So it was precisely that perspective that led me into a relationship to the left.

O'Dell's story is a common one. I heard dozens of variations on the theme as a young writer in the 1980s and 1990s, when I conducted oral histories with aging veterans of the Abraham Lincoln Brigade, the "premature anti-fascists"—most of them Communist Party members or allies, but also socialists and anarchists—who traveled from America in the 1930s to fight with Spanish Republican forces against Francisco Franco and the allies of Hitler and Mussolini. The Communist Party's influence was greatest in the labor movement and international solidarity campaigns. For the most part, it did not extend to the broader political stage although, prior to and during World War II, Communists got close enough to the political mainstream so that the Republican Borough President of Manhattan hired Simon Gerson, a prominent writer for the party's *Daily Worker* newspaper, as one of his top aides, and two Communists were elected to the New York City Council. One of them, a young Harvard Law School graduate named Benjamin Davis, Jr., who in the 1930s had become a prominent civil rights and labor lawyer, would declare: "I am proud to be an American, proud to be a Negro, and proud to be a Com-munist! And there is no contradiction between the three. I am proud to be an American because I have an abiding confidence in the creative capacity of the American people to set our country right in all respects and keep it so, and to move it to higher levels of happiness and peace."

Davis's service on the city council of the nation's largest city was fol-lowed by a prison sentence, as he and other members of the CP's national leadership were convicted of violating a contemporary variation on John Adams's anti-democratic Alien and Sedition Acts, the Alien Registration Act, which made it illegal for anyone in the United States to "organize any society, group, or assembly of persons who teach, advocate, or encourage the overthrow of [the] government by force or violence." While Davis's election and service on the city council seemed to confirm that he had opted for a non-violent and admirably civic approach, the point of the law—which had been pushed through Congress by a virulently anti-labor southern segregationist, Virginia Democrat Howard Smith—was never to protect the United States from foreign "threats." Smith wanted to weaken the resolve of the labor movement to press for radical reforms, especially for desegregation in the south. To a substantial degree, Smith and his successors (Richard Nixon and Joe McCarthy, among others) achieved their goal.

Pressure on the most militant unions—from the government and from the CIO's increasingly cautious leadership—heightened exponentially after former Vice President Henry Wallace campaigned for the presidency in 1948, with backing from left-led unions and leading Communists, on a platform that castigated the Democrats and Republicans as "old parties" willing to "impose a universal policy of Jim Crow and enforce it with every weapon of terror. They refuse to outlaw its most bestial expression—the crime of lynching. They refuse to abolish the poll tax, and year after year they deny the right to vote to Negroes and millions of white people in the South." Wallace and his running-mate, Idaho Senator Glen Taylor, did not come close to beating the old parties. But they shook a lot of powerful people up, by campaigning at integrated rallies in the deep south and asserting the radical view that "it is the first duty of just government to secure for all the people, regardless of race, creed, color, sex, national background, political belief, or station in life, the inalienable rights proclaimed in the Declaration of Independence and guaranteed by the Bill of Rights."

In the late 1940s, congressional committees pressing for full implementation of the anti-labor Taft-Hartley Act (which among other things required union officials to sign affidavits that they were not Communist Party members) began holding hearings where union leaders were grilled about their political beliefs, while at the same time prosecutors and immigration officials began preparing legal strategies to go after radical trade unionists and civil rights activists. The CIO responded by expelling affiliates that had backed Wallace or that were portrayed as being "Communist-dominated" or "Communist-influenced"—among them

Bridges's ILWU, the Mine, Mill, and Smelter Workers, the United Electrical and the United Farm Equipment unions. There remained in the CIO a nucleus of unions that were deeply committed to fighting segregation, notably the Chicago-based United Packinghouse Workers of America and the United Automobile, Aerospace and Agricultural Implement Workers of America (whose leader, Walter Reuther, was a former Socialist Party activist who had wrangled bitterly with the Communists but always maintained a deep personal commitment to the cause of civil rights). The battles took their toll, however, especially in the south, where the CIO's "Operation Dixie" had attempted in the post-war era to battle the segregationists by organizing multiracial units operating along the lines of the 10,000-member Food, Tobacco, Agricultural, and Allied Workers Local 22 in Winston-Salem, North Carolina. "[The] effects of the domestic Cold War and the break-up of the left-center alliance in labor sealed the fate of the campaign," veteran labor activist Bill Fletcher said of "Operation Dixie." The former president of TransAfrica Forum and co-founder of the Black Radical Congress argued: "There was no way, even under optimal conditions, that a movement suspicious of itself would be able to gain the enthusiasm and will to go up against the obstacles faced in a Southern organizing drive." And the expulsions, purges, finger-pointing and fear factors of the second "red scare" made the fight for civil rights a harder one, something Dr. King would recognize in the mid-1960s when he affirmed: "Our irrational obsessive anti-communism has led us into too many quagmires to be retained as if it were a mode of scientific thinking."

A. Philip Randolph knew a thing or two about red scares. He had been a target in the first one, which unfolded in the waning days of World War I and lasted into the early 1920s. A son of the segregated south who came north at the beginning of the great migration to Harlem, Randolph joined the Socialist Party in 1916, as a young militant inspired by the rhetorical power of Eugene Victor Debs and his "great admiration [for] Debs's position on the Negro, his belief that the best chance for the elimination of racial injustice, which was rooted in the competitive economic system, lay in the socialization and democratization of the system."

"The Republicans knew they had the Negroes in their pockets, and the Democrats looked down at them," Randolph said of the party of Lincoln and the party of the southern segregationists (including then President Woodrow Wilson). "Neither party thought it had to offer Negroes elective office, and neither party had a program for the Negro. The Socialist Party was the only party that had a philosophy that took account of the race problem and whose economic analysis addressed itself to the solution of the Negro's problems." Over the next sixty-three years, until his death in 1979, Randolph would hold to this view, a position that would put him at odds not just with Republicans and Democrats but with the Communists, who he frequently charged were too cautious and calculating in making demands on power. Ultimately, Randolph would wrangle with all of them—the CP in the 1940s, when he argued (in the paraphrase of Ralph Bunche) that: "it would be foolish for [the African American] to tie up his own interests with the foreign policy of the Soviet Union or any other nation of the world"; the Republicans in the 1950s, when Randolph complained they were collecting African-American votes as the "Party of Lincoln" but delivering little in return; the Democrats in the early 1960s, when he said they talked a good line on civil rights but continued to allow their party to be defined by the southern segregationists who dominated congressional committee chairmanships. In the mid-1960s, as a man of the "old left," he would wrestle in his own mind, and sometimes publicly, with the tactics of a younger "new left" that included Black Panthers and Students for a Democratic Society—in particular, he would echo the worries of many older leftists about "the aspect of utilizing violence as a method of social change." Yet he would close that turbulent decade on a note of solidarity, recalling, "I was probably the first Negro to go to jail for encouraging Negroes to oppose the draft," declaring his "love [for] the young black militants" and explaining that he understood "why they are in this mood of revolt." Randolph could find common ground, he could compromise, and often did, with partisan and ideological foes; it was a necessary requirement of his day-to-day work of organizing the poorest transportation workers and his broader mission of tearing down the infrastructure of segregation and economic inequality.

Yet, in the early years of his Socialist Party membership, he was in no mood for compromise.

In November 1917, Randolph and his Socialist comrade Chandler Owen launched a party-aligned magazine, the *Messenger*, as "the only magazine of scientific radicalism in the world published by Negroes." The country was six months into World War I and the Wilson administration's draconian crackdown on dissent was accelerating, but the *Messenger* did not follow W. E. B. Du Bois' call for African Americans to "close ranks" and support the war effort. As internationalists who bowed to Thomas Paine rather than the rhetoric of "my country right or wrong," Randolph and Chandler rejected the notion that fighting a British king's war against a German Kaiser would "make the world safe for democracy." Indeed, Randolph explained, the very notion was "a tremendous offense to the intelligence of the Blacks because at that time the Blacks were being lynched and denied the right to vote, in the South especially, and were the victims of segregation and discrimination all over the nation."

Like the most militant suffragettes who questioned why women who were denied the franchise should support a war that was supposedly being waged in defense of distant democracies, the *Messenger*'s editors questioned why African Americans who were not afforded full citizenship in their home country should sacrifice their lives on its behalf in a European war. Ridiculing the notion that African Americans were volunteering for the military because they were enthusiastic about the project, Randolph wrote in a *Messenger* article: "the Negro may be choosing between being burnt by Tennessee, Georgia or Texas mobs or being shot by Germans in Belgium. We don't know about this pro-Germanism among Negroes. It may be only their anti-Americanism—meaning anti-lynching."

That language did not win Randolph any friends in the Wilson White House. The Justice Department would label the *Messenger* as "by long odds the most dangerous of all the Negro publications," and its editors became the target of steady surveillance by the emerging Federal Bureau of Investigation. On a speaking tour in the summer of 1918, Randolph and Owen were arrested by agents in Cleveland, just up the road from where Eugene Victor Debs had delivered the anti-war "Canton Speech" that would land him in jail for two and a half years. Randolph was luckier. The nation's leading Socialist lawyer, Seymour Stedman, raced to the defense of the young editors and secured their release, only to have Randolph turn around and write a column in which he recalled with relish—and without apology—his run-in with the Cleveland courts:

The judge was astonished when he saw us and read what we had written in the *Messenger*. Chandler and I were twenty-nine at the time, but we looked much younger. The judge said, why, we were nothing but boys. He couldn't believe we were old enough, or, being black, smart enough, to write that red-hot stuff in the *Messenger*. There was no doubt, he said, that the white socialists were using us, that they had written the stuff for us.

He turned to us: "You really wrote this magazine?" We assured him that we had. "What do you know about socialism?" he said. We told him we were students of Marx and fervent believers in the socialization of social property. "Don't you know," he said, "that you are opposing your own government and that you are subject to imprisonment for treason?" We told him we believed in the principle of human justice and that our right to express our conscience was above the law.

Randolph's commitment—as well as his genius as an organizer, strategist and speaker—was well recognized by the Socialist Party, which in 1920 nominated the thirty-one-year-old editor for statewide office. The New York Socialists got serious about integrating and expanding the appeal of their New York ticket that year, nominating not just a prominent African-American radical, Randolph, but also a woman, Jessie Wallace Hughan, in that first year of women's suffrage. A prolific author, Hughan's "Facts of Socialism" was among the most widely circulated and influential radical texts of the era. Both nominations were bold gestures, as the characterization by federal authorities of Randolph as "the most dangerous Negro in America" was paralleled by the fact that Hughan's name had in 1919 been included by a US Senate committee on a list of sixty-two "dangerous radicals."

On a ticket led by Debs and Stedman, the New York Socialists ran up one of their most impressive votes yet and Randolph earned particular note by securing more than 200,000 votes, 7 percent of the statewide total, on the strength of the surge in support from Harlem. Impressed, the Socialists would nominate Randolph again two years later as their candidate for Secretary of State. On that occasion he won more than 5 percent of the vote—and as much as a quarter of the vote in some Manhattan and Brooklyn precincts.

The party would have kept running Randolph, and more than a few comrades predicted that he might by the 1930s be a presidential or vice-presidential nominee—perhaps on a ticket with his close friend Thomas. (It was not idle speculation; in 1944 the Socialists wanted to nominate Randolph for vice president, but he refused to be distracted from the struggles to integrate the labor movement and the military.) In the mid-1920s, however, the young editor had something other than a political career on his mind. Frustrated as much with the "Back-to-Africa" and "black capitalism" proposals of Marcus Garvey's United Negro Improvement Association, which he thought were drawing African Americans away from the serious work of improving their economic and political circumstances in New York and across the United States, as he was with the conciliatory approaches of prominent African Americans in the tradition of Booker T. Washington, who he dismissed as "me-too-boss-hat-in-hand Negroes," Randolph determined to organize African-American trade unionists with the purpose of forging a base from which to demand civil rights.

It would not be easy. The IWW, Randolph's favored organization, had lost much of its membership and muscle during the post–World War I "red scare," and Samuel Gompers's American Federation of Labor was only beginning to address the "color line" that barred African Americans from membership in many unions. Randolph called for "a new leadership for Negro workers. It is a leadership of uncompromising manhood. It is not asking for a half loaf but for the whole loaf. It is insistent upon the Negro workers exacting justice, both from the white labor unions and from the capitalists or employers." Ultimately, he explained, working people of all races and nationalities needed to organize, and work in coalition, on the theory that:

> Organized labor cannot afford to ignore any labor factor of production which organized capital does not ignore … If the employers can keep the white and black dogs, on account of race prejudice, fighting over a bone; the yellow capitalist dog will get away with the bone—the bone of profits. No union man's standard of living is safe so long as there is a group of men or women who may be used as scabs and whose standard of living is lower.
>
> The combination of black and white workers will be a powerful lesson to the capitalists of the solidarity of labor. It will show that labor, black and white, is conscious of its interests and power. This will prove that

unions are not based upon race lines, but upon class lines. This will serve to convert a class of workers, which has been used by the capitalist class to defeat organized labor, into an ardent, class-conscious, intelligent, militant group.

But Randolph was not holding his breath waiting for Gompers to do the right thing when it came to the civil rights fights of the 1920s, just as, forty years later, he would not wait for Gompers's heirs to do the right thing when it came to the civil rights fights of the 1960s. He was going to go out and organize a union, and he would call it the Brotherhood of Sleeping Car Porters.

In the mid-1920s, the Pullman Car and Manufacturing Co. was one of the largest employers of African Americans in the United States. Its fleet of 9,800 sleeping cars rolled along the rail lines of a nation that was only beginning to anticipate super-highways and commercial air travel. More than 12,000 African-American men worked for the company as porters. Dressed in crisp uniforms, they were at the beck and call of passengers who generally referred to every porter, no matter what his actual name, as "George"—a reference to the first name of the company's authoritarian founder that seemed to suggest the porters were extensions of their Pullman cars rather than human beings. "No matter who you were, or how old, most everybody wanted to call you 'George,'" recalled a veteran porter. "It meant that you were just George Pullman's boy, same as in slave days when if the owner was called 'Jones' the slave was called 'Jones.'" The first porters were ex-slaves who George Pullman and his associates were confident had been trained on antebellum plantations "to perform their duties under circumstances which necessitate unfailing good nature, solicitude and faithfulness." As the years passed, however, porters became something of an elite among the African-American working class. They traveled extensively, got to read the newspapers and magazines that were left in the sleeping cars, and formed a national network of working men who celebrated and encouraged education and community service. While their circumstance was better than that of most African-American workers—especially when tips were added to their base wage—the porters had to put up with appalling demands from the company.

As Jervis Anderson, a Randolph biographer and the great historian of the African-American working-class and civil rights experiences, recalled:

> The basic work month consisted of 400 hours or 11,000 miles, whichever was logged first. No overtime was paid until a porter exceeded one of these figures—and then at the rate of only 60 cents for every extra 100 miles. It is hardly surprising that few porters—a favored handful who were given extra runs—managed to log either 400 hours or 11,000 miles a month, let alone qualify for overtime. Out of his salary and tips, a porter paid for his own meals and bought his own uniforms and equipment—down to the polish he used to clean the passengers' shoes. And if he ran out of polish on the job, he was reported by the white conductor, and penalized.
>
> A porter was expected to ride … hundreds of miles a month without pay. This was called "deadheading." It worked this way. A porter scheduled to leave New York at 12:30 a.m. on a train for Washington, DC, say, was required to report for duty at 7:30 p.m. He spent these hours preparing the car for departure and welcoming passengers. His paid time, however, did not begin until 12:30, when the train pulled out. And if, at 12:30, there were no passengers, the porter was required to "deadhead" into Washington, in the hope that there would be passengers coming back.
>
> Then there were the times when the porter had to "double out," whether he liked it or not. That is, whenever he returned from a long run—which may have lasted for as long as a week—he could be ordered out on the very next train, without a rest period, and at a lower rate of pay. This, of course, gave him no time to see his family, or even to shower, shave or change his clothes. But if, while "doubling out," he was found untidy, unclean or asleep, he was either docked, suspended or fired.

The porters were ripe for unionization.

But the existing railroad labor organizations, many of which maintained rigid color lines, were not about to organize African Americans. And even if they had been so inclined, the Pullman bosses were more determined than most employers to prevent independent unions from upsetting an arrangement that essentially allowed the company to make any demand it wanted on its employees. Even the hint of a serious organizing effort brought reprisals, reassignments and firings.

So the porters who wanted to form a union knew they were going to need an outside man for their organizer. As many of them lived in Harlem, they were familiar with Randolph as an agitator who was, in his own words, "insistent upon the Negro workers exacting justice, both from the white labor unions and from the capitalists or employers." In the summer of 1925, a group of porters asked Randolph to be their man. For a dozen years, he would, in the words of historian John Edgerton, travel among a "scattered contingent of overworked and underpaid black men who did all the hard labor on a chain of rolling hotels" and forge a union that, with its leader, would "become a beacon of strength in labor, race relations and the reformation of the south."

On August 25, 1925, at the Imperial Lodge of Elks hall on Harlem's West 129th Street, 500 porters and their allies gathered to hear Randolph address what New York's *Amsterdam News* described as "the greatest labor mass meeting ever held of, for and by Negro workingmen." Promising a battle for better pay, fewer hours, fairer work rules and, "by no means least, that porters will be treated like men," Randolph would sign up the first union members before the end of the following day. By October, more than half of the porters in the city were carrying the card of the Brotherhood of Sleeping Car Porters.

Randolph knew that organizing in Harlem was different from organizing in St. Louis, Omaha, Jacksonville and the rest of the United States. With a small grant that had been arranged with the help of Socialist allies such as Norman Thomas, Randolph began riding the rails himself, traveling thousands of miles each year to speak, usually in African-American churches, to porters who wanted to join the union but feared the consequences. Pullman company spies infiltrated union meetings, and porters who attended them were dismissed by the dozens. African-American business leaders, political "ward healers" and newspaper editors found their accounts padded with Pullman money if they attacked the "Bolshevik" Randolph and his radical allies. Pullman executives used their connections with the Republican administrations of Calvin Coolidge and Herbert Hoover to thwart the drive—a task made easier by the fact that the nation's railroad labor laws did not extend protections to the employees of sleeping car companies. (Pullman lobbyists had argued successfully that their company was an "innkeeper," not a rail enterprise.)

The AFL refused the Brotherhood's application for a national charter and the segregated halls of all-white unions were closed to Randolph and his organizers—as were hotels and restaurants in many of the cities on his route. Randolph faced death threats and physical violence, and the Brotherhood's southern organizer was pulled out of Florida when a judge threatened him with lynching. (The organizer, Bennie Smith, only quit Jacksonville after his wire to the New York headquarters of the fledgling union—which read: "I'M WILLING TO MAKE THE SUPREME SACRIFICE. HAVE SACREDLY DEDICATED MY ALL TO THE BROTHERHOOD'S NOBLE CAUSE. ADVISE AT ONCE"—brought an order from Randolph and his lieutenants for the young man to head north.) What money the union had was soon spent on lawyers and lobbyists, and Randolph often had to pass the hat at the end of meetings in order to raise the fare to get to the next stop. Despite the tough times that accompanied the onset of the Great Depression, there was always just enough money to keep Randolph on the rails because, as Chicago activist George Lancaster put it, the porters knew: "If we lose him we lose the cause." One of the oldest of the early union members, Dad Moore, sent a letter just before his death in 1930 with a message to the younger porters: "Tell all the men in your District that they should follow Mr. Randolph as they would Jes Christ."

The porters did just that, against what seemed to be insurmountable odds, so insurmountable that even allies of the union came to believe there might be some truth to the words of a Pullman superintendent who told the union's Chicago leader, after firing him: "Remember, this is a white man's country, white people run it, will keep on running it, and this company will never sit down around the table with Randolph as long as he's black." Worse yet, Randolph was a black socialist. "It is known that American capital will not negotiate with socialists," warned the *Pittsburgh Courier*, a widely-circulated African-American newspaper that allied itself with the Brotherhood's cause in the early days but began to doubt the organizing drive's potential as the years passed. "It has ever been so where white people were concerned," the *Courier* continued. "Mr. Randolph has been informed that the Company will not deal with him because of his history as a socialist." Randolph countered such sentiment with an argument that would be echoed in the 1960s by Dr. King when he was told to purge the ranks of the civil rights movement of Socialists, Communists and freelance radicals: "Never again," Randolph declared, "will Negroes permit white people to select their leaders for them. I would make it very emphatic that upon that principle we shall not compromise, not only with respect to the Pullman porters but with any Negro movement."

As it happened, American capital did negotiate with socialists. After the coming of the New Deal, following the swing from Herbert Hoover's Republicans to Franklin Roosevelt's Democrats in 1932, the balance began to shift in favor of the Brotherhood. The union had finally gained a place within the AFL. And Roosevelt's National Recovery Act and Emergency Railroad Transportation Act, though initially vague on the issue, were at the urging of the Brotherhood amended to afford rights and protections to sleeping car employees. This was the tipping point and, despite Pullman attempts to undermine the union with mass firings and the establishment of a pliant "company union," a federally-supervised union recognition vote began in May of 1935 at the sixty-one porter terminals across the country. "This is the first time that Negro workers have had the opportunity to vote as a national group in an election, under federal supervision, for their economic rights. It is an extraordinary occasion. It is the result of ten years of militant, determined and courageous fighting by a small band of black workers against one of the most powerful corporations in the world," Randolph wrote to National Association for the Advancement of Colored People president Walter White. "It may be interesting for you to know that on the Pullman board sit J. P. Morgan, R. K. Mellon, Alfred P. Sloan, George F. Baker, Harold S. Vanderbilt, George Whitney, and others. These men rule Wall Street, America and practically the world of capitalist finance and industry. And yet the Brotherhood of Sleeping Car Porters has, in the face of nameless opposition and terror, stood its ground through one of the worst depressions ever witnessed in America, and has come to the point where it has caused a national election to be called to determine the organization the porters really want."

"The porters," he declared, "are the vanguard of the black workers of America."

That was not just the fancy wordplay of a Socialist editor turned organizer. When the Brotherhood won the election by an overwhelming margin, the Urban League's *Opportunity* magazine declared: "No labor leadership in America has faced greater odds. None has won a greater victory." That victory was not fully realized until, after two years of hard negotiations, mediation and court battles, the Pullman executives recognized the Brotherhood of Sleeping Car Porters—twelve years to the day after Randolph called the union into being, and twenty-six years to the day before A. Philip Randolph would arrive in the nation's capital to meet with members of the US Senate and begin the final preparations for the 1963 March on Washington for Jobs and Freedom.

Randolph might not, on that day, have been anticipating the march itself. But he did know, as historian John Edgerton put it, "that bigger battles lay ahead." As he had fought for the principle "that porters will be treated like men"—not "boys" named "George"—he would now position the porters and their 15,000-member Brotherhood at the forefront of the cause of civil rights. "There was no other group of Negroes in America who constituted the key to unlocking the door of a nationwide struggle for Negro rights as the porters," Randolph recognized. "Without the porters, I couldn't have carried on the fight for fair employment, or the fight against discrimination in the armed forces."

As the president of the Brotherhood, Randolph now had a place at the table in the House of Labor. The union was accepted as a full member of the AFL, and its president became, in the words of New York Mayor Fiorello LaGuardia, "one of the foremost progressive labor leaders in America." He used the resources of his union and others to help organize more African-American rail workers, assisting in the formation of the Joint Council of Dining Car Employees, the International Brotherhood of Red Caps and the Provisional Committee for the Organization of Colored Locomotive Firemen. He pressured both the AFL and the break-away Congress of Industrial Organizations to require affiliated unions to remove explicit restrictions against integrated locals, to address discriminatory practices in workplaces and to launch aggressive organizing projects such as the CIO's "Operation Dixie." But the labor movement was also a base from which to organize local and regional civil rights groups, to put pressure on political parties to embrace civil rights platform planks and, ultimately, to force state and federal officials to strike down "Jim Crow" laws and to guarantee equal accommodation, access to education and voting rights. These were the baseline demands of the civil rights movement of the 1940s, 1950s and 1960s. But, always bringing a socialist analysis to the struggle, Randolph recognized long before Dr. King that the promise of civil rights would never be realized unless economic rights were guaranteed and poverty was made history.

With his ambitious agenda, Randolph had a long march ahead of him. But he also had an army. The porters, finally secure in their employment and empowered by some of the best pay packages available to African-American workers, became rolling ambassadors of the labor and civil rights movements. Invariably well read and worldly because of their extensive travels and contacts with cross-sections of society, the porters now received regular missives from Randolph and supporters such as Norman Thomas. Members of the Brotherhood soon recognized their essential role in the civil rights movement and used the fact that they were constantly traversing the country, including the segregated south, to spread the word.

Porters would collect newspapers that had been left behind on trains, as well as the labor, Socialist or African-American publications they had been reading, roll them up and tie strings around them. Then, as the trains passed through the "wrong side of the tracks" neighborhoods of urban America and through the countryside of the rural south, porters would toss the papers onto the porches or into the yards of African-American families. Thus, people who rarely came into contact with news of the labor or civil rights movements—and might have had trouble affording big-city papers and liberal magazines—had it delivered to their doorsteps.

When porters came home, they took leadership roles in churches, fraternal groups, political parties and African-American organizations. They became radical role models in their communities, influencing and inspiring new generations of activists. Congressman Ron Dellums, who during his years in Washington became a leading member of the Democratic Socialist Organizing Committee and Democratic Socialists of America, took cues from his uncle, C. L. Dellums, one of the key organizers of the Brotherhood on the west coast. "These were guys that came out of the twenties, these were the old left-wing guys in the twenties. They came together and organized the first African-American trade union in the history of America, the Brotherhood of Sleeping Car Porters," the congressman recalled in an oral history several years ago:

> These were guys who placed a great premium on the spoken word as a way of organizing, to be impressive when they challenged people. You know, people thought A. Philip Randolph and C. L. Dellums and these guys were Harvard graduates, because they developed an affect that challenged the system to deal with them intellectually, at an eyeball-to-eyeball level. Well, my uncle: here's this beautiful, erudite, incredibly well-groomed, impeccable person with extraordinary articulation who, on Seventh Street, had an office over the pool hall. So in my life there was this magnificent success model, and wherever I went, people when they'd hear my last name would say, "Is C. L. Dellums your father?" And I'd say "No, my father is Verney Dellums, but C. L. Dellums is my uncle." But I immediately began to realize that C. L. was the man and that he commanded respect across the broad spectrum of people in the Bay Area. And going to his office, he had a staff person, he had an office, he smoked a pipe, he dressed elegantly. He was a fighter, he was strong, he was courageous. So this success model in my life was very important in shaping my life, because here I knew that you could succeed, that you could be successful. You did not have to be intimidated, and you could be respected by people, because the politics of that community came through him: union activity, civil rights activity, et cetera. He was just this incredible, larger-than-life person who continued to push me to pursue my education.

In the south, members of the Brotherhood worked with Socialist Party campaigners such as H. L. Mitchell, who had organized the integrated Southern Tenant Farmers Union in the 1930s, and with Christian socialist intellectuals including the Rev. James Dombowski, Myles Horton and the remarkable Zilphia Horton—an Arkansas native who reworked an old gospel tune to serve as the civil rights anthem, "We Shall Overcome." With contributions from Norman Thomas and other New York educators, religious leaders and activists they had met while studying at the Union Theological Seminary in New York, Horton, Dombowski and educator Don West set out to develop a southern education center inspired by the Danish *folkehøjskole*, or "folk high school" movement that began in the nineteenth century as an extension of the revolutionary fervor of the 1840s and its passion for popular education. The point of the project, as explained by Horton, was to "get behind the common judgments of the poor, help them learn to speak and act for themselves, help them gain control over the decisions affecting their daily lives ... The sooner the poor were trusted to develop and express their own ideas—their own creative ideas—the sooner America would begin to achieve the social structure that could end poverty and racial prejudice, set aside exploitation and the reasons for war." They called their radical initiative the Highlander Folk School, and among its "graduates" were the Rev. Martin Luther King, Jr.; his successor as head of the Southern Christian Leadership Council, Dr. Ralph Abernathy, who would preach that "the key to the salvation and redemption of this nation lay in its moral and humane response to the needs of its most oppressed and poverty-stricken citizens"; Student Nonviolent Coordinating Committee (SNCC) chairman and future congressman, John Lewis; Mississippi Freedom Democratic Party vice chair Fannie Lou Hamer, who taught that "nobody's free until everybody's free"; and SNCC's Stokely Carmichael, the man who would popularize the term "Black Power."

E. D. Nixon, a porter working out of his native Montgomery, who historian Taylor Branch described as "a homespun Alabama copy" of Randolph, had organized the Montgomery Division of the Brotherhood of Sleeping Car Porters after hearing the union's leader speak in the late 1920s. Nixon "got" Randolph's vision of the Brotherhood as a tool for building the broader civil rights and economic justice movements. "The civil rights movement saw to it that black people were able to do things legally, like ride on a Pullman car. But the labor movement saw to it that black people had the money to buy the ticket to ride on the Pullman cars," explained Nixon, who began working with Myles Horton in the 1930s to organize Alabama cucumber pickers. When he became president of the Alabama Conference of the NAACP, Nixon arranged for bright young African-American activists to attend Highlander classes. In 1955, he dispatched the secretary and youth director of the association's Montgomery affiliate to the school. The woman, Rosa Parks, returned with a passion to do more, and Nixon had a project for her—as the face of the struggle to integrate the city's bus system. On December 1, 1955, when

Parks refused an order to give up her seat to a white man on the Cleveland Avenue bus, she was arrested and charged with a violation of Chapter 6, Section 11 of the segregation law of the Montgomery City code. E. D. Nixon went to the jail to bail her out, along with a local white lawyer, Clifford Durr—a Roosevelt administration aide who had quit his post as a member of the Federal Communications Commission to protest redbaiting in the late 1940s and served as president of the National Lawyers Guild—and his wife, Virginia Foster Durr, a friend of Eleanor Roosevelt's who shared the former First Lady's passion for racial justice and who had sought a Virginia US Senate seat in 1948 as a candidate of Henry Wallace's Progressive Party.

That night, Jo Ann Robinson, an English professor at Alabama State College and the president of the Women's Political Council of Montgomery—who a year earlier had pointedly defended Virginia Durr when she was hauled before a Senate subcommittee investigating alleged Communist Party involvement with the burgeoning civil rights movement—drafted a call to action. Robinson, an ally of Nixon's who had been formulating the idea of a bus boycott for several years, wrote:

> Another woman has been arrested and thrown in jail because she refused to get up out of her seat on the bus for a white person to sit down. It is the second time since the Claudette Colvin case that a Negro woman has been arrested for the same thing. This has to be stopped. Negroes have rights too, for if Negroes did not ride the buses, they could not operate. Three-fourths of the riders are Negro, yet we are arrested, or have to stand over empty seats. If we do not do something to stop these arrests, they will continue. The next time it may be you, or your daughter, or mother. This woman's case will come up on Monday. We are, therefore, asking every Negro to stay off the buses Monday in protest of the arrest and trial. Don't ride the buses to work, to town, to school, or anywhere on Monday. You can afford to stay out of school for one day if you have no other way to go except by bus. You can also afford to stay out of town for one day. If you work, take a cab, or walk. But please, children and grown-ups, don't ride the bus at all on Monday. Please stay off all buses Monday.

Nixon convinced the new pastor of Dexter Avenue Baptist Church to head the group that would call the boycott; and on that Monday night, after 42,000 African-American men, women and children had refused to ride the buses, the Rev. Martin Luther King, Jr. told a cheering crowd of 7,000 boycotters:

> We are not wrong in what we are doing. If we are wrong, the Supreme Court of this nation is wrong. If we are wrong, the Constitution of the United States is wrong. If we are wrong, God Almighty is wrong. If we are wrong, Jesus of Nazareth was merely a utopian dreamer that never came down to Earth. If we are wrong, justice is a lie, love has no meaning. And we are determined here in Montgomery to work and fight until justice runs down like water and righteousness like a mighty stream …
>
> There is never a time in our American democracy that we must ever think we are wrong when we protest. We reserve that right. When labor all over this nation came to see that it would be trampled over by capitalistic power, [there] was nothing wrong with labor getting together and organizing and protesting for its rights. We, the disinherited of this land, we who have been oppressed so long, are tired of going through the long night of captivity. And now we are reaching out for the daybreak of freedom and justice and equality.

Randolph liked what he heard. He sent Bayard Rustin—who had become his most trusted point man, and whose experience organizing civil disobedience against southern segregation dated to the 1947 "Journey of Reconciliation" that established a model for the "Freedom Rides" of the 1960s—from New York to Montgomery. There, the student of Gandhi's non-violent tactics gave strategic advice to Nixon and King. But Rustin, an ex-Communist and a gay man, would quickly be targeted as a "northern infiltrator" by local authorities. He headed back to Harlem, where Rustin continued to counsel King by phone and raised funds to support the boycott. That was fine by Randolph, who had confidence in Nixon and who quickly recognized King as a gifted communicator and potential leader of the movement. An agile organizer who understood that it was always wise to let a successful movement keep on succeeding, Randolph cautioned, "We should learn from them rather than assume we know it all."

The mutual respect that would develop between Randolph and King proved to be a powerful force over the next decade, as the older man handed off his title as the nation's most visible spokesman for civil rights.

Randolph had achieved that status fifteen years earlier with what was, at that point, the as-yet ill-defined movement's most audacious challenge to power.

In 1941, as it became increasingly clear that the United States would enter World War II, President Roosevelt was vitally concerned with developing the "arsenal of democracy" that would be used by the Allied powers to mount an international "defense of freedom" in the fight against the forces of fascism. Yet, for all the presidential preachments about the vital role that every American had to play in the struggle, the federal government acknowledged that "over 500,000 Negroes who should be utilized in war production are now idle, because of the discriminatory hiring practices of the war industries. Several million other Negroes engaged in unskilled occupations are prevented from making greater contributions." Major corporations, such as Standard Steel, refused to hire African-American workers, while some of the nation's largest unions collaborated with factory owners to maintain "whites-only" employment barriers. In the south, federal money was turned away after local officials agreed with the mayor of Shreveport, Louisiana, who claimed: "Of equal importance to winning the war is keeping Negroes out of skilled jobs."

Throughout 1940, Randolph worked with leaders of the NAACP, the Urban League, and prominent African Americans who had White House contacts, such as Mary McLeod Bethune and the young Thurgood Marshall, to address concerns about segregation in the military and defense industries. They had gotten a hearing from Eleanor Roosevelt. But the War Department made a series of announcements in the fall of that year that indicated a clear intent to maintain strict segregation policies. In December, a frustrated Randolph was on a train headed south from Washington to visit the Brotherhood's locals in the region. He and Milton Webster, the no-nonsense organizer who served as the Brotherhood's vice president, were talking about the intransigence of the White House. "We are going to have to do something about it," Randolph said. By the time they got to Georgia, Randolph had hatched a plan to "get 10,000 Negroes to march on Washington to protest."

When Randolph announced the plan that night in Savannah, Webster recalled, "It scared everybody to death." By the time the pair returned to

New York several weeks later, however, the idea was front-page news in the nation's African-American newspapers, which breathlessly reported that the head of the sleeping car porters' union was telling African Americans: "Power and pressure are at the foundation of the march of social justice and reform ... power and pressure do not reside in the few, and intelligentsia, they lie in and flow from the masses. Power does not even rest with the masses as such. Power is the active principle of only the organized masses, the masses united for a definite purpose."

Sounding every bit the tribune of "scientific radicalism" he had proclaimed himself to be almost a quarter-century earlier as the young editor of the *Messenger*, Randolph declared: "Negro America must bring its power and pressure to bear upon the agencies and representatives of the Federal Government to exact their rights to National Defense employment and the armed forces of the country ... I suggest that TEN THOUSAND Negroes march on Washington, DC, with the slogan: WE LOYAL NEGRO AMERICAN CITIZENS DEMAND THE RIGHT TO WORK AND FIGHT FOR OUR COUNTRY."

"One thing is certain," Randolph concluded, "and that is, if Negroes are going to get anything out of this national defense, which will cost the nation 30 or 40 billions of dollars that we Negroes must help pay in taxes as property owners and workers and consumers, WE MUST FIGHT FOR IT AND FIGHT FOR IT WITH GLOVES OFF."

"No mightier pressure had ever been brought to bear in the political history of the American Negro," recalled the sympathetic *New York Post*.

Randolph got the usually cautious NAACP and Urban League on board, as well as key leaders of religious and fraternal organizations across the country, along with an emerging generation of young Socialist activists such as Bayard Rustin. But the Brotherhood remained the backbone of the effort, as union officials and members donated portions of their salaries to create a $50,000 fund to pay for organizing the march, printing signs and renting buses. Randolph, who wanted the movement to be "of, by and for" the African-American community—as opposed to a white-led or even white-assisted project—hit the road himself, talking up the march not just in churches and union offices but in Elks clubs, pool halls, beauty parlors and restaurants. And the old radical who was still being trailed by federal agents went out of his way to encourage the FBI to record his "Let the Negro masses march, let the Negro masses speak" calls not just for 10,000 marchers but, as the enthusiasm grew, for 100,000. He wanted the Roosevelt administration to be alerted to the fact that the march was a serious proposition.

The White House got the message, especially after Randolph invited Eleanor Roosevelt to address the march, which was scheduled for July 1. The First Lady asked NAACP President Walter White to talk the union leader out of the project. But White said he had no control over Randolph. She then met with Randolph and, while expressing sympathy for the cause, urged him to soften his demands. He would not. New York Mayor LaGuardia was then charged by the White House with the task of talking Randolph down. It didn't work.

Finally, Randolph was invited to the White House. Roosevelt greeted Randolph with a hearty "Hello, Phil" and, making a common mistake with the well-spoken union leader, asked which class he had graduated with from Harvard.

"I never went to Harvard," replied Randolph.

"I was sure you did," the president came back, pouring on all the charm he could muster. "Anyway, you and I share a kinship in our great interest in human and social justice."

"That's right, Mr. President."

Roosevelt was sympathetic. He offered to call the CEOs of defense contractors and ask them to integrate their factories. Randolph said he wanted an executive order banning discrimination and a federal board charged with enforcing it.

"Questions like this can't be settled with a sledgehammer," said the president, urging a compromise to avert the march, which was to step off in barely ten days.

"I'm sorry, Mr. President, the march cannot be called off."

"How many people do you plan to bring?"

"One hundred thousand, Mr. President."

The NAACP's White, who was at Randolph's side, echoed the union leader. "One hundred thousand, Mr. President."

"You can't bring one hundred thousand Negroes to Washington. Somebody might get killed."

Not, Randolph suggested, if the president would greet the marchers and address the rally as a friend of the struggle.

Roosevelt was a friend of the struggle, but he was reluctant about expending the political capital it would require to make so great a leap. The politician in him feared the reactions both of his own party's southern flank and of the captains of industry he was asking to join in the war effort.

"Call it off and we'll talk again," the president said, thinking he was making his final offer.

Randolph said he could not go back to the Negro masses without something real. "I have to stand by the pledge I've made to the people," he declared.

LaGuardia who, uncharacteristically, had sat quietly on the sidelines of the discussion, intervened. "Gentlemen," he said, "it is clear that Mr. Randolph is not going to call off the march, and I suggest we all begin to seek a formula."

The "formula," worked out across a week of wrangling in which Randolph repeatedly rejected compromise proposals, was Executive Order 8802:

> WHEREAS it is the policy of the United States to encourage full participation in the national defense program by all citizens of the United States, regardless of race, creed, color, or national origin, in the firm belief that the democratic way of life within the Nation can be defended successfully only with the help and support of all groups within its borders; and
>
> WHEREAS there is evidence that available and needed workers have been barred from employment in industries engaged in defense production solely because of considerations of race, creed, color, or national origin, to the detriment of workers' morale and of national unity:
>
> NOW, THEREFORE, by virtue of the authority vested in me by the Constitution and the statutes, and as a prerequisite to the successful conduct of our national defense production effort, I do hereby reaffirm the policy of the United States that there shall be no discrimination in the employment of workers in defense industries or government because of race, creed, color, or national origin, and I do hereby declare that it is the duty of employers and of labor organizations, in furtherance of said policy and of this order, to provide for the full and equitable participation

of all workers in defense industries, without discrimination because of race, creed, color, or national origin ...

> Franklin D. Roosevelt
> The White House,
> June 25, 1941

Randolph was far from satisfied. He knew the order fell short of what he had hoped for, and far short of what was needed, to break the grip of segregation and racism on a country where the majority of African Americans were still denied the basic rights guaranteed them by the Constitution—let alone the economic rights he argued were needed to give that citizenship meaning. But the organizer in him told Randolph that it was time to claim a victory. So the order went out from the Brotherhood's headquarters in New York. The buses would not roll. The March on Washington would not take place. The fight—not the war, but the fight—had been won.

Eleanor Roosevelt wrote Randolph, promising that "from this first step, we can go on to others." And, though Rustin and a few of the younger comrades grumbled, this was the general sentiment. A crowd of 20,000 packed Madison Square Garden to celebrate the March on Washington Movement. New York's *Amsterdam News* compared Randolph with Frederick Douglass. Other newspapers would refer to him as "the American Gandhi," while columnist Murray Kempton would allow that he had emerged as "a paladin of the Negro community." History would, if anything, be kinder. John Egerton, in his epic examination of the roots of the civil rights movement, *Speak Now Against the Day*, notes that Randolph's March on Washington Movement had offered a signal that "race, once an ignored topic thought to involve only poor people in the South, was about to become a major public issue in the United States." Even though, as Egerton notes, "segregation would remain the order of the day" in much of the country for another quarter century, Randolph had begun to construct the framework for the federal interventions of the future. And, as another historian of the civil rights era, Lenore Bennett, tells us, he had framed the strategy that was to come: one of "unrelenting pressure on the government."

Randolph might well have been able to fight the battle from the inside, or as a national candidate. Not just the Socialists but also Democrats and

Republicans urged him to seek a newly-drawn congressional seat representing Harlem. And the Socialists were serious about making him their 1944 vice-presidential nominee. But in both cases he declined, telegraphing regrets to his party comrades in which he explained that, but for the struggle in which he was already engaged, "nothing would give me greater pleasure than to share the national campaign as part of the Socialist ticket, not to achieve immediate office, but to build the intellectual and spiritual foundation for the development of a broad political movement in America in the pattern of and comparable to the Canadian Commonwealth Federation." That spring, in Saskatchewan, the Cooperative Commonwealth Federation had swept provincial elections and formed the first explicitly socialist state or provincial government in North America. The premier was Tommy Douglas, who would come to be known as "the father of the Canadian national health-care system." (From his base in western Canada, Douglas would over the next two decades lead a successful campaign to get other provinces and finally the federal government to embrace a single-payer model for assuring that all Canadians would receive quality care. It was part of a broader push to develop a Scandanavian-style social welfare state that, while never fully realized, made Douglas an epic and beloved figure far beyond his base of supporters in the labor and farm movements that would eventually form what is now Canada's social-democratic third party, the New Democrats.)

Randolph cheered the election of Douglas in Canada, where the Brotherhood would the following year win a collective bargaining agreement with the Canadian Pacific Railway that, among other things, would address the issue of passengers and white employees calling union members "George" or "boy" by requiring that plaques with the actual names of porters be placed on the walls of the Pullman cars where they worked. Even as Randolph celebrated his union's victories abroad, the labor leader's focus remained on the civil rights struggle in the United States.

Randolph kept building the Brotherhood but, in many senses, his primary public role became that of the radical champion of desegregation. In the late 1940s, he led a movement to integrate the military that saw him unsettle official Washington when he told a Senate panel discussing a peacetime draft: "This time Negroes will not take a Jim Crow draft lying down. The conscience of the world will be shaken as nothing else when thousands and thousands of us second-class Americans choose imprisonment in preference to permanent military slavery ... I personally will advise Negroes to refuse to fight as slaves for a democracy they cannot possess and enjoy." Randolph did just that. As liberal Democrats were congratulating themselves in the summer of 1948 for adopting a civil rights plank muscular enough to force the Dixiecrats to flee the party convention in Philadelphia, Randolph and a circle of Socialists, young civil rights activists and pacifists allied with his friend A. J. Muste stood outside the convention hall holding signs that announced: "Don't Serve in a Jim Crow Army" and "We Demand an Executive Order Outlawing Military Segregation." The union leader carried a sign with big bold letters declaring: "Prison is Better Than Army Jim Crow Service." Other union leaders urged him to "get on the team" and back President Truman, but Randolph was not on the Democratic team. That year he endorsed his friend Norman Thomas on the Socialist ticket. In truth, Truman was less concerned with securing Randolph's endorsement than he was with the fact that he could not afford—in an election year where southern Democrats were defecting to Strom Thurmond's State's Rights Party, and northern lefties were aligning with Henry Wallace's Progressive Party—to have Randolph, Bayard Rustin and their League for Nonviolent Civil Disobedience Against Military Segregation reminding African-American voters that, for all the kind words in the Democratic platform, segregation remained in force in the armed services.

Less than two weeks after the Democratic convention closed, and following a meeting between Randolph and the president every bit as contentious as the 1941 session with his predecessor, Truman issued Executive Order 9981: "It is hereby declared to be the policy of the President that there shall be equality of treatment and opportunity for all persons in the armed services without regard to race, color, religion or national origin. This policy shall be put into effect as rapidly as possible, having due regard to the time required to effectuate any necessary changes without impairing efficiency or morale."

The front page of the *Chicago Defender*, beneath a headline that blared "President Truman Wipes Out Segregation in Armed Forces," featured a large box urging readers to "SAVE this PAPER, It Marks HISTORY." For his part, however, Randolph was interested in more than history. He was almost sixty years old. He had seen and made substantial social progress. He had the ear of presidents, the Congress and a powerful labor movement. He had built movements that could force changes in programs and agencies that were under federal control. But in his native Jacksonville, Florida, he still was not allowed to sit at the lunch counter of the local Woolworth's.

Even as he spent much of the 1950s fighting frustrating battles to get the AFL-CIO to end discrimination within its own unions, Randolph was watching the south and thinking, planning and plotting for the March on Washington that was his dream deferred.

Randolph followed the news of the Montgomery bus boycott on a daily basis, taking calls and telegrams from the Brotherhood's Alabama leader E. D. Nixon, Rustin and others. Randolph, as a veteran orator and organizer, recognized that a remarkable new leader had come on the scene. He and Dr. King formed an instantaneous alliance, with Coretta Scott King recalling years later that the young pastor saw Randolph as his "great inspiration" and regularly sought "advice and counsel" from the senior statesman of the civil rights movement.

Randolph was not merely drawn by King's charisma, nor even by the fact that the Baptist preacher was leading a new generation of southern churchmen to throw off the caution that had made the union leader so frustrated with the religious leaders of the 1930s and 1940s. He especially respected the fact that King mingled his preachments about morality and the rule of law with practical economics and a social-democratic vision for the nation's future.

King never joined the Socialist Party or other explicitly socialist groupings. Yet, while he might not have been the "Marxist-Leninist" advocate of the "official philosophy of communism" and "action-oriented Marxism" that North Carolina Senator Jesse Helms decried when he tried to block a national holiday honoring King, the doctor of philosophy was plenty familiar with the radical thinking of the previous century. C. L. R. James, the Marxist novelist and historian who met him in London in 1957, declared King to be "a man whose ideas were as advanced as any of us on the Left." The pastor was an agile commentator on the writings of the author of *The Communist Manifesto*, and liked to say, "I always look at Marx with a yes and no." He was a critic of the totalitarian excesses of communist regimes and of what he deplored as "false assumptions and evil methods." In his view, "You don't have to go to Karl Marx to learn how to be a revolutionary. I didn't get my inspiration from Karl Marx; I got it from a man named Jesus, a Galilean saint who said he was anointed to heal the broken-hearted." For King, Jesus was "the greatest revolutionary that history has ever known."

The young pastor would nevertheless concede, in an essay on religion and Marxism:

> Communism arose as a protest against the injustices and indignities inflicted upon the underprivileged. *The Communist Manifesto* was written by men aflame with a passion for social justice. Karl Marx, born of Jewish parents who both came from rabbinic stock, and trained, as he must have been, in the Hebrew Scriptures, could never forget the words of Amos: "Let judgment roll down as waters, and righteousness as a mighty stream." Marx's parents adopted Christianity when he was a child of six, thus adding to the Old Testament heritage that of the New. In spite of his later atheism and anti-ecclesiasticism, Marx could not quite forget Jesus' concern for "the least of these." In his writings, he champions the cause of the poor, the exploited, and the disinherited.

"Christians," King argued, "are bound to recognize any passionate concern for social justice." And that included Marx's writings. Ultimately, however, King was more influenced by "Social Gospel" thinkers such as Baptist preacher Walter Rauschenbusch, who believed that "Christianity is in its nature revolutionary," and held to the Blakean notion of "building Jerusalem" such that the Kingdom of God "is not a matter of getting individuals to heaven, but of transforming the life on earth into the harmony of heaven."

Outlining the principles of Christian socialism, Rauschenbusch and other religious radicals formed the Brotherhood of the Kingdom movement in 1892 to spread the idea that "the force of religious spirit should be bent toward asserting the supremacy of life over property." King would channel Rauschenbusch when, in a 1967 presidential address to the SCLC, he proposed: "[Communism] forgets that life is individual. Capitalism forgets that life is social, and the kingdom of brotherhood is found neither in the thesis of communism nor the antithesis of capitalism but in a higher synthesis."

The search for that higher synthesis might begin with asking questions, said King. He himself suggested a few:

> There are forty million poor people here. And one day we must ask the question, Why are there forty million poor people in America? And when you begin to ask that question, you are raising questions about the economic system, about a broader distribution of wealth. When you ask that question, you begin to question the capitalistic economy. And I'm simply saying that more and more, we've got to begin to ask questions about the whole society. We are called upon to help the discouraged beggars in life's marketplace. But one day we must come to see that an edifice which produces beggars needs restructuring. It means that questions must be raised. You see, my friends, when you deal with this, you begin to ask the question, Who owns the oil? You begin to ask the question, Who owns the iron ore? You begin to ask the question, Why is it that people have to pay water bills in a world that is two-thirds water? These are questions that must be asked.

Such questions, he said, would force sincere civil rights activists "to honestly face the fact that the movement must address itself to the matter of restructuring the whole of American society." This was a constant theme of King's in his last years, when he would tell his aides at a retreat in Frogmore, South Carolina: "You can't talk about solving the economic problem of the Negro without talking about billions of dollars. You can't talk about ending the slums without first saying profit must be taken out of slums ... we are treading in difficult water, because it really means that we are saying that something is wrong ... with capitalism ... There must be a better distribution of wealth and maybe America must move toward a democratic socialism."

There is a tendency today to suggest that King evolved toward an embrace of democratic socialism after the experience of the civil rights struggles of the late 1950s and early 1960s—or perhaps under the influence of radicals like the ex-Young Communist Rustin and the ex-CPer Jack Odell. But Coretta Scott King, who had attended the Progressive Party convention of 1948 as a student campaigner for Henry Wallace's presidential bid, would explain in her book *My Life With Martin Luther King, Jr.*—and in biographical works and interviews—that her husband always "knew that the basic problem in our society had to do with economic justice" and "the contrast of wealth between the haves and the have-nots." "Believe it or not, he spoke these words to me when I first met him," she wrote. "It wasn't something that he learned later and developed." In 1952, she recalled, the young scholar had talked to her "about working within the framework of democracy to move us toward a kind of socialism." His wife explained that King believed, even in the middle of the McCarthy era, that "a kind of socialism has to be adopted by our system because the way it is, it's simply unjust. He looked at the poor and that so many people were in ill health with no way for them to pay their medical expenses. He asked how to catch up on all these things. There's got to be some kind of concern in the nation."

Randolph knew the concern. A dozen years before King's birth he had been standing on the soap boxes of Harlem, shouting about the need to move toward a kind of socialism. He, too, had read and respected Marx while rejecting the orthodoxy of the Communist Party. And, though the union leader was almost four decades older than the pastor, the pair shared a sense of urgency and a recognition that a new era demanded new tactics.

Randolph's old idea of a mass March on Washington now seemed like more than mere strategy. It was, he began to argue, a necessity. "We must develop huge demonstrations, because the world is used to big dramatic affairs. They think in terms of hundreds of thousands and millions and billions ... Billions of dollars are appropriated at the twinkling of an eye," he said. "Nothing little counts."

It was in this spirit that Randolph made his call on that January night in 1960, with King at his side and with a presidential election on the horizon—an election that would replace the decent if cautious Dwight Eisenhower (the last president born in the nineteenth century) with a much younger man who might fully embrace Lincoln's understanding that a house divided cannot stand. King was challenging segregation in the belly of the beast, and building a non-violent movement to make real the promises—social and economic—that had been offered a century earlier. Now, the new generation of civil rights campaigners needed something more than rulings from the Supreme Court. They needed the full force of the federal government to declare, once and for all, that the Constitution applied to every state and to every American. And they needed a new economic order that would declare war not just on Jim Crow but on poverty.

The plan was to start with the political parties, which would gather that summer for national conventions that were themselves "dramatic affairs" but that would—because of the intensifying scrutiny of television news cameras—form ideal backdrops for the "huge demonstrations" Randolph envisioned. Party conventions, particularly Democratic conventions, had since 1948 been important policy battlegrounds in the national civil rights war. But the battles had generally taken place on the floor of the conventions, with northern and southern delegations facing off over platform planks. In 1960 Randolph's plan was to march thousands of demonstrators to the door of the convention hall, and then place explicit demands before the delegates and the nation.

This was not a project that enthused the more conciliatory African-American organizations or the AFL-CIO, especially as formal statements from Randolph and his allies pressured the Democratic Party—with which the labor movement was increasingly linked—"to repudiate and condemn the segregationists, white supremacists, racists and Dixiecrats in your ranks—and to unseat and expel them. The Negro people nor any other democratic-minded Americans can have any confidence in a Party which seats a [Arkansas Governor Orval] Faubus or an [Mississippi Senator James] Eastland, or that contains within its ranks those who make alliances with such racists. We demand a pledge to unseat Senator Eastland from the United States Senate as being elected from the state of Mississippi, where Negro citizens—the majority of the state's population—are disfranchised in violation of the 13th, 14th, and 15th Amendments."

King, however, was on board as the co-chairman of what Randolph and Rustin dubbed—with a bow to their past projects—the "March on the Conventions Movement." To organize the protests, Randolph and Rustin turned to a new cadre of Socialist comrades who had been drawn to the movement in recent years, especially thirty-two-year-old Michael Harrington.

Harrington, who had begun writing the series of articles that would form the basis for his groundbreaking examination of economic inequality, *The Other America*, was dispatched to Los Angeles, where Democrats would meet to nominate a moderate New Englander with a mixed record on civil rights, Massachusetts Senator John Kennedy, for president and, many liberals hoped, Randolph's friend and the author of the party's pattern-shifting 1948 civil rights plank, Minnesota Senator Hubert Humphrey, for vice president. As it happened, the No. 2 spot on the ticket went to a southerner, Senate Majority Leader Lyndon Johnson, a Texan whose compromises and calculations had allowed southern Democratic committee chairs to take the teeth out of the Civil Rights Acts of 1957 and 1960. Randolph, King, Harrington and their comrades were less concerned with the make-up of the ticket, however, than with the platform, which they sought to rewrite so that there was no longer any doubt about the commitment of the Democrats to defend "the Constitutional rights and human dignity of 18 million Negro Americans" or the party's determination to address "the decisive domestic issue of our time."

The demands of the demonstrators were as ambitious as the moment required. The very first of them asked the party, which remained the political home of the south's cruelest county sheriffs and local police chiefs, to go on record in favor of civil disobedience against segregation. "We demand that this convention go on record as fully endorsing the great, peaceful democratic sit-in movement in the South, led by the heroic Negro students, supported by increasing numbers of their white fellow students. This movement seeks not alone the constitutional rights of Negroes; but it aims at the moral regeneration of America. It should be endorsed by this convention both as to its non-violent methods and to its ennobling spirit," declared Randolph and King. "It is the responsibility of this convention and of its representatives in the federal government in Washington to speak out against, and to halt, the lawless terror, intimidation, brutality, false arrests and violence upon these students as they seek to exercise their constitutional rights against the degradation of segregation, discrimination and Jim Crow."

They also sought a genuine and immediate commitment to voting rights, declaring: "The 1960 elections will be a farce unless more than 10 million Negroes in the South have the opportunity to vote. We demand that this convention go on record for establishing a federal registration apparatus in the deep South, in which the victims—the Negro people—shall serve. This apparatus should be put into effect now for the 1960 elections—and not be postponed until after the elections when the Negro people will have been effectively disfranchised in this year's election. Moreover, the entire federal apparatus should be drawn into guaranteeing the right of the Negro people in the South to vote."

There were, as well, calls for commitments on the part of the party and the next president to lead the fight to desegregate the schools and to "issue an executive order barring all discrimination in government employment, in all employment policies of firms doing business with the government and in all forms of public supported housing." And, as Randolph had insisted upon since his youthful days as a Socialist Party soap-box speaker on the streets of Harlem, there was a bow to international solidarity, in the form of a "demand that this convention and its candidates take a clear moral stand against colonialism and racism of all kinds, everywhere, and especially in Africa where apartheid has led to the massacre of hundreds of people seeking only to live in freedom in their own land."

Getting the Democratic National Convention to go on record in support of these positions—or even gentle rewrites of them—would force a breaking point in a party which its two-time presidential nominee in the 1950s, Adlai Stevenson, had struggled to keep together with platform language and policies that were often less specific or progressive than those of Eisenhower's Republicans. It would take more than just a powerful presentation by Randolph, a labor leader who was at the time engaged in a bitter public dispute with AFL-CIO President George Meany, or even a rhetorical masterstroke from King. And it would take much, much more than the small symbolic demonstrations that had been organized outside past conventions.

Twelve years earlier, when Democrats convened in Philadelphia, Randolph and his small band had quietly marched on behalf of integrating the military. But on the Saturday before the Democratic National Convention in Los Angeles, when Harrington collected King at the airport, he would outline a dramatically more aggressive plan for the following day's march and rally that would realize the call Randolph had made in

New York six months earlier: "The Negro people must stand up before these conventions and say to the nation and the world: 'We want to be free.'"

Five thousand marchers, most of them African-American but with sizable contingents of white students such as the young Tom Hayden (who would make his own history eight years later outside the Democratic National Convention in Chicago), marched through the streets of the city to the Sports Arena, where the convention would open the following day. The rally that followed became a major news story when Senator Kennedy appeared to declare his commitment to the civil rights agenda—albeit in language so restrained that the response from the crowd was described by reporters as "tepid." The success of the march was such that a decision was made to mount a round-the-clock vigil at the gates of the Sports Arena, where delegates and television camera crews were confronted as they came and went from the convention by crowds of mostly young activists singing the movement's songs, chanting its slogans and demanding that the Democratic Party finally make a commitment to small-"d" democracy. "Day after day during convention week, hundreds of chanting picketers kept the cause visible to the delegates and to the nation," notes historian Maurice Isserman, who argues that the modern tradition of protesting outside conventions was established on the streets of Los Angeles that summer. "Journalists who had come to Los Angeles thinking the only story worth covering was inside the convention hall were surprised by the size and spirit of the demonstrations. The 1960 picketers thus helped rewrite the script for this and future political conventions as places where activists could bring issues of importance to public attention."

The convention adopted a platform that followed the outlines—if not the full agenda—laid out by Randolph and King. Remarkably, the delegates even approved an embrace of the sit-down demonstrations, declaring: "The peaceful demonstrations for first-class citizenship which have recently taken place in many parts of this country are a signal to all of us to make good, at long last, the guarantees of the American Constitution."

"The time has come to assure equal access for all Americans to all areas of community life, including voting booths, schoolrooms, jobs, housing, and public facilities," the document declared in a section that detailed specific commitments never before seen in a Democratic platform. It closed with a bow to Randolph's internationalism and Tom Paine's radical vision of the Rights of Man:

> The Democratic President who takes office next January will face unprecedented challenges. His Administration will present a new face to the world.
>
> It will be a bold, confident, affirmative face. We will draw new strength from the universal truths which the founder of our Party asserted in the Declaration of Independence to be "self-evident."
>
> Emerson once spoke of an unending contest in human affairs, a contest between the Party of Hope and the Party of Memory.
>
> For 7 1/2 years America, governed by the Party of Memory, has taken a holiday from history.
>
> As the Party of Hope it is our responsibility and opportunity to call forth the greatness of the American people.
>
> In this spirit, we hereby rededicate ourselves to the continuing service of the Rights of Man—everywhere in America and everywhere else on God's earth.

Coming from a virtually all-white convention, and in the context of an election campaign when Democrats were making a bid for the votes of African-American and white liberal voters who were increasingly focused on the civil rights issue, it is easy—and, ultimately, appropriate—to be skeptical about the extent of the investment by key Democrats in anything more than rhetorical flourishes. But Isserman suggests that the commitments made at the convention—coupled with the influence of the demonstrations on Kennedy and his more liberal aides—would play a critical role in tipping one of the closest elections in American history to the Democrats:

> The convention over, delegates and protesters alike dispersed. Yet the full effects of the civil rights protest at the Democratic convention were still to be felt. A month before the November election, a group of student activists in Atlanta, Ga., persuaded King to join them at a sit-in at a segregated restaurant. They were arrested for disturbing the peace, but all were soon released—except King. Georgia authorities hustled the civil rights leader off to a state penitentiary on a charge of violating probation from an earlier traffic citation.

When King was jailed, neither Kennedy nor his Republican opponent, Richard M. Nixon, initially offered any comment. Kennedy had kept the volatile issue of civil rights at arms-length ever since the Los Angeles convention; the last thing Kennedy's staff wanted the presidential nominee to do before election day was anything that might alienate the party's traditional base among Southern white voters.

Yet a few of Kennedy's maverick advisers urged him to make a gesture that would, at least, show his concern for King's safety. Finally deciding to take the risk, Kennedy telephoned King's wife, Coretta Scott King, to offer his sympathies. Also, his brother, Bobby Kennedy, successfully pressured a Georgia judge to order King's release.

On election day, black voters rewarded Kennedy, giving him 70 percent of their vote, significantly more than given to the Democratic presidential nominee in 1952 or 1956. Arguably, the black vote made the difference in Kennedy's extremely narrow margin of victory in 1960.

Given the political risks, however, why did ultra-cautious Kennedy make the decision in October to help King against the advice of most seasoned advisers? I believe that memories of the march and picket line at the Los Angeles Democratic convention prompted him to pay attention to an issue that, before then, had little engaged him. A consummate old-school politician, Kennedy was learning to operate in a new political environment in which movements that were armed with little political clout but a strong moral claim would have an increasing say in setting the nation's priorities.

Randolph knew that campaigning was different from governing. While Kennedy peopled his administration with some serious supporters of civil rights (especially young lawyers like William vanden Heuvel in Attorney General Robert F. Kennedy's Department of Justice), Randolph and his allies did not expect quick action from the new administration, or from a Congress where key committee chairs were still held by sons of the south and where a new breed of right-wing Republicans, led by Arizona Senator Barry Goldwater, were claiming that federal civil rights laws represented an unfair intrusion on the states. Even before Kennedy took office, Randolph wrote in a cover article for a fall 1960 issue of the Socialist Party's *New America* magazine (which was edited by Harrington) that both major parties remained unreliable allies of the civil rights movement. According to Randolph, "Idealism and vision were not to be found within the convention halls but outside, among the thousands of civil rights supporters who marched on both conventions demanding Negro freedom now."

Instead of waiting for politicians to act, Randolph argued that it was time for the movement to initiate "the kind of physical, and essentially non-violent, assault on reactionary institutions that the labor movement developed in its finest days."

Randolph was writing of King's campaigning in the south, but he was also outlining a plan to finally realize the promise of the March on Washington Movement of 1941.

Over the next three years, Randolph and Rustin would frame out the vision for such a march, with the idea that it would make the linkage between civil rights and economic justice. The AFL-CIO, while increasingly sympathetic, would not endorse the march, although the United Auto Workers (led by Walter Reuther, a former Socialist Party member) and powerful union locals that had been dogged by red-baiters during the 1950s but survived, such as New York's District 1199 (led by the radical Leon Davis) and District 65 (led by the equally radical David Livingston), were fully on board. So, too, this time, were the major civil rights organizations. That said, Randolph kept a tight grip on the organizing program. As Jervis Anderson recalls in his masterful retelling of the events leading to what remains the most historic of a thousand historic civil rights demonstrations, Roy Wilkins of the NAACP was unhappy that Randolph wanted Rustin as the chief organizer of the march. To quiet the concerns about putting an ex-Communist, the subject of constant rumor-mongering about his sexuality, in so sensitive a position, Randolph agreed to accept the title of "national director." Then he explained that in this new capacity he would be responsible for naming an organizer, "and I want you to understand that I'm going to select Bayard." Even when White House aides urged the removal of Rustin, and when South Carolina segregationist Strom Thurmond shouted from the Senate floor that the march's lead organizer was a "Communist, draft-dodger, and homosexual," Randolph held firm. And rightly so. The march that Rustin devoted a year to planning and managing—with the help of a young Eleanor Katherine Holmes, the future Congresswoman Eleanor Holmes Norton—would exceed all expectations.

The initial plan was to muster 100,000 people for a "March on Washington for Jobs and Freedom" on August 28, 1963. But it did not take long for Rustin to realize that the turnout goal of the cancelled 1941 march would be exceeded. In fact, it would be more than doubled. On the morning after the march, the *New York Times* would declare—not in an editorial but in the news article of the day: "It was the greatest assembly for a redress of grievances that this capital has ever seen." President Kennedy, who just weeks earlier had met with Randolph and suggested that the timing of the march was wrong, and potentially threatening to his legislative agenda, would declare on the evening of August 28: "History has seen many demonstrations—of widely varying character and for a whole host of reasons. As our thoughts travel to other demonstrations that have occurred in different parts of the world, this Nation can properly be proud of the demonstration that has occurred here today." More importantly, Kennedy would explicitly embrace the call for both jobs and freedom, announcing his commitment to advance civil rights legislation and his conviction that: "This Nation can afford to achieve the goals of a full employment policy—it cannot afford to permit the potential skills and educational capacity of its citizens to be unrealized."

The memory of the march, still vivid for those aging Americans who made the trek on the more than 2,000 buses, 21 special trains and ten airliners Rustin enlisted, and maintained to some extent by textbooks that offer a frequently sanitized version of events, has for most Americans softened with the passage of years. There are a great many citizens of good intention and spirit who know only that the Rev. Martin Luther King, Jr., fresh from Georgia's "Albany Movement" and Alabama's Birmingham campaign and on his way to Selma and Memphis, electrified the crowd with his declaration: "I have a dream." But King was not the only speaker on August 28, 1963. After Marian Anderson sang the National Anthem, it was A. Philip Randolph—the fiery young radical champion of the IWW and the anti-colonial struggle, the "most dangerous Negro in America," the proud Socialist soap-box campaigner for Eugene Victor Debs and the "cooperative commonwealth," the man who used the threat of a mass mobilization to force the integration of the defense industries of World War II and the threat of a mass refusal to serve to force the integration of the military, now the white-haired counselor of presidents but still a self-declared "radical militant"—who opened the program with a call for progress "in service of human needs, not at the service of profits" and a declaration that "private property takes second place to the sanctity of the human personality."

"Fellow Americans," the seventy-four-year-old Randolph told the crowd massed at precisely the sort of March on Washington he had imagined on that train ride with Milton Webster all those years before, "we are gathered here in the largest demonstration in the history of this nation. Let the nation and world know the meaning of our numbers. We are not a pressure group. We are not an organization or a group of organizations. We are not a mob. We are the advance guard of a massive moral revolution for jobs and freedom."

As the 250,000 Americans cheered, he continued:

> This revolution reverberates throughout the land, touching every city, every town, every village where black men are segregated, oppressed, and exploited. But this civil rights revolution is not confined to the Negro nor is it confined to civil rights, for our white allies know that they cannot be free while we are not; and we know we have no future in a society in which six million black and white people are unemployed and millions more live in poverty. Nor is the goal of our civil rights revolution merely the passage of civil rights legislation.
>
> Yes, we want all public accommodations open to all citizens, but those accommodations will mean little to those who cannot afford to use them. Yes, we want a Fair Employment Practices Act, but what good will it do to millions of workers, black and white? We want integrated public schools, but that means we also want federal aid to education—all forms of education. We want a free democratic society dedicated to the political, economic, and social advancement of man along moral lines. Now, we know that real freedom will require many changes in the nation's political and social philosophies and institutions. For one thing, we must destroy the notion that [a white person's] property rights include the right to humiliate me because of the color of my skin. The sanctity of private property takes second place to the sanctity of the human personality.
>
> It falls to the Negro to reassert this proper priority of values, because our ancestors were transformed from human personalities into private property. It falls to us to demand new forms of social planning, to create full employment, and to put automation at the service of human needs,

not at the service of profits—for we are the first victims of unemployment. Negroes are in the forefront of today's movement for social and racial justice, because we know we cannot expect the realization of our aspirations through the same old anti-democratic social institutions and philosophies that have all along frustrated our aspirations.

Meticulous as ever about making the economic connections between working-class whites and working-class minorities, Randolph told his audience to "Look for the enemies of Medicare, of high minimum wages, of social security, of federal aid to education, and there you will find the enemy of the Negro—the coalition of Dixiecrats and reactionary Republicans that seeks to dominate the Congress." "The March on Washington," he promised, "is not the climax of our struggle but a new beginning, not only for the Negro but for all Americans who thirst for freedom and a better life."

At the end of that historic day, after he had introduced King and cheered the younger man's announcement that "we refuse to believe that the bank of justice is bankrupt," Randolph sent the marchers home—but first, all those present pledged in thunderous unison to give "my heart, and my mind, and my body, unequivocally and without regard to personal sacrifice, to the achievement of social peace through social justice."

Randolph, King and countless others took the pledge as a deeply personal commitment. The sacrifices would be immense. But so too would be the victories. The Civil Rights Act of 1964. The National Voting Rights Act of 1965. The confirmation of Thurgood Marshall (the son of a sleeping car porter) to serve as the first African-American justice on the United States Supreme Court. The election of Ed Brooke, a Republican more liberal than most of today's Democrats, as the first African-American senator since Reconstruction. The rise of movements for the liberation of women, Hispanics, the disabled and gays and lesbians that took their inspiration from the successful interventions of all those who pledged to pursue "the achievement of social peace through social justice." Yet, as Randolph had said, the aim of the March was never "merely the passage of civil rights legislation." The journey's goal was not a statute, it was "a free democratic society dedicated to the political, economic, and social advancement of man along moral lines." And to get there, Randolph and King focused increasingly in the mid-1960s on making those "many changes in the nation's political and social philosophies and institutions."

Working with Michael Harrington, who with the publication of *The Other America* found himself advising members of the Kennedy and Johnson administrations on how to mount a "war on poverty," Randolph focused on the challenge of moving from rhetoric to specifics, touring the country with the purpose of transitioning the campaign for civil rights into a broader campaign for economic rights. When the Johnson White House organized the "To Fulfill These Rights" conference in the spring of 1966, he outlined a plan to "call upon the leaders of the Freedom Movement to meet together with economists and social scientists in order to work out a specific and documented 'Freedom Budget.'"

Written by former President Truman's chief economic advisor, Leon H. Keyserling, with input from Harrington, sociologist Herbert Gans, and a circle of economists and activists who had been working on poverty issues, the "Freedom Budget for All Americans" was a plan to spend an estimated $185 billion to end poverty in ten years, with policy and spending shifts. Specifically, it proposed:

1. To provide full employment for all who are willing and able to work, including those who need education or training to make them willing and able.
2. To assure decent and adequate wages to all who work.
3. To assure a decent living standard to those who cannot or should not work.
4. To wipe out slum ghettos and provide decent homes for all Americans.
5. To provide decent medical care and adequate educational opportunities to all Americans, at a cost they can afford.
6. To purify our air and water and develop our transportation and natural resources on a scale suitable to our growing needs.
7. To unite sustained full employment with sustained full production and high economic growth.

"[In] the richest and most productive society ever known to man, the scourge of poverty can and must be abolished—not in some distant future, not in this generation, but within the next ten years!" declared

Randolph in his muscular introduction to the Freedom Budget. "The tragedy is that the workings of our economy so often pit the white poor and the black poor against each other at the bottom of society." Developing a message that would eventually underpin the Rev. Jesse Jackson's Rainbow Coalition campaigns of 1984 and 1988, the union leader argued: "all Americans are the victims of our failure as a nation to distribute democratically the fruits of our abundance. For, directly or indirectly, not one of us is untouched by the steady spread of slums, the decay of our cities, the segregation and overcrowding of our public schools, the shocking deterioration of our hospitals, the violence and chaos in our streets, the idleness of able-bodied men deprived of work, and the anguished demoralization of our youth."

Herculean efforts by Randolph and Rustin, who toured the country on behalf of the Freedom Budget, secured support from a multiracial coalition of more than 200 prominent Americans. They included leading civil rights activists such as Nobel Peace Prize winner Ralph Bunche, the NAACP'S Roy Wilkins, the National Urban League's Whitney Young, Jr., the Congress of Racial Equality's Floyd McKissick, outgoing SNCC leader John Lewis (a future congressman) and a young Vernon Jordan; cutting-edge economists such as Clark College president Vivian Henderson (the great scholar of southern economic conditions) and John Kenneth Galbraith (fresh from his service in the Kennedy and Johnson administrations, and busy developing his theory of a "new socialism" that would see the state acting to protect "the health and well-being" of society in a mixed economy); labor leaders such as the UAW's Reuther and Steelworkers' chief I. W. Abel, religious leaders such as the Rev. Robert Drinan (a prominent figure on the religious left and another future congressman), and even celebrities such as Dr. Benjamin Spock (the renowned pediatrician who might well have been the nation's most prominent democratic socialist of the moment).

Launched in New York City and accepted by White House officials in Washington, the "Freedom Budget" earned national attention and serious consideration from Americans who were willing—in that last moment of so much possibility—to listen as Randolph explained:

The "Freedom Budget" spells out a specific and factual course of action, step by step, to start in early 1967 toward the practical liquidation of poverty in the United States by 1975. The programs urged in the "Freedom Budget" attack all of the major causes of poverty—unemployment and underemployment; substandard pay; inadequate social insurance and welfare payments to those who cannot or should not be employed; bad housing; deficiencies in health services, education, and training; and fiscal and monetary policies which tend to redistribute income regressively rather than progressively. The "Freedom Budget" leaves no room for discrimination in any form, because its programs are addressed to all who need more opportunity and improved incomes and living standards—not just to some of them. ...

The "Freedom Budget" ... is not visionary or utopian. It is feasible. It is concrete. It is specific. It talks dollars and sense. It sets goals and priorities. It tells how these can be achieved. And it places responsibility for leadership with the Federal Government, which alone has the resources equal to the task.

King was one of the most ardent advocates for the initiative, writing the introduction to a twenty-page pamphlet detailing the budget's proposals, and preaching that "the ultimate answer to the Negroes' economic dilemma will be found in a massive federal program for all the poor along the lines of A. Philip Randolph's Freedom Budget, a kind of Marshall Plan for the disadvantaged." In the spring of 1967, he would deliver the second most famous speech of his life to a meeting of Clergy and Laity Concerned—held one year to the day before his assassination—at New York's Riverside Church. The Riverside Church speech, rightly remembered for its precise condemnation of the war in Vietnam and its broader critique of military and economic imperialism, unsettled Rustin, who had grown increasing deferent to insider Washington when it came to foreign policy debates, and a number of other leading civil rights advocates. In the initial struggle to advance the Freedom Budget, both Rustin and Randolph had gone out of their way to maintain good relations with the Johnson administration—echoing White House lines on foreign policy and distancing themselves from the demands of younger and more militant campaigners. Randolph made no secret of the fact that he was ill at ease with slogans like "Black Power," which he feared would divide the working class and made it harder to place effective demands upon Washington and Wall Street. For a time, especially during the period from 1965 to 1967, there was a genuine tension between the old radical and the new radicals, with younger militants dismissing Randolph as "leader emeritus" and even an "Uncle Tom." Randolph would say of Stokely Carmichael, the former Student Nonviolent Coordinating Committee leader who popularized the "Black Power" slogan and increasingly advanced a black nationalist position: "He's vigorous, he is brilliant, but I think he is wrong."

By the time of King's 1967 speech, however, Randolph was entertaining his own deep doubts about the Vietnam War and about the commitment of the Johnson administration to mount a genuine "war on poverty" at home. And he was coming to the conclusion—as King was—that efforts had to be made to reach out to the militants. King would appear with Carmichael at a New York event on April 15, 1967, to denounce the draft. For his part, Randolph would eventually tell *Ebony* magazine: "I love the young black militants. I don't agree with all their methodology, and yet I can understand why they are in this mood of revolt, of resort to violence. I was a young black militant myself, the angry young man of my day. As a Socialist, an advocate of trade unionism and the editor of a radical magazine called *The Messenger*, I didn't agree with anything that was supposed to be respectable, that was supposed to be a part of the American ideal and the American system. I believed that the old political, economic and social order had to be changed and changed immediately!" While he eventually came to believe in non-violent civil disobedience and the power of protest to make social progress "inevitable," Randolph argued: "Whereas, at the present time, the demands of the black militants and the black nationalists for immediate change will not bring about immediate change, their condemnation, their general rejection of the social order nevertheless has value in that it shakes the country to the recognition that here is a grave social injustice that is being done to a great people, a social injustice that must be changed and it must be changed immediately." Some older civil rights leaders, like some older socialists, grew increasingly ill at ease with a new left, but Randolph had already begun to try and build bridges and focus what he saw as "a new social force" on the work of creating a new economic order.

King remained close personal and political allies. Randolph recognized the importance of pointing out that money spent on distant and unnecessary wars robbed the Treasury of funds that could be spent to fight poverty at home. And he could not help but be moved by the portions of the preacher's Riverside Church address that reprised language the union leader had been using for years. "I am convinced that if we are to get on the right side of the world revolution, we as a nation must undergo a radical revolution of values," said King. "We must rapidly begin the shift from a 'thing-oriented' society to a 'person-oriented' society. When machines and computers, profit motives and property rights are considered more important than people, the giant triplets of racism, materialism, and militarism are incapable of being conquered."

King had cast caution aside when it came to economic debates. "Call it democracy, or call it democratic socialism, but there must be a better distribution of wealth within this country for all God's children," he told the Negro American Labor Congress in 1965. By 1967, he was framing a new message that had at its heart the Freedom Budget. "It didn't cost the nation one penny to integrate lunch counters," King said as he toured Mississippi in February 1968 in preparation for the "Poor People's Campaign" in which he planned to lead marchers from the deep south to Washington. "[But] now we are dealing with issues that cannot be solved without the nation spending billions of dollars and undergoing a radical redistribution of economic power."

King's assassination did not end the push for the Freedom Budget. An attempt was made to carry the Poor People's Campaign through. And Michael Harrington found himself swept into the presidential campaign of Bobby Kennedy, who as the Democratic Senator from New York had discussed the Freedom Budget with Randolph and had encouraged the Poor People's Campaign with a suggestion to Marian Wright (Edelman) that it was time to "bring the poor to Washington." Kennedy's campaign evolved through the tortured spring of 1968 into a passionate crusade that held out the promise of uniting working-class whites, African Americans, Asian Americans and Latinos in a coalition capable of imagining the politics that would advance a Freedom Budget for All Americans. On April 5, Kennedy spoke to the City Club of Cleveland "On the Mindless Menace of Violence." He addressed King's assassination, which had shocked the nation only hours earlier, and the riots that threatened American cities. But he counseled his elite audience to see further. "For there is another kind of violence, slower but just as deadly destructive as the shot or the bomb in the night," the senator explained. "This is the violence of institutions; indifference and inaction and slow decay. This is the violence that afflicts the poor, that poisons relations between men because their skin has different colors. This is the slow destruction of a child by hunger, and schools without books, and homes without heat in the winter."

Had Kennedy survived to be nominated and elected, it is not so difficult to think that a Freedom Budget might have been enacted—and with it an advance toward the democratic socialism which Randolph had championed. After the senator's assassination, the suppression of dissent inside and outside that summer's Democratic National Convention and the defeat of Randolph's friend Hubert Humphrey, however, the presidency fell to Republican Richard Nixon, who had rejected the Freedom Budget and the whole idea of spending "billions of dollars for the poor." By the spring of 1969, Randolph would admit to *Ebony* that: "There has been a decided lack of interest on the part of the government in facing this problem realistically."

It was true. But it was no less true that A. Philip Randolph's socialist faith, the American Socialist faith of Eugene Victor Debs, Norman Thomas, Jessie Wallace Hughan, Bayard Rustin, Jack O'Dell, Michael Harrington and so many others with whom he had struggled across the decades from the days when he began to organize the sons of slaves to the days when he sat in the White House, from the day when he was jailed in Cleveland to the day when he stood before 250,000 marchers for jobs and freedom in Washington, was unwavering. "I have always considered myself part of the democratic Socialist movement," he would say in the spring of 1970, when he accepted the honorary chairmanship of the Socialist Party.

What that meant to Randolph was what it had meant ever since he stepped onto the Socialist soap box on a street corner in Harlem more than half a century earlier.

"The tragedy is that the workings of our economy so often pit the white poor and the black poor against each other at the bottom of our society. The tragedy is that groups only one generation removed from poverty themselves, haunted by the memory of scarcity and fearful of slipping back, step on the fingers of those struggling up the ladder," he explained toward the end of a lifetime of working to link the struggles for racial and economic justice so that all Americans could climb the ladder. "The question is not whether we have the means. Before 1975, we will have a $1 trillion economy. The question is whether we have the *will*. Ten years from now, will two-fifths of our nation still live in poverty and deprivation? This is, above all, a moral question. And upon the answer hangs not only the fate of the Negro—weighed down by centuries of exploitation, degradation and malice—but the fate of the nation."

"But What About Democratic Left Politics?"

The Other America *by Michael Harrington was the book that had the greatest influence on the Kennedy and Johnson Administrations, leading to the policies of the Great Society ...*
> —Michael Kaufman, "The Dangers of Letting Presidents Read,"
> *New York Times*, 1999

Socialism [is] no longer a dirty word to labor.
> —*Business Week*, 1979

We will not settle for a tomorrow in which we become a lesser people in a lesser land.
> —Senator Edward Kennedy, 1987

Let me talk about the broader issue, this whole notion that I am shifting to the center or that I'm flip-flopping or this or that or the other.
> —Senator Barack Obama, 2008

"Socialism" Not So Negative, "Capitalism" Not So Positive.
> —Pew Research Center for the People and the Press finding, 2010

A year into Barack Obama's presidency, the annual Conservative Political Action Conference convened to cheer the likes of Iowa Congressman Steve King, a fire-and-brimstone Republican right-winger who told the crowd: "I want to define that enemy. They are liberals, they are progressives, they are Che Guevarians, they are Castroites, they are socialists ... Gramsciites ... Trotskyites, Maoists, Stalinists, Leninists, Marxists. They are all our enemies. Who'd I leave out? How about I go to: democratic socialists? And I'm going to ask you to go to the dsausa.org website and take a look and see what you find there. The Democratic Socialists of America. They are the socialists. There is a game plan on there. That game plan looks suspiciously like President Obama's game plan." If King didn't get the CPACers stirred up with his talk of Che Guevarians and democratic socialists, surely former House Speaker Newt Gingrich did, with his warning: "we are now in a struggle over whether or not we are going to save America. I believe the radical left is a secular, socialist machine so dedicated to values destructive of America that if it is allowed to remain in power ... that machine is antithetical to the survival of America as a prosperous, healthy country."

But what really stirred the American conservatives as they gathered in the nation's capital was an "investigative" report from behind "enemy" lines.

With time to kill before the ranting about the suspiciously socialist outlines of "Obama's game plan" was to begin, conservative activist and talk-radio host Rob Port took a guided tour of the Obama White House.

In no time, "North Dakota's Most Popular Political Blogger" had uncovered the socialist menace that was lurking there—on a bookshelf.

"One of the stops on the tour (which was wonderful by the way) was the White House library," explained the developer of North Dakota's aptly-labeled "Say Anything" blog. "Now, according [to] the person who guided our tour, the library is [stocked] with books picked out by the First Lady, Michelle Obama. Being a bit of a bibliophile, I started to peruse some of the books on the shelves ... and lookie, lookie what I found ..."

Port posted a photograph which he labeled "Photo Evidence: Michelle Obama Keeps Socialist Books in the White House Library."

On a rather too tightly packed shelf, amid the books on the organization of political parties, were *The American Socialist Movement 1897–1912* ("the epic story of the struggle to build a mass socialist movement in ragtime America," by Ira Kipnis, an exceptionally eclectic historian who later became a corporate lawyer) and *The Socialist Party of America* (David Shannon's "standard scholarly history," according to the Conservapedia.com website). Next to the "socialist books" was Nathan Glazer's *The Social Basis of*

American Communism (never mind that Glazer is considered an intellectual godfather of neoconservatism).

Troubling? Perhaps not to Americans who had neglected the "signs" of socialist slinking within the Obama White House, Port fretted. "But in the context of [former communications aide] Anita Dunn saying Chairman Mao is her favorite political philosopher? In the context of the Mao ornament on the White House Christmas tree? In the context of Obama's economic policies?"

Well, the right-wing blogosphere was certainly troubled. Make that apoplectic. Port's post rocketed around the Internet and became fodder for fevered fulminations on talk radio. Surely, this was the: "See! See! We told you so! Obama really *is* the Manchurian candidate and now the fellow-traveling First Lady is turning the White House library into a propaganda mill" moment.

"Figures. Michelle Obama Stocked White House Library with Books on Socialism," read the headline on www.freerepublic.com, where the more feckless—and grammatically challenged—commentators chirped about "Something we all have known … Her and her Husband are the Julius and Ethel Rosenberg of the 21st century." The "All American Blogger" asked, presumably with an arched eyebrow: "I wonder if the liberals who mock conservatives who refer to Obama as a socialist still find it funny?"

The *Washington Post* announced that the "socialist books" scandal had started a "blog wildfire," while *New York* magazine smirked: "The conservative blogosphere is having a collective climax today because a blogger from sayanythingblog.com snapped a photo of some old reference books about socialism in the White House Library—which the tour guide said was stocked by Michelle Obama. Surely this means that every time President Obama is in the midst of important policy deliberations, he goes into the library, dusts off *The American Socialist Movement, 1897–1912*, and uses it to help him figure out what the most socialist policy would be."

That may read like parody. But on the edge of the wildfire, commentators were getting extra marks for flaming the ideology and the intelligence of the First Couple by asking: "How else could they 'fundamentally change America forever' without some written instruction?"

"Know your enemy!" roared a "Free Republic" commentator on the books.

Another declared ominously: "The Obamas BELIEVE in their commie/socialist books."

And by their books shall ye know the commies!

Or maybe not.

Excited by a burgeoning book controversy, literary editors started inquiring into the story that had the socialist-hunters on the right salivating.

"The only problem is the books Port photographed have been sitting in the library since 1963," the *Washington Post* explained. "The library came into being during the presidency of Franklin Roosevelt. In 1961, First Lady Jacqueline Kennedy asked Yale University librarian James T. Babb to oversee a committee that would select books for the library. In 1963, 1,780 were placed on the shelves."

An amused Marjorie Kehe, book editor of the *Christian Science Monitor*, relayed a salient detail in the online paper's "Chapter & Verse" blog: "Apparently they have been sitting quietly on the White House shelves for several decades now, including throughout the administrations of Ronald Reagan, George H. W. Bush, and George W. Bush."

But the wisest insight came from a description of the collection written almost five decades earlier by the librarian James Babb, after he had finished the year-long task of assembling the titles—with the assistance of a small committee that included the editors of the Thomas Jefferson and John Adams papers and a young White House aide and historian named Arthur Schlesinger, Jr.

Babb explained the physically constrained collection's ambitious purpose as follows: "It is intended to contain books which best represent the history and culture of the United States, works most essential for an understanding of our national experience."

Even in the shadow of the Cold War, at a time when the Cuban Missile Crisis was a current event and Frank Sinatra and Janet Leigh had just finished production on *The Manchurian Candidate*, it was considered both historically and culturally correct to include books that respected the role that the Socialist Party and socialist thinkers had played in shaping the United States. President Kennedy was something of a scholar of political dissent, being the Pulitzer Prize–winning author (with an assist from Ted Sorensen and others) of *Profiles in Courage* and the chair of a committee that named as one of the five greatest senators the chamber's most radical alumnus (and the only member to seek the presidency with the endorsement of the Socialist Party), Robert M. La Follette.

Kennedy was worldly enough to joke comfortably, and reasonably knowledgeably, about Karl Marx, even in the midst of the Cold War. As the future president told the annual awards dinner of the Overseas Press Club in 1957:

> I gained a new appreciation for the lot of the foreign correspondent when the April issue of American Heritage revealed that, in 1851, the *New York Tribune* under Horace Greeley employed as its London correspondent an obscure journalist by the name of Karl Marx. (Some of the copy he filed, it seems, was ghost-written by his friend and patron, Friedrich Engels—but that practice no doubt is as thoroughly discredited today among overseas correspondents as it is among practicing politicians.) In any event, we are told that foreign correspondent Marx, stone-broke and with a family ill and under-nourished, constantly appealed to Greeley and managing editor Charles Dana for an increase in his munificent salary of $5 per installment—a salary which he and Engels ungratefully labeled as "the lousiest petty-bourgeois cheating." But when all his financial appeals were refused, Marx looked around for other means of livelihood and fame, eventually terminating his relationship with the *Tribune* and devoting his talents full-time to the cause that would bequeath to the world the seeds of Leninism, Stalinism, revolution and Cold War. If only this capitalist New York newspaper had treated him more kindly, if only Marx had remained a foreign correspondent, history might have all been different, our taxes today might be lower—and I hope all publishers will bear this lesson in mind the next time they receive a poverty-stricken appeal from abroad for a small increase in the expense account.
>
> Perhaps it was the *Tribune* that made Marx an expert on capitalist exploitation—for he used to scream to Engels, in language exceedingly inappropriate to the gentlemanly traditions of foreign correspondents, that this "lousy rag," as he called the *Tribune*, run by two "lousy bums," Greeley and Dana, was exploiting Engels and himself like "paupers in a workhouse."

This soliloquy preceded a declaration by Kennedy that he was preparing a proposal to ease restrictions on US relations with communist countries such as Poland, explaining, just four days after the death of Joe McCarthy: "The basic laws governing our foreign economic policies ... recognize only two categories of nations in the world: nations 'under the domination or control' of the USSR or the world Communist movement—and 'friendly nations.' I suggest to you that there are more shades of gray than these black and white definitions would indicate—that there are and will be nations such as Poland, that may not yet be our allies, or even friendly, but which are at least beginning to move out from Soviet domination and control. I suggest that these Acts be rewritten accordingly ..."

Kennedy was no "red," despite the claims of the John Birch Society—which went to the sort of rhetorical extremes that were denounced by prominent Republicans and conservative commentators of the late 1950s and early 1960s, but that are now the *lingua franca* of Republican leaders of the US House and Senate. In fact, Kennedy was more on the side of the red baiters than many Democrats; he was relatively friendly with McCarthy and famously avoided taking a stand even when other senators finally got around to condemning the dishonest and destructive reign of political terror that the senator from Wisconsin did so much to foster in the early years of the Cold War era. No less a figure than Eleanor Roosevelt, the former First Lady and grand dame of liberal Democrats, was disgusted by Kennedy's compromises, writing in 1958 that:

> During the lively contest for the vice-presidential nomination between Sen. Estes Kefauver and Sen. John Kennedy, a friend of Senator Kennedy came to me with a request for support. I replied I did not feel I could do so because Senator Kennedy had avoided taking a position during the controversy over Sen. Joseph McCarthy's methods of investigation. Senator Kennedy was in the hospital when the Senate condemned Senator McCarthy and, of course, could not record his position. But later, when he returned to the Senate, reporters asked him how he would have voted and he failed to express an opinion on McCarthyism.
>
> "Oh, that was a long time ago," the senator's friend told me. "He was unable to vote and it is all a thing of the past. It should not have anything to do with the present situation."
>
> I replied that I thought it did. "I think McCarthyism is a question on which public officials must stand up and be counted," I added. "I still have not heard Senator Kennedy express his convictions. And I can't be sure of

the political future of anyone who does not willingly state where he stands on that issue."

Later, Senator Kennedy came to see me. I told him exactly the same thing. He replied in about the words he had previously used in talking to reporters, saying that the McCarthy condemnation was "so long ago" that it did not enter the current situation. But he did not say where he stood on the issue and I did not support him.

Mrs. Roosevelt would continue to refuse to support Kennedy in 1960, going so far as to appear at the Democratic National Convention to urge the renomination of Adlai Stevenson, expressing concerns about whether Kennedy was courageous and experienced enough to defend civil liberties at home and to establish "new policies in our foreign relations"—which she saw as an "overriding" issue. As was so often the case in that era, the former First Lady proved to be correct in her concerns. Kennedy may have softened some of the rhetoric, but he remained very much a Cold Warrior, embracing policies that were as unnecessary as they were indefensible with regard to Latin America, Asia, Africa and the Middle East. It ought never be forgotten that Nelson Mandela was arrested, tried, convicted and jailed— for the crime of encouraging workers to strike—during Kennedy's presidency, and that US officials continued to maintain warm relations with South Africa's apartheid government because it was anti-communist. And then there is the matter of Vietnam, where Kennedy increased the US military presence from 900 advisors at the close of the Eisenhower years to more than 16,000 in 1963.

Yet, in the midst of the Cold War, when the Soviet Union was a superpower with genuine ambitions, Kennedy was comfortable making distinctions between different kinds of communists, between communists and socialists and between different kinds of socialists—all the "shades of gray" that give clarity to a worldview and to domestic policymaking. He even joked about Marx.

Yet, a half century later, with the Cold War finished and the Soviet Union gone, and with the *Economist* magazine hailing "Marx the economist," America hears more ranting and raving about the perils of socialism —and the welfare state, anti-colonialism and "social justice"—than we have since the John Birchers were going after Kennedy. The only difference is that the Bircher fantasies of fifty years ago are now spouted on the floors of Congress by Republican Party leaders and provide the subtext for hyper-ventilating talk radio and television programs that crowd a 24/7 news cycle in which there is all the time in the world for debate, but very little inclination to make it mean much.

If a Joe McCarthy or a young Richard Nixon arrived on the current scene, they'd fit right in. In fact, McCarthy and Nixon might take some hits from contemporary Republicans and their media echo chamber for being too moderate, too sympathetic to big government.

Is this too negative an assessment of our times?

Let's test the theory.

Imagine if Barack Obama were to deliver a humorous rumination on Marx and Engels before launching into a proposal to build better relations with Hugo Chávez in Venezuela, Evo Morales in Bolivia or Raúl Castro in Cuba. It wouldn't just be a field day for Fox News and Rush Limbaugh's ultimate "I told you so!" show. The fevered discussion would dominate the discourse for days, perhaps weeks, with supposedly main-stream media outlets—which increasingly take their cue from right-wing bloggers and broadcasters, as the supposed "controversies" about ACORN in 2009 and Department of Agriculture aide Shirley Sherrod in 2010, reveal—bludgeoning surely bludgeon us with speculations about whether Obama is a "secret socialist," a "fellow traveler," or an actual "Manchurian Candidate" for the post–Cold War era. We know this because major media outlets have already carried the "Obama's-putting-us-on-the-road-to-socialism" story to absurd lengths. During the health-care reform debate, erstwhile citizens did not need to listen to Limbaugh or watch Fox in order to get an earful and an eyeful of key players in the GOP congressional cau-cuses and their amen corner in the commentary class fretting that buried somewhere in a plan to help people with pre-existing conditions was a blueprint for Stalinism.

The obsessive use of the "S" word by Republican operatives who wanted to prevent Obama from becoming president and who, after the fact, wanted to prevent his presidency from getting traction, created by the middle of his first term an "Alice in Wonderland" moment where socialism is more dis-cussed and less embraced by American political leaders than at any time in a quarter century.

That quarter-century mark is a rough measure, but an important one.

Go back half a century and you will find that socialism was both discussed and embraced—or, at the very least, respected—by Democrats and Republicans. After the 1960 presidential election, at a forum in New York, Republican Senator Jacob Javits amiably dissected the results with the man who was arguably the nation's most prominent Socialist, Norman Thomas. Around the same time, former Republican presidential candidate Alf Landon would join Eleanor Roosevelt and Thomas at major events promoting disarmament. The economist John Kenneth Galbraith, when he was not writing leisurely essays about the contributions made by Marx to the understanding of capitalism, or proposing "new socialist" models for economic planning, was penning speeches for Adlai Stevenson and accepting appointment as Ambassador to India under John Kennedy and Lyndon Johnson. After Michael Harrington finally finished writing *The Other America*—with its argument, as much poetic as statistical, about how the poor live "beyond history, beyond progress, sunk in a paralyzing, maiming routine"—President Kennedy came across Dwight Macdonald's massive January 1963 review (in truth, a celebration) of the book in the *New Yorker*. Kennedy called Walter Heller, the chairman of his Council of Economic Advisers, into the Oval Office. Was there anything to this notion that tens of millions of Americans lived in the "invisible poverty" of an "other America"? And could steps be taken by the government to address their plight—and that of a republic that would never fully realize its promise in the face of broad and unyielding inequality? Heller answered the president's questions by finding him a copy of Harrington's book and, as the author recalled with a measure of amazement years later: "Shortly thereafter, Kennedy decided to make the elimination of poverty a major domestic goal."

Thirty-five years later, Michael Kaufman would declare in the *New York Times*: "*The Other America* by Michael Harrington was the book that had the greatest influence on the Kennedy and Johnson Administrations, leading to the policies of the Great Society ..."

Harrington was invited to the White House, beginning a process that would see him move in and out of the inner circle of "War on Poverty" organizer Sargent Shriver and contribute proposals that—although bolder than the plans that were finally implemented—provided rough sketches for the prime domestic-policy initiatives of at least two presidencies. The centerpiece of Lyndon Johnson's first State of the Union message was a presidential expression of solidarity with Americans who "live on the outskirts of hope—some because of their poverty, and some because of their color, and all too many because of both."

Johnson added a new phrase to the national lexicon, declaring: "This Administration today, here and now, declares unconditional war on poverty in America." With a big budget, congressional support and a presidential imprimatur, Shriver developed the Office of Economic Opportunity that *Time* magazine described as "a direct spiritual heir of the New Deal's Works Progress Administration." Harrington remained an inside-outside counselor and critic, contributing memos on what should be done and making *New York Times* headlines when he noted what was not being done. There was never any question, however, that Harrington's language, a language rooted in socialist ideals of the past and social-democratic initiatives of the moment, was being echoed in the White House. Describing his determination to cure the causes of poverty, Shriver explained to Americans: "It will be impossible to end completely the culture of poverty until opportunity is equal for all. The programs of this agency are designed to alleviate permanently the conditions that have for so long kept the poor 'in their place.'"

The experience was a heady one for Harrington, and it would influence the remaining twenty-five years of his public life. A relatively young member of the "remnant of a remnant" that was the Socialist Party, he was seen by more than a few comrades as an intellectual, ideological and stylistic heir to Thomas. But Harrington's recognition that he—and other Socialists such as A. Philip Randolph and Bayard Rustin—were not just gaining the attention of the powerful, but actually shaping the agenda, caused him to question whether it was any longer necessary, or wise, to shout from the political sidelines. Harrington still wanted to shout, loudly, aggressively and without apology, about the need to address economic and social injustices that he believed to be the by-products of capitalism. But he was starting to think that doors left slightly ajar by liberals could be thrown open by socialists.

Reasonable people will debate whether Harrington was right to believe that it was possible to work within the Democratic Party, or even within the political process, to forge fundamental change. There are, after all, many socialisms. In the 1960s and 1970s, Harrington's distinct brand of "democratic socialism," with its emphasis on party politics and elections, working within the labor and civil rights movements and promoting a mixed economy—with a robust public sector and public ownership of some major industries but also a good deal of private enterprise—was rejected by much of what was then referred to as the "New Left." Though Harrington was a relatively young man, he ended up wrangling with leaders of Students for a Democratic Society and more radical groupings, and that wrangling remains the stuff of legitimate debate over the limits of electoral politics, reform movements and the prospects for reforming capitalism.

Viewed from today, Harrington's activism (with its criticism of Democratic "New Deal," "Fair Deal" and "Great Society" programs as tepid and insufficient) seems radical—and what he sought to accomplish seems even more so. In fact, compared to what was seen at the same time in many other western democracies, it was a rather mild intervention. Yet it illustrates the extent to which our public discourse has been narrowed and dumbed down over the past several decades. Today it is difficult to imagine an avowed socialist engaging with and influencing the process as Harrington did. And that should unsettle every American, no matter what their ideology, because our range of national options has narrowed. What Harrington was about, especially in the 1970s and early 1980s, was expanding those options.

As the unbounded optimism of the 1960s gave way to the bounded optimism of the 1970s, Harrington framed an argument that the place for socialists was within the Democratic Party: no longer on the outside running educational campaigns, but in the thick of the process by which presidents and congresses would be chosen, on the primary trail and at the conventions, supporting the most progressive contenders, fighting platform battles and more generally defining "the left wing of the possible." Much did seem possible at that moment, both in the United States and internationally. A new generation of democratic socialist leaders, invariably described by US media as "Kennedy-esque" was taking the world stage and renewing the image of the old movement as the fresh face of the future. They were winning elections, from Britain to Germany, from Sweden to Australia, from Costa Rica to Jamaica. They were inspiring reggae songs like Max Romeo's "Socialism Is Love" and Nueva Canción Chilena lyrics like Victor Jara's "Plegaria a un labrador," in a time when the student leader Tariq Ali proclaimed that "the whole culture has been radicalized ..." Some of the most prominent of the new-generation socialists were even American-educated, like Swedish Prime Minister Olof Palme, who fashioned in his country what my colleague Robert W. McChesney, writing with John Bellamy Foster, has described as "the dream world" for reformers seeking to describe what social democracy in an advanced western state might look like. For all its challenges and flaws, McChesney and Foster note in their wise contemporary essay "Capitalism, the Absurd System," it is undeniable that "Sweden, during the decades of relative prosperity following the Second World War, was, in many ways, an enviable society. It enjoyed a degree of economic equality that has rarely been approached in a capitalist society, associated with high wages, superior social programs, and progressive taxation. It provided high-quality universal health care and free education up through university. The condition of women—described by Marx, after Fourier, as the measure of all human progress—was much better in Sweden, in that period, than in most capitalist societies."

This "enviable society," with its charming prime minister who happened to speak eloquent English, became a reference point for American socialists who saw in the strength of the post-war labor movement, the rise of the civil rights movement and the "war on poverty" the outlines of a coming political and ideological realignment of the United States. Harrington, who moved within the circles of the Socialist International, could be pardoned for looking at ambitious young liberals such as New York Mayor John Lindsay or New York Senator Robert F. Kennedy and imagining the prospect of an American social democracy that would borrow ideas about industrial policy and land-use planning, about education and housing, about transportation and environmental protection, about cooperation and commonwealth, from the likes of Palme and Harrington's friend Willy Brandt. The Kennedys were friendly, welcoming Harrington onto their campaign planes and buses as a policy wonk and a strategist; and in Ted Kennedy's case, openly celebrating him as a hero who had "made more Americans more uncomfortable for more good reasons than any other person I know."

And yet Harrington was never satisfied that Bobby or Ted Kennedy was sufficiently social democratic—let alone socialist in any conventional sense. Even George McGovern fell short of the mark, although in his last years the Democratic Socialists of America leader was reasonably enthusiastic about the Rev. Jesse Jackson and the Rainbow Coalition. The point was not a person, however. The point was a process. Harrington believed that the ambitious liberalism of leading Democrats—who had pretty much cornered the ideological energy after the exit from the GOP fold of genuinely liberal Republicans, such as Mayor John Lindsay and Michigan Congressman (and future Senator) Don Riegle—needed to be recognized as a way station on the path to social democracy. He even suggested that liberals, particularly in the New Deal era and its aftermath, had begun to construct "a social democracy that did not speak its name" in the United States. This argument has since been advanced well and wisely by labor historian Joshua Freeman, who argues in his book *Working-Class New York: Life and Labor Since World War II* that across the arc of the twentieth century liberal reformers and radicals fashioned something akin to a social democracy in the nation's largest city. Harrington would have loved Freeman's book, not merely for its conclusions but for its recognition of the prospect that liberals—even liberal Republicans—can make common cause with socialists. As Harrington's friend and ally Irving Howe explained it (in a fresh introduction to *The Other America* for an edition published three decades after its initial release), the author began to believe that: "Liberals and socialists can work together in harmony, to enact reforms that decent men and women will endorse." More importantly, he argued that those initiatives could establish the framework of official planning and social investments to deal with poverty, "even" if initially they did so only "in a reformist way."

To this end, in the early 1970s Harrington left the old Socialist Party with its seemingly endless sectarian squabbles—and a streak of anti-communism that ran so deep that some of its leading members defended the Vietnam War long after its folly had been exposed—and worked with a widening circle of old comrades and new allies that included literary critic Howe, progressive educational reformer Deborah Meier, sociologist Bogdan Denitch, labor leaders such as William Winpisinger of the Machinists union and Victor Reuther of the UAW, California

Congressman (and future Oakland Mayor) Ron Dellums, San Francisco Supervisor and nationally-recognized gay rights champion Harry Britt, feminist writer and organizer Gloria Steinem and actor Ed Asner, to forge the Democratic Socialist Organizing Committee and then—following a merger with the New American Movement—Democratic Socialists of America. Harrington worked tirelessly to build a broad-based movement that would get liberals and democratic socialists cooperating, even if they did not always agree on an endgame. "The Democratic Socialists envision a humane social order based on popular control of resources and production, economic planning … and racial equality. I share an immediate program with liberals in this country because the best liberalism leads toward socialism," explained Harrington. "I want to be on the left wing of the possible." What made DSOC remarkable was the extent to which the group—especially when it worked under the "Democratic Agenda" umbrella in alliance with major labor unions such as the United Auto Workers, the International Association of Machinists and the American Federation of State County and Municipal Employees—became a powerful presence within the Democratic Party.

DSOC's "Democracy '76" project and the ensuing Democratic Agenda initiative, pulled together with the help of brilliant young organizers such as Marjorie Phyfe Gellermann and Jack Clark, responded to Harrington's premise that: "It was not enough … to be abstractly right." The author was tired, he wrote in a *New York Times* opinion piece, of gathering "to celebrate ceremonial socialism at occasional banquets." The point, he argued, was to join the New Left of the 1960s with the Old Left and the labor movement in a "united political movement of the liberal-left" that would operate within the Democratic Party not to rally it once more as the "party of Roosevelt," but to "look beyond the New Deal, the Fair Deal, the New Frontier and the Great Society."

"The crying necessity for democratic left programs and ideas is, then, clear enough. But what about democratic left politics?" Harrington asked, before answering: "We believe that the left wing of realism is today found in the Democratic Party. It is there that the mass forces for social change are assembled; it is there that the possibility exists for creating a new first party in America."

Though even Harrington may not have fully recognized the analogy, he was proposing that the left maneuver within the Democratic Party as what would come to be known as the "new right" was beginning to operate within the Republican Party—making itself a presence to be reckoned with on platform committees, within campaigns and ultimately at the side of congressional leaders and Cabinet aides. Harrington hit the road in the Bicentennial year with a speech titled "Challenging the New Tories: A Politics of Hope or a Politics of Fear," and a new mission to transform the Democratic Party. Former Georgia Governor Jimmy Carter was not Harrington's first, second or third choice for the party's nomination in 1976. But Minnesota Senator Walter Mondale, the vice-presidential nominee, was a steady liberal, and the platform fights at that summer's Democratic National Convention in New York's Madison Square Garden seemed to prove Harrington's point about the power an organized left could wield within the party. "[Carter] instructed his point man on the platform committee, Joe Duffy, to do what he could to satisfy the concerns of the Democratic Agenda caucus," recalled Harrington biographer Maurice Isserman. "As a result, the campaign platform the Democrats adopted in July was full of promises of support for full-employment legislation and national health insurance, as well as pledges to institute limits on defense spending and nuclear arms development—in Michael's judgment 'probably the most liberal [platform] in the history of the Democratic party.'"

Carter would not, however, be the most liberal president in the history of the Democratic Party. By the summer of 1977, Democratic Agenda was working closely with organized labor to pressure the new administration to back full-employment legislation proposed by Minnesota Senator Hubert Humphrey and California Congressman Augustus Hawkins. The partnership between DSOC and the leaders of major unions grew so strong that *Business Week* would soon observe: "Socialism [is] no longer a dirty word to labor." Democratic Agenda conferences were held in halls crowded with as many as 2,000 activists. An able observer of the era, Harold Meyerson, suggests that one of the largest of them—a 1977 session in Washington—"was a landmark in American liberalism chiefly because of the strategic reconciliations it signified. The conference marked a coming together of leaders of the left movements that had emerged in the 1930s—that is, the progressive unions—with the leaders of the left movements that had emerged in the 1960s—feminist, civil-rights, and environmental."

By December 1978, Democratic Agenda's organizing in advance of the party's mid-term convention in Memphis was causing such a stir that the national media provided breathless coverage of what was portrayed by the *New York Times* as "a virtual vote of confidence [regarding] the president." While the shorthand for the fight over the direction of the party held that the duel was between Carter and Ted Kennedy, White House spokesman Jody Powell told reporters: "The dispute which appears to be on the horizon in Memphis is not between the President and Senator Kennedy but between the Administration and Democratic Agenda."

Forty percent of the delegates to the conference—a formal Democratic proceeding established as part of the reforms initiated in the late 1960s and early 1970s to open up the party—backed Democratic Agenda reso-lutions calling for the establishment of public power production to counter the economic and environmental excesses of the oil and gas companies, national health insurance and the abandonment of budget policies that cut social-service spending while increasing Pentagon alloca-tions. The Carter administration and its floor leaders at the convention, including a young lawyer named Hillary Rodham, were shaken by the votes, as they were by the prolonged standing ovation accorded Kennedy's call for "health care as a matter of right and not a privilege." Less than a month after the conference, the White House rescinded pro-posed cuts in federal health-care spending and the *Times* suggested that "the political pressures generated by Kennedy and others in the liberal wing of the Democratic party played a role in the restoration of health funds. The impact is likely to be seen in other social programs, as well, when those budgets are made public."

For Harrington, DSOC and the broader Democratic Agenda move-ment, this was evidence that the party could be moved. And they imagined moving it much further. "At Memphis," Meyerson recalled years later, "Carter delivered a lackluster speech that won a tepid response, but Kennedy absolutely electrified the delegates with a passion-ate address on the need for universal health care. The delegates stood and cheered straight through the last two minutes of Kennedy's delivery—his voice was so resonant that he concluded, rightly, that he could be heard even over the din. The speech laid out and created the momentum for his coming challenge to Carter." That 1980 challenge would have the early and enthusiastic backing of Harrington and some of his union allies. But Kennedy's campaign was a mess, and the left was divided. The Campaign for Economic Democracy, a California-based movement organized by Tom Hayden—with whom Harrington had sparred over ideology and tactics in the early 1960s, but who now was on a similar page regarding the need to organize politically to challenge corporate power—cheered on California Governor Jerry Brown in the early primaries. Scientist Barry Commoner was mounting a relatively high-profile presidential campaign on the line of the Citizens Party, which in many senses would anticipate the Green Party of a quarter century later. And Illinois Congressman John Anderson's run for the Republican nomination as a reasonably liberal presidential candidate—as well as his fall campaign as an independent partnered with former Wisconsin Governor Patrick Lucey, a Kennedy ally—attracted significant support from college students and young professionals who were drawn to its reform message.

The 1980 election season was a disaster for Democrats, and for the broader progressive movement. Harrington had failed to fully recognize that he was in a race against time. As he and his allies struggled to move the Democratic Party to the left, so that it might provide a coherent response to the challenges of a new decade and a new era, an equally energetic and far better funded conservative movement was working just as hard and rather more successfully to move the Republican Party to the right. Ronald Reagan assumed the presidency in January of 1981 and the Democratic Party went into retreat. Mid-term conventions were scaled back and eventually eliminated, with the purpose of preventing future fights over policy. And instead of recognizing that the compromises of the late 1970s had weakened the party, the lobbyists and corporate contributors who would come to dominate the party hierarchy in following decades began to spin the fantasy that the party was too liberal. It was a laughable argument, but one that a media that was less and less inclined to cover politics in a serious way embraced. Harrington, his allies and some of his old foes responded astutely by completing the merger of DSOC and the New American Movement to form DSA, a move that added some of the smartest socialists in the country, including writer Barbara Ehrenreich and veteran west coast activist Dorothy Healey, to the organization. But the Reagan era was a hard time for Harrington, whose health was declining and whose ability to muster the coalitions needed to move the Democratic Party to the left was undermined by the growing reluctance of those who once identified themselves as "liberal" to employ even that term—let alone the "S" word. Most frustrating of all for Harrington, who I got to know during this time, was the tendency of top Democrats to imagine that they could win elections simply by not being the Republicans; after Reagan and his vice president, George Herbert Walker Bush, were brought low by the Iran-Contra scandal, Harrington warned against the false premise "that Iran-gate will take Reagan down, so that the Democrats won't even have to think."

When Jackson's "Rainbow Coalition" campaign of 1987 and 1988 renewed hopes that the Democratic Party might again stand for something, DSA proposed an endorsement of the civil rights leader who had appeared at a number of events organized by the group and its labor allies in the mid-1980s. Jackson was, Harrington said, "the only candidate who is talking any kind of sense" on economic issues and foreign policy. DSA's Patrick Lacefield acknowledged that while "Jackson's certainly no Social-ist," the candidate was "articulating the gut economic issues that appeal to working people and merits our support." As talk of the DSA expected endorsement began to circulate, however, Jackson's campaign manager told the media that it "wasn't necessary." "We want everybody's help, but we don't need everybody endorsing," explained Gerald Austin. Jackson only learned about Austin's machinations when he read about them in the *New York Times.* He immediately called Harrington to say he wanted endorsement, and that he was unwilling to be swayed by the threat of red-baiting. As Harrington recalled, "[Jackson] was upset that people might get the impression that he was turning his back on any part of his coalition."

That coalition would make the DSA-backed candidate the second-place finisher in the race for the 1988 Democratic presidential nomina-tion. But Jackson was not selected; nor was he offered a place on the ticket headed by Massachusetts Governor Michael Dukakis, who lost badly after being attacked both as a "card-carrying member of the ACLU," and for initially declaring as a "proud liberal" and then seeming to spend the remainder of the campaign trying to avoid the label. Many in the Democratic establishment—and a media that was now openly and unapologetically more interested in "the lifestyles of the rich and famous" than it was in the work that needed to be done to end poverty—would take the result as an indication that Reagan had transformed the nation into a place where even technocratic liberalism was now unwelcome, and where socialism was beyond the pale. Yet, just two years later, a Jackson campaigner named Paul Wellstone was elected to the US Senate from Minnesota as an enthusiastic liberal, while independent socialist Bernie Sanders was elected to the US House from Vermont (a state that had voted twice for Reagan and in 1988 backed Bush). Both men beat Republican incumbents and ran well in supposedly conservative regions of their states, suggesting that Dukakis's problems had far more to do with his colorless campaign than any ideological excesses. That was a point Harrington had always made, and that Kennedy would touch upon in the summer of 1988 when 600 fans of the nation's most prominent socialist gathered to celebrate his sixtieth birthday at New York's Roseland Dance Hall. The senator from Massachusetts told a crowd that included Ed Asner, Bella Abzug, Gloria Steinem and Harrington's labor pals like Machinists president William Winpisinger and Cesar Chavez of the United Farmworkers: "In our lifetime, it is Mike Harrington who has come the closest to fulfilling the vision of America that my brother Robert Kennedy had, when he said: 'Some men see things as they are and say, Why? But I dream things as they never were and say, Why not?'"

While he acknowledged that "some call it socialism," Kennedy said of the honoree's message: "I see Michael Harrington as delivering the Sermon on the Mount to America."

The senator still heard the sermon, and echoed its message. He argued during the period of transition from Reaganism to what was supposed to be a "kinder, gentler" America—and an international winding down of the Cold War—that Democrats needed to steer clear of "ideologies such as laissez-faire and survival of the fittest." "Full employment for our workers, compassion for our needy, first-class education for our children, quality health care for all Americans are not a dying dream," Kennedy declared in a late 1980s call for his party to be bold in responding to the impatience of Americans for "leadership on the unmet needs, on the unfinished agenda."

But while Harrington's death in 1989 inspired an outpouring of goodwill and warm editorial comment, the rising generation of Democratic leaders was disinclined to consider liberal ideas, let alone to listen to the sort of socialists that Franklin Roosevelt, Harry Truman, John Kennedy and Lyndon Johnson had so frequently consulted, debated and sometimes embraced.

Dukakis was the last Democratic presidential nominee to allow himself to be defined as a liberal and, by most measures, this was appropriate. Having excluded grass-roots Democrats from the party processes, the Washington elites and their allies were moving the party further from Main Street and closer to Wall Street. Bill Clinton, a leader of the noxious Democratic Leadership Council (Jackson would say its initials, DLC, really referred to "Democrats for the Leisure Class"), would imagine— wrongly—that he won the presidency in 1992 because of a series of "Sister Souljah" moments in which he distanced himself from the party's African-American, trade union, socially liberal and economically social-democratic base. The modestly more liberal Al Gore would win the presidency eight years later by half a million votes—only to lose after he and his aides told the base to stay home rather than battle in the court of public opinion against the transparently partisan interventions of Florida officials and a Supreme Court determined to confirm the old Socialist Party premise that the judiciary's main purpose was to thwart democracy. During the Republican interregnum that followed, the Democratic Party showed signs of life, but they were invariably throttled by party bosses in Washington who presumed that the best way to win back the White House and the Congress was to stand for nothing more than "not George Bush, not Dick Cheney." After the death in 2002 of Paul Wellstone, who had emerged as the leader of what he called "the Democratic wing of the Democratic Party," and the defeat of Howard Dean's mildly insurgent presidential campaign of 2004, the politics of positioning so trumped the politics of principle that the old "yellow-dog Democrat" values of the Deep South—basically that "any Democrat, no matter how uninspired intellectually or ideologically, will do"—came to define a party that voted first and asked questions later.

Liberals and social democrats still remained at the base of the party—polls of Democratic National Convention delegates invariably suggested that substantial numbers of them would have been just as comfortable at a Democratic Socialists of America conference or a Socialist Party picnic.

All the same, over the two decades following the fading of Jackson's Rainbow and the failure of Dukakis, the defining elites of the party moved so far to the right—especially on economic issues—that Harrington's notion of liberalism as a way station on the road to socialism had to be called into question. For most of the twentieth century, Democrats had been open to ideas proposed by socialists—just as Republicans had been in the nineteenth and early twentieth centuries. But under Bill Clinton and Barack Obama, it became increasingly difficult to accept Harrington's premise that "a Democratic administration always opens up a space for those who stand on the left."

Certainly, those who stand on the left, or at least a good many of them, hoped that Obama's election in 2008 would open up that space. After all, he knew the territory. He had met enough radicals as a kid growing up in Hawaii and as a student at Columbia and Harvard to stir up the conspiracy theorists of the right. And he had attended enough events with Chicago socialists and radicals of varying stripes to inspire Republican John McCain's semi-hysterical claim late in the race that Obama "began his campaign in the liberal left lane of politics and has never left it."

By any honest measure, however, Barack Obama was never the Che Guevara in pinstripes that the right-wing attack machine conjured up. It was comical to suggest that his record on Capitol Hill was "more liberal than a Senator who calls himself a socialist [Vermont's Bernie Sanders]," as McCain wheezed on the last stops of a dying campaign. And Obama certainly did not deserve the title bestowed upon him by former Senator Fred Thompson in a speech to Republican National Convention delegates: "the most liberal [Democratic] nominee to ever run for president." Thompson had apparently forgotten not just George McGovern but Walter Mondale and Michael Dukakis, all of whom sought the presidency as more left-leaning contenders than did Obama in 2008. And, as McGovern, an able historian, reminds us: Franklin Roosevelt put contemporary Democrats to shame when it came to embracing and advancing radical notions.

But while the fears of Obama tended toward the delusional, so too did the hopes inspired by his candidacy. Obama was a classic Baskin-Robbins candidate, presenting America with an ideological flavor for every day of the month. Neither a tried-and-tested veteran of "the good fight" nor a Clintonesque compromiser or DLC corporatist, he offered Democratic primary voters whatever alternative they preferred in a race with presumed front runner Hillary Clinton. After he had secured his party's nomination, Obama blurred the ideological lines even more. The task was not a difficult one. Obama was young, new to Washington, not exactly a blank slate but an unknown enough quantity so that Marxists and libertarians found ways to back him. The children and grandchildren of civil rights leaders could couple their endorsements of his candidacy with those of the children and grandchildren of Dwight Eisenhower, Richard Nixon, Barry Goldwater and Ronald Reagan. Arguably the most comical moment of the 2008 presidential campaign came when Republican operatives and their media echo chamber "revealed" that Obama's pastor was a "radical." That was supposed to hurt the Democrat. In fact, as the eventual nominee drifted more and more toward the right, "base" Democrats clung to the memory of the controversy involving the Rev. Jeremiah Wright, Jr. in order to reassure themselves that Obama really might represent a break from the dull continuum of ever more ideologically extreme Republicans and managerial Democrats who never quite cleaned up the messes they inherited. Maybe Obama sounded like a centrist in interviews with *Fortune* magazine, the liberals assured themselves, but surely this was just election-season positioning—not a serious indication of the man's caution and penchant for compromise.

The faith that Obama stood for something more than his own election was not entirely romantic or irrational. Dr. Manning Marable—founding director of the Institute for Research in African-American Studies at Columbia University, and a wise and worldly veteran of the American left's struggles of the late twentieth and early twenty-first centuries— argued that "there are a number of people with left histories who were early participants in Obama's mobilization. They have a strong belief in Obama as a candidate with the possibility of changing the tenor of politics within the Democratic Party."

Obama made some effort to reinforce that belief. Though he avoided mention of the "S" word, except to declare that it certainly did not apply to him, candidate Obama used the language of social and economic justice movements to reassure the left. Having secured the delegates required to claim the Democratic nomination, Obama found himself at a town hall meeting in suburban Atlanta, where he was grilled about whether—having run as a primary-season progressive—he was now shifting to the center.

The senator was clearly offended by the suggestion. "Let me talk about the broader issue, this whole notion that I am shifting to the center or that I'm flip-flopping or this or that or the other," he began. "You know, the people who say this apparently haven't been listening to me."

Obama continued: "I am somebody who is no doubt progressive. I believe in a tax code that we need to make more fair. I believe in universal health care. I believe in making college affordable. I believe in paying our teachers more money. I believe in early childhood education. I believe in a whole lot of things that make me progressive."

Those were not casually chosen words. Barack Obama knows what it means to say he is a "progressive." When he does so, he is not merely avoiding the word "liberal," as the sillier of his right-wing critics have so frequently imagined. Obama actually understands the subtle nuances of the American left. This is a man who moved to Chicago to be part of the political moment that began with the 1983 election of Congressman Harold Washington—a genuine man of the left, who rarely missed Chicago DSA's annual Debs–Thomas Dinner—as the city's first African-American mayor. Obama really did study the organizing techniques of Saul "Rules for Radicals" Alinsky. He worked with proudly radical labor leaders to defend basic industries and avert layoffs; he used his Harvard-minted legal skills to fight for expanded voting rights; he was mentored by a former civil libertarian legislator and federal judge, Abner Mikva; he discussed the intricacies of Middle East policy with Edward Said and Rashid Khalidi; he learned about single-payer health care from his old friend and neighbor Dr. Quentin Young, the longtime coordinator of Physicians for a National Health Program. And, famously, Obama did not just make anti-war sounds before Iraq was invaded; he appeared at an anti-war rally in downtown Chicago with a "War Is Not an Option" sign waving at his side.

Obama came on the national stage as someone who knew not just the rough outlines of the left, but the specifics. He did not need to be presented with progressive ideas for responding appropriately to an economic downturn, to environmental and energy challenges, to global crises and democratic dysfunctions. He had, over the better part of a quarter century, spoken of, written about, and aligned with those who campaigned for such ideas. That did not mean, however, that he had fully embraced them—or that he would have the confidence to advance them as president.

I first covered Obama in late 1995 and early 1996, when he was running for the Illinois state senate as a Democratic candidate endorsed by the New Party, the labor-left movement of the era that declared "the social, economic, and political progress of the United States requires a democratic revolution in America—the return of power to the people." At New Party events in those days, Obama was clear, if not overly aggressive, about his desire to move the Democratic Party out of the cautious center where Bill Clinton had wedged it. Carl Davidson, a veteran Chicago progressive, recalled that the young candidate was invariably measured in his responses to questions: "Even then, he was careful. You got a sense that he was thinking through his answers, trying not to say anything too controversial." That said, Obama was sufficiently left-leaning in his politics to secure the endorsement of the New Party and of the Chicago DSA chapter, which states, in the Debs–Thomas–Harrington tradition:

> Our mission is to establish democratic socialism as a political force in the United States and around the world by training and mobilizing socialist activists to participate in a vibrant and diverse socialist organization at both the local and the national level. DSA both educates the public about democratic socialist values and policies and builds progressive coalitions to win victories that move the US and the world toward social democracy. In the near term, democratic socialists struggle for reforms that shift power and resources away from corporate elites and put them in the hands of ordinary citizens. In the long term, democratic socialists fight for a world in which all people share equally in the governing of the economic, political and cultural institutions and relationships that shape their lives.

My sense a decade and a half ago was that, even in his supposedly radical young manhood, Barack Obama was a good deal more interested in the "build progressive coalitions to win victories" end of the equation than in the "establish democratic socialism as a political force in the United States" part. But it was certainly possible to imagine him, then and over the next few years, as a member of Wellstone's "Democratic wing of the Democratic Party." When I interviewed him as his prominence grew, especially in 2004 as he pursued an Illinois US Senate seat, Obama told me that he saw Wisconsin Democrat Russ Feingold—the lone dissenter against the Patriot Act, the Senate's most steadily anti-war member and an old-school battler against big banks and corporate-sponsored "free trade" deals who would lose his seat in the 2010 Democratic debacle—as the best role model in the chamber.

Once he got to the Senate, however, Obama established a voting record that was a good deal less progressive than that of Feingold, and dramatically more tepid than that of independent socialist senator Bernie Sanders or the Congressional Black Caucus and Congressional Progressive Caucus members in the House who still worked with DSA, groups like Progressive Democrats of America and leftie unions. Since reaching Washington, Obama has been clearly wary of getting too near individuals—or ideals—that might be brushed with the scarlet "S." That has made him a lesser president, with fewer ideas and fewer prospects. It has, as well, given ammunition to his critics, who capitalize on the caution of Obama and the Democrats to denigrate ideas which, not so many years ago, were being peddled by moderate Republicans as tools for economic renewal—such as increased education spending and infrastructure investment—and present them as Marxist shibboleths.

It would be reassuring if the problem began and ended with Obama, or even with the right's over-the-top reaction to the country's first African-American president. But, of course, Obama is a rather typical high-ranking Democrat of this era: overly-careful, obsessive about covering himself in the cloak of "consensus"—even if that consensus must be achieved at the cost of principle. His rhetorical flourishes have always been bolder than his practical deeds, which is to say that he remains what he has been since I started covering him: a very predictable politician.

So be it.

Presidents rarely lead. They operate within the parameters of the periods in which they serve. Thus, a patrician from Hyde Park, New York, governed as something of a social democrat, while a humble son of Hope, Arkansas, undid FDR's regulations on big banks and allowed Wall Street to engage in an orgy of excess that would have made the robber barons blush. The Supreme Commander of the Allied forces in Europe dialed down the Korean War, while a Quaker from southern California extended the Vietnam quagmire into Laos and Cambodia. Social welfare programs expanded under a series of increasingly right-wing Republican presidents, while Bill Clinton signed a "welfare reform" bill so draconian that his own Assistant Secretary for Health and Human Services resigned in protest.

Worrying about presidents is pop politics. Worrying about parties is a more serious, and necessary, endeavor. And there is much to worry about with regard to a Democratic Party that now promotes platforms so conservative that Jimmy Carter—the man with whom Harrington and the Democratic Agenda engaged in ideological conflict—is today seen by party bosses as an ideological outlier, so far out on the leftie fringe (particularly when it comes to foreign policy issues such as the Middle East peace process) that he is denied a speaking slot at national conventions.

Harrington might have been right when he argued, in the afterglow of the policy and political breakthroughs of the 1960s and 1970s: "I share an immediate program with liberals in this country because the best liberalism leads toward socialism." But he was thinking of the muscular domestic liberalism of such men as Franklin Roosevelt, who said:

> For too many of us the political equality we once had won was meaningless in the face of economic inequality. A small group had concentrated into their own hands an almost complete control over other people's property, other people's money, other people's labor—other people's lives. For too many of us life was no longer free; liberty no longer real; men could no longer follow the pursuit of happiness. Against economic tyranny such as this, the American citizen could appeal only to the organized power of government. The collapse of 1929 showed up the despotism for what it was. The election of 1932 was the people's mandate to end it. Under that mandate it is being ended.

He was thinking of Ted Kennedy, who stood before the 1980 Democratic National Convention and declared:

> Let us pledge that we will never misuse unemployment, high interest rates, and human misery as false weapons against inflation.
>
> Let us pledge that employment will be the first priority of our economic policy.
>
> Let us pledge that there will be security for all those who are now at work, and let us pledge that there will be jobs for all who are out of work; and we will not compromise on the issues of jobs.
>
> These are not simplistic pledges. Simply put, they are the heart of our tradition, and they have been the soul of our Party across the generations. It is the glory and the greatness of our tradition to speak for those who have no voice, to remember those who are forgotten, to respond to the frustrations and fulfill the aspirations of all Americans seeking a better life in a better land.
>
> We dare not forsake that tradition.

Unfortunately, the liberalism of the mid-to-late twentieth century in the United States has, for the most part, been replaced by a "liberalism" that barely (and rarely) dares to speak its name, and that when it actually does so speaks a language that owes more to the Gladstonian liberalism of the nineteenth century, with its unquestioning embrace of free trade, horror at nationalization and much-discussed but never quite realized promise of "equality of opportunity." American liberalism, as it is today expressed, bears scant resemblance temperamentally or ideologically to the program promoted by Franklin Roosevelt in 1935, John Lindsay in 1965, Bobby Kennedy in 1968, George McGovern in 1972, Lowell Weicker in 1982 or Paul Wellstone in 1992.

Drowned in the toxic mix of compromise, confusion and apologia that has defined discussions of "liberalism" since the 1980s, the word as it is now used means far less than it did to FDR or the Kennedy brothers for whom, Ted said, Michael Harrington "bats three for three." The same goes for the word "progressive," which historically defined my political faith as a Wisconsin-born heir to the rural populist tradition of Robert M. La Follette and the anti-imperial, anti-corporate crusades that he and his campaign manager in rural Blue River, Wisconsin—my great-grandfather—pursued on their own and in alliance with the Socialists of Milwaukee.

Today, cautious politicians who do not want to be called "liberals" dub themselves "progressives"—as if the terms were interchangeable. And the corporate-friendly Democratic Leadership Council's "think tank" labels itself the "Progressive Policy Institute."

It may well be that the only word of the left that still has any meaning is "socialism."

Were Obama the tortured intellectual that we all should wish him to be, he might wrestle with this prospect. Were Democrats serious about not just winning elections but doing something with their mandates, they too might ask themselves whether they have steered their party away from the ideals and ideas that might best inform responses to the most pressing questions of the moment. But no one who is serious about the debates that must be had in the twenty-first century can afford to wait for Obama or the Democrats to sort out their relationship with the "S" word.

For those who are serious, however, for genuine liberals and progressives who want the Democratic Party to be as robust a political grouping as the Republicans, or who are ready to form new and more robust groupings to the left of the Democrats, something greater than mere intellectual curiosity should draw them to a new consideration of the place of socialist ideas in America's history, its present and its future. This does not mean that they must follow a particular platform or line of analysis, nor even that they must declare themselves to be something more than what they are. The point here is not to say that everyone on the left needs to embrace every aspect of socialism—or even more modestly social-democratic ideals. But if the experience of the past quarter century in general, and the first years of Barack Obama's presidency in particular, have taught those who stand on the left anything, it is that they would do well to consider their relationship with the one word that still has the power to frighten, inform and inspire Americans.

It is no secret that battles of consequence are won with a politics of meaning, not mumbled apologies. That America's slef-defined liberals and progressives lack a politics of meaning—as outlined in the 1990s by *Tikkun* magazine editors Michael Lerner and Peter Gabel—has been well illustrated by the inability even of independent movements to force Democrats to deliver on the promise of the "hope and change" election of 2008. That failure produced an "enthusiasm gap" that would leave Obama and the Democrats politically isolated—abandoned even by many of their "base" voters—in the disastrous 2010 mid-term election.

The problem has not been with the left asking for too much—despite the fact that former White House chief of staff Rahm Emanuel crudely characterized even modest liberal activism as "fucking retarded." It is that activists are being trained to play a PR game they cannot win. If they ask for anything at all, they are branded as "socialists." So they ask for less and less. In effect, the fear of the "S" word steers our politics steadily further to the right.

As the national discourse has collapsed into the center, or even to the right of it, what passes for debate in the United States is most often a vague and passionless recitation of slightly different takes on the latest free-market mantras and imperial excesses. So it is that President Obama, elected on a promise of "change," kept Bush-era mandarins in positions of authority at both the Pentagon and the Federal Reserve. Our national debates tend toward dull and seemingly (though never really) pointless hair-splitting, with opponents of health-care "reform" wailing about how they "don't want a government takeover" while the supposed standard-bearers for "reform" announce that they certainly are, um, well, er … "not proposing any kind of government takeover." The fact is that Teddy Roosevelt and the Republicans of an earlier era were right: there are some things that a government of, by and for the people can do better than banks and corporations that are of, by and for their own bottom lines. When that option of "government takeover" is taken off the table by supposed reformers, then "reform" often becomes a slogan rather than a reality. And an "enthusiasm gap" opens, as even the most committed liberals and progressives wonder whether it matters to win elections. It is that enthusiasm gap, not some genuine turn to the right on the part of the great mass of Americans, that explains the political peril Democrats now find themselves in. And it is that enthusiasm gap that raises the question of whether our politics will, after the movement-like Obama deviation of 2008, become more and more of a spectator sport.

This is a lousy place to end up as a country that got its start with Tom

Paine preaching revolution and agrarian justice, that progressed at the call of Fanny Wright and Horace Greeley, that confronted its demons at the behest of Eugene Victor Debs and A. Philip Randolph, and that not so long ago dared to imagine a war on poverty.

No wonder Americans are dissatisfied with what passes for politics these days.

They should be.

This country, which was founded on a radical interpretation of enlightenment ideals, which advanced toward the realization of those ideals with an even more radical assault on the southern aristocracy, which was made more humane and responsible by the progressive reforms, the New and Fair Deals and the wars on poverty and inequality of the first three quarters of the twentieth century, is now tinkering around the edges of the challenges posed by the twenty-first century. Our dumbed-down debate is narrower, more constrained, and more meaningless than at any time in our history. One need not embrace socialism ideologically or practically to recognize that public-policy discussions ought to entertain a full range of ideas—from right to left, not from far right to center right. Historically, America welcomed that range of ideas, and benefited by the discourse. Where Michael Harrington once promised a country which still believed in the possibility that "under socialism, there will be no end to history—but there may be a new history," we have since been told that we have reached an "end to history" in which neoliberal economics and neoconservative foreign policies are our fate—no matter how frequently they fail. And we can't even mention the "S" word.

Well, at least reasonable people aren't supposed to mention it.

Unreasonable people mention it all the time. Since the summer of 2008, the word "socialism" has re-entered the American political lexicon—with a vengeance. It is mentioned more today than at any time in decades. Google "libertarianism"—not exactly a neglected ideology—and you get eight million hits; google "liberalism" and the number goes to 14.6 million; "conservatism" takes it to 15.7 million. Google "socialism" for the same period and you get twenty-four million hits. It just would be hard to find a conservative talk-radio or talk-television personality who has not used "socialism" as his or her epithet of choice—not in the last month or the last week, but every day. Former Arkansas Governor Mike Huckabee, a Fox TV host and a frequent front runner in polls assessing the strengths and weaknesses of 2012 GOP presidential prospects, told conservative activists that "the Union of American Socialist Republics is being born" and dismissed the Obama administration's Wall Street–friendly agenda with the line: "Lenin and Stalin would love this stuff"— seemingly oblivious to the fact that Goldman Sachs and the Bank of America loved it more. The former Speaker of the US House of Representatives Newt Gingrich, who fancies himself something of a conservative intellectual, published in the spring of 2010 a book entitled *To Save America: Stopping Obama's Secular-Socialist Machine*. Right-wing radio host Aaron Klein was out with *The Manchurian President: Barack Obama's Ties to Communists, Socialists and Anti-American Extremists*. And North Carolina Senator Jim DeMint offered up *Saving Freedom: We Can Stop America's Slide into Socialism*. DeMint, the ablest red-baiter since Joe McCarthy and the pointman for the Tea Party right in the Republican primary fights and fall campaigning of 2010, tells his audiences that President Obama is now "the world's best salesman of socialism."

The notion that a centrist Democrat who governs more cautiously than Richard Nixon on most domestic issues could be any kind of "salesman of socialism" is, of course, absurd. The real salespeople of socialism are people like Huckabee, Gingrich, DeMint and Sarah Palin who reject the notion that the great American debate pits Republican versus Democrat, liberal versus conservative, or Obama versus the opposition. It is, says Palin, between "those who love America" and "those who support such a thing: socialism."

It is the political right that has put the word "socialism" into play.

But a funny thing happened on the way to the Tea Party.

Instead of scaring people, the cringing conservatives have reintroduced their fellow citizens to an ideological thread that has stretched across the history of the American experiment.

In July 2010, the Fox Business channel announced: "It's Official: Obama Is a Socialist." There had been no White House press conference or eight p.m. address to the nation. In fact, Obama had spent the day discussing a national HIV/AIDS strategy that had a decent measure of bipartisan support and was not, at least as far as the White House press corps was concerned, a secret socialist scheme. What was "official" was a poll conducted a month earlier by the Democracy Corps, which asked 1,000 voters how well the term "socialist" fit President Obama. Fifty-five percent of those surveyed answered "well" or "very well." "Fair and balanced" Fox Business commentator David Asman surmised: "This must scare the hell out of the elites in the media and academe, who think such talk is just the province of Glenn Beck, not the majority of voters. But, yes, and yes again. It is Glenn Beck and it is the American people who think that. And when you look at the evidence, it's hard to dispute."

Something else is hard to dispute. At around the same time as the Democracy Corps survey was released, polls conducted by CNN, Associated Press and Ipsos/McClatchey all found that roughly 50 percent of Americans approved of Obama's presidency, while the ABC News/*Washington Post* poll put the figure at 52 percent. So it might be said that at least half, and perhaps a clear majority of Americans approve of a president who is well or very well defined as a "socialist."

It does not follow, of course, that half of Americans are socialists. But it is the case that most Americans are more comfortable with the word and with the ideology—at least to the extent that they know its rough outlines—than the American media or political class acknowledge.

That point was confirmed by a national survey conducted by the Pew Research Center for the People and the Press in the spring of 2010. The Pew folks summed up their findings with the headline: "'Socialism' Not So Negative, 'Capitalism' Not So Positive." After the better part of two years of over-the-top fear-mongering, with the condemnation and mischaracterization of socialism as something very foreign and frightening, roughly 30 percent of Americans said they had a positive view of socialism (25 percent of men, 33 percent of women).

Among African Americans, 53 percent of those surveyed by Pew rated socialism positively, as opposed to the 35 percent who held it in disregard. In fact, socialism was viewed at least as favorably—and in many instances more favorably—than capitalism by tens of millions of Americans. The most striking figures in the survey reveal the openness of the rising generation to an ideology that they have heard decried and dismissed for all of their lifetimes. Among voters aged eighteen to twenty-nine, Pew found that 43 percent viewed socialism positively, exactly the same percentage that felt favorable toward capitalism.

An anomaly? Hardly. Spring 2009 polling by Rasmussen Reports, a Republican-friendly survey research group, found that 20 percent of all Americans believed socialism to be a superior system to capitalism. Another 27 percent were not sure whether socialism or capitalism was preferable. Rasmussen also found that younger Americans were more inclined toward socialism, with 33 percent of adults under the age of thirty identifying with the "S" word while 30 percent suggested that they were undecided between socialism and capitalism.

These young people may not know much about socialism, but their experience of capitalism in an era of high unemployment and unprecedented economic inequality has made them open to an alternative to capitalism. What they should be aware of is that in seeking that alternative, they are not embracing a foreign ideology. They are considering a very American "ism," one that in reality if not always in name has been a part of our experience from the first days of the republic. A century and a half ago, on the eve of the Civil War, the most radical opponents of human bondage in the south and wage slavery in the north called themselves "socialists"—or "Republicans." A century ago, champions of civil rights and civil liberties, of peace and a renewal of the anti-colonialist spirit that summoned the United States into being, called themselves "socialists." Fifty years ago, writers, organizers and marchers for jobs and freedom and a "war on poverty" called themselves "socialists." This is the history of America. It is a history reflected in the White House library— and not just in the books photographed by our blogger friend on his way to the CPAC conference. On a nearby shelf, a few feet away from the volumes placed there by James Babb and his committee, sits a first edition of Michael Harrington's *The Other America*.

Perhaps it is the very copy that Walter Heller handed to John F. Kennedy when the president asked whether there was anything to this talk of rampant poverty in a land of plenty. Certainly it is a reminder of a time, not so very long ago, when presidents who were not socialists were wise enough to recognize that socialists and socialist ideas had much to contribute to a country still seeking to realize the promise of Tom Paine that in turn inspired Tom Jefferson, who in turn inspired Frances Wright to tell Americans that they were engaged in a struggle distinguished from all that had come before. It was "the red harlot" of Walt Whitman's "sweetest of sweet memories" who preached on behalf of a "common cause against oppression." Where was Fanny Wright's hope and change? "It is the ridden people of the earth who are struggling to throw from their backs the 'booted and spurred' riders whose legitimate title to starve as well as to work them to death will no longer pass current," she announced. "It is labor rising up against idleness, industry against money, justice against law and against privilege." Those were words too radical to be uttered in most countries in 1829. But not too radical for her adopted land, a land of revolutions, where it was possible to imagine that "liberty and justice for all" was not just a polite turn of phrase but the blueprint for an American ideal called "socialism."

A Note on Sources

The richest and most appealing source for a book on mainstream socialism and social democracy in the United States would have to be my dear friend and comrade of many years, Frank Zeidler, who throughout his long life was an activist, an archivist and a historian. I got to know Frank in the late 1970s and was especially close to him from the mid-1990s to his passing in 2006 at age ninety-three. Frank and I spent long afternoons in the old Socialist Party headquarters on Milwaukee's Old World Third Street, just a few blocks from the City Hall, where he governed one of America's largest cities for a dozen years as a proud Socialist. The office, with its posters of Eugene Victor Debs and Norman Thomas on the walls, its stacks of campaign posters from the 1948 race for state treasurer and pins from Frank's 1976 run for president, was arguably the finest living museum I have ever visited. And Frank was its greatest exhibit. His personal recollections, shared with me in formal interviews and informal conversations offered a personal connection to Victor and Meta Berger, Helen Keller, Jessie Wallace Hughan, Dan Hoan, Norman Thomas, A. Philip Randolph and literally hundreds of his other Socialist comrades in Milwaukee and across the country. Frank informs the whole of this book.

So, too, did interviews and conversations over the years with Michael Harrington, Bayard Rustin, Victor Reuther, Bernie Sanders, Huck Gutman, Tom Hayden, Tim Carpenter, Barbara Ehrenreich, Carl

Davidson, Harold Meyerson, Steve Cobble, Jesse Jackson, Cornel West, Bill Fletcher, Jr., David McReynolds, Gus Hall, Angela Davis, Myrtle Kastner, Shaun Richman, Bob Kimbrough, Lottie Gordon, my dear friend Clarence Kailin and dozens of other socialists, social democrats and radicals of every stripe that I came to know as a political writer covering conventions and conferences of the Socialist Party, Democratic Socialists of America, the International Socialist Organization, the Committees of Correspondence and other socialist and social democratic groupings. Scholars such as Howard Zinn, Allen Ruff, Paul Buhle, Linda Gordon, Allen Hunter, Paul Le Blanc, Phil Gasper and, above all, Bob McChesney expanded my understanding, as did authors such as Paul Foot and Naomi Klein. History ought never be merely from the page. It must be felt and experienced wherever possible, and these people helped me to do that. Though my primary work is in covering the political campaigns of Democrats and Republicans, I have, always gone out of my way to write about third, fourth and fifth party presidential and vice-presidential candidates of the left and right. This endeavor has allowed me to spend time with candidates of the Socialist Party going back to Zeidler in 1976 and McReynolds in 1980. I've also interviewed Communists, independent socialists and candidates of other socialist and social democratic tendencies, as well as Libertarians, Constitutionalists and Ralph Nader (who waxes quite poetic regarding his youthful meeting with Norman Thomas). Invariably, my conversations with the Socialist Party contenders had a historical undercurrent that made them at least as interesting—and often far more meaningful—than the interviews I have conducted with George H. W. Bush, Bill Clinton, George W. Bush and Barack Obama. They also helped me to recognize the constant, if frequently neglected, socialist presence in our politics—as well as the several distinct American socialist traditions that exist within the Democratic Party and outside of it, and within the labor, civil rights and environmental movements of the past and present.

Ultimately, however, this book is defined by the documentary evidence of that American socialist tradition—or perhaps I should say "traditions." Most of the primary sources for this book's chapters are original documents, found in the archives of socialist groups and publications, as well as mainstream journals and newspapers. I was especially concerned about breaking patterns of misquotation and misinterpretation, which in an odd way have contributed to the caution with which contemporary commentators approach this country's history. To give an example, I have long loved a quote attributed to Abraham Lincoln, which was supposedly written in the waning days of the Civil War. It reads:

> We may congratulate ourselves that this cruel war is nearing its end. It has cost a vast amount of treasure and blood … It has indeed been a trying hour for the Republic; but I see in the near future a crisis approaching that unnerves me and causes me to tremble for the safety of my country. As a result of the war, corporations have been enthroned and an era of corruption in high places will follow, and the money power of the country will endeavor to prolong its reign by working upon the prejudices of the people until all wealth is aggregated in a few hands and the Republic is destroyed. I feel at this moment more anxiety for the safety of my country than ever before, even in the midst of war. God grant that my suspicions may prove groundless.

This is a line very much in keeping with Lincoln's letters and speeches of the era, and I can imagine that he might well have written these words, as is claimed, in a November 21, 1864, letter to Col. William F. Elkins. I certainly would have liked to have included it in the chapter of Lincoln and Marx. Unfortunately, there is no reference to the letter in the many fine collections of Lincoln's correspondence, and I am afraid that I am convinced by Merrill Peterson's able research and commentary in his book *Lincoln in American Memory* (Oxford University Press, 1994) that the sixteenth president did not issue such a prophesy. It is not necessary to put words in Lincoln's mouth. After all, as Peterson recounts: "It was easy to understand Lincoln's appeal to social radicals, said [socialist William J.] Ghent, for he held very advanced views of the rights of labor. As early as 1847 he had written, 'To secure to each laborer the whole product of his labor, or as nearly as possible, is a most worthy object of any good government,' which was remarkable for a prairie lawyer of that time. Speaking in New England in 1860, he praised the right to strike, as then being exercised by the shoemakers of Lynn. His clear assertion of the labor theory of value in the 1861 message—'Labor is prior to, and … superior to capital'—and his answers to the addresses of workingmen abroad and at home gave a color of Marxism to his thinking. He was, surely, the best friend labor ever had in the White House."

The point of this book is to get precise details of history right while at the same time enriching the national narrative with a fresh understanding of the extent to which socialists and other radicals have always been a part of the American story. As such, it follows in the footsteps of the great scholars who have unearthed and highlighted so much of our hidden history. There are a number of books that are essential to understanding that history, beginning with the canon produced by my friend and mentor Howard Zinn, who died during the writing of this book. Howard was the best teacher, collaborator and proponent any young writer could ask for, and his *A People's History of the United States: 1492–present* (Harper Perennial Modern Classics, 2005 edition) is where so many of us begin our journey. But Zinn's long list of books and essays, especially his writing on the political careers of Fiorello La Guardia, Vito Marcantonio and other leading figures on the left provide essential insights with regard to the frequently forgotten electoral successes of radical candidates. *The Zinn Reader: Writings on Disobedience and Democracy* (Seven Stories Press, 2003) serves as a touchstone, as is the urgent collection *Declarations of Independence: Cross-Examining American Ideology* (Perennial, 1991). As points of embarkation, I would also recommend several of Michael Harrington's books, especially *Socialism* (Saturday Review Press, 1972), *Fragments of the Century: A Social Autobiography* (Saturday Review Press, 1973) and *Socialism: Past & Future* (Arcade Publishing, 1989).

For the purposes of this project, Eric Foner's canon was invaluable. No historian has delved so deeply and so well into the political history of the country's critical junctures, especially the periods leading up to and following the Civil War. Books such as *Free Soil, Free Labor, Free Men: The Ideology of the Republican Party Before the Civil War* (Oxford University Press, 1995 reissue with a new preface), *Politics and Ideology in the Age of the Civil War* (Oxford University Press, 1980) and *Nothing but Freedom: Emancipation and Its Legacy* (Louisiana State University Press, 1983) give us much more than the mere details of a particular era and are necessary to understanding the American experience, as is Foner's *Tom Paine and Revolutionary America* (Oxford University Press, 1976). I am also indebted to the work of Foner's uncle, Philip, a fierce and freewheeling radical historian whose books, packed with details about early labor and socialist struggles, guide researchers toward vast archives of original documentation that might otherwise be forgotten.

Two other agile and engaged historians who focused on particular individuals and eras produced books that are broadly informative and essential to the whole understanding of the story of American socialism: Nick Salvatore, the author of *Eugene V. Debs: Citizen and Socialist* (Reprinted by University of Illinois Press, 1984) and Maurice Isserman, the author of *The Other American: The Life of Michael Harrington* (Public Affairs, 2000), a book that is often quoted here. Isserman wrote two other definitional texts: *Which Side Were You On? The American Communist Party during the Second World War* (University of Illinois Press, 1993) and *If I Had a Hammer… The Death of the Old Left and the Birth of the New Left* (Basic Books, 1987).

Finally, I am indebted to the books, the inspiration and encouragement provided by the late Jeanne Boydston, the historian of women and gender in the early republic who died just a few days before the 2008 election. On long walks in all seasons, she introduced me to historical facts and features that inform this book at many turns, and that were essential to the chapters dealing with the pre–Civil War era. Jeanne's essays and books, especially *Home and Work: Housework, Wages, and the Ideology of Labor in the Early Republic* (Oxford University Press, 1994), will guide historians and scholars for generations to come. And, like all the best radicals, she had a wicked sense of humor and a warm gift for friendship.

Now, to the individual chapters and their sources:

PREFACE AND ACKNOWLEDGEMENTS: WHITMAN, SYLVIE AND THE EMMAS

You can read Emma Lazarus's best writing on Liberty Island, in big print. One of the finest of the many collections of her work is *Emma Lazarus: Selected Poems and Other Writings* (Broadview Press, 2002), edited by Gregory Eiselein. Esther Schor's excellent biography *Emma Lazarus* (Schocken, 2006) is an invaluable resource. A solid interview with Schor was broadcast by National Public Radio on October 21, 2006. It is archived at www.npr.org.

The World of Emma Lazarus (Schocken, 1949; Kessing Publishers, 2007), a pioneering biography by H. E. Jacobs, is useful—and quite charming.

The Jewish Women's Archive contains a good deal of material on Lazarus at http://jwa.org/historymakers/lazarus. It is also a source for background on the Emma Lazarus Federation of Jewish Women's Clubs, including Joyce Antler's thoughtful article on the group. The records of the federation are maintained by the American Jewish Archives, which features a useful background essay on the clubs at www.americanjewisharchives.org.

I also relied on the archives of the *New York Times*, which reported on the threat to deport June Gordon on August 13, 1960. Gordon remained in the United States, continuing as executive director of the federation until her death in 1967.

CHAPTER 1: "MORE OF A SOCIALIST THAN I THOUGHT"

All quotes from Whitman's poetry are from *The Complete Poems* (Penguin Classics, 1977); prose quotes are from *The Complete Prose Works of Walt Whitman* (Nabu Press, 2010). The Whitman Archive, edited by Ed Folsom and Kenneth Price and online at www.whitmanarchive.org, provides useful and precise chronologies and timelines, as well as a detailed biography of Whitman by Folsom and Price. Three of the many shelves of Whitman biographies proved especially useful in the writing of this book: Justin Kaplan's *Walt Whitman: A Life* (Simon and Schuster, 1979), Jerome Loving's *Walt Whitman: The Song of Himself* (University of California Press, 1999), and David Reynolds's *Walt Whitman's America: A Cultural Biography* (Vintage Books, 1995). I also commend to readers Jason Stacy's *Walt Whitman's Multitudes: Labor Reform and Persona in Whitman's Journalism and the First Leaves of Grass, 1840–1855* (Peter Lang Publishing, 2008) and, of course, Newton Arvin's *Whitman* (Macmillan Company, 1938)—along with Wilson Follett's November 27, 1938, *New York Times* review, "Walt Whitman as the Poet of Socialism."

Horace Traubel's *With Walt Whitman in Camden* (edited by Jeanne Chapman and Robert MacIsaac), a massive work, is published by W. L. Bentley Rare Books in Oregon House, California. It's a treasure, and you will find much good material on it at the Whitman Archive site and the publisher's www.wlbentley.com site. A fine condensed version of the materials can be found in *Intimate With Walt: Selections from Whitman's Conversations with Horace Traubel, 1882–1892* (University of Iowa Press, 2001), edited by Gary Schmidgall . One biography of Traubel, an understudied figure, is William English Walling's *Whitman and Traubel* (Haskell House, 1969).

The transcript of the Hannity/Gingrich interview from March 24, 2010, can be found at http://www.foxnews.com/story/0,2933,589882,00. html. The transcript of the Hannity/Palin interview from June 9, 2009, can be found at http://www.foxnews.com/story/0,2933,525542,00.html. *New York Times* writer Jeff Zeleny's article "The President Is on the Line to Follow Up on Socialism" was published March 7, 2009. A transcript of the entire Zeleny/Obama interview can be found at http://www. nytimes.com/2009/03/08/us/politics/08obama-text.html?ref=politics. The *New York Times* article describing the influence of Norman Thomas on American politics, "Norman Thomas: Sparkling at 70," appeared November 20, 1954.

With regard to the section on GOP efforts to rebrand the Democrats as socialists, the article "Proposed RNC Resolution Recognizing the Democrats' March Towards Socialism" can be found at http://www.repconcaucus. com/content/proposed_rnc_resolution_recognizing_democrats_ march_towards_socialism, and a good reflection on the initiative is the *Christian Science Monitor* piece, "RNC drops resolution to call Democrats 'Socialists,'" from March 20, 2009. The *New York Times* provided extensive coverage of the 1950 effort by conservative Republicans to frame a "Liberty Versus Socialism" campaign that year; the key articles are "G.O.P. Poses Issue for '50 as Liberty Versus Socialism," February 7, 1950; "Text of Truman's Address to Jefferson-Jackson Day Dinners," February 17, 1950; and "GOP Digest Trims 'Socialism' Issue," April 3, 1950. Margaret Chase Smith's "Declaration of Conscience" was delivered on the US Senate floor June 1, 1950, and can be found in the Congressional Record; it is reprinted in Robert C. Byrd's *The Senate, 1789–1989: Classic Speeches, 1830–1993* (Government Printing Office, 1994). A biography of Smith which deals with the speech and issues surrounding it is Janann Sherman's *No Place for a Woman: A Life of Senator Margaret Chase Smith* (Rutgers University Press, 2000).

Historian Terrance Ball's essay "Socialists as Patriots," which discussed Medicare's progress during the Cold War, appeared September 14, 2009, as part of a *New York Times*–sponsored debate on the topic: "What is Socialism in 2009?" So, too, did Patrick Allitt's essay "What's All the Fuss?" Details regarding Harrington and the Kennedys can be found in Isserman's *The Other American* and Scott Stossel's *Sarge: The Life and Times of Sargent Shriver* (Smithsonian Books, 2004). More material can be found in the outstanding Sargent Shriver Collection at the John F. Kennedy Presidential Library and Museum in Boston.

For more on the amazing Edward Carpenter and his links to Whitman, read Sheila Rowbotham's *Edward Carpenter: A Life of Liberty and Love* (Verso, 2008). Carpenter's own *Days with Walt Whitman* first appeared in 1906, while his *Friends of Walt Whitman* was published in 1924. The Edward Carpenter Archive is at www.edwardcarpenter.net. The Bolton Museum and Archive, in Bolton, England, has a fine collection of materials relating to James William Wallace and Whitman. Good information and links can be found at http://www.boltonmuseums .org.uk/bolton-archives/walt-whitman/.

Whitman's references to Fanny Wright are found in Traubel's *With Walt Whitman in Camden*. There are several sound biographies of Wright; I was impressed by Celia Morris Eckhardt's *Fanny Wright: Rebel in America* (University of Illinois Press; revised edition, 1992). Ralph Thompson's *New York Times* review "The True Whitman" appeared October 25, 1938. The communications between Debs and the Whitman Fellowship can be found in another *New York Times* article, "Debs Name Cheered: Walt Whitman Fellowship Approves…," which was published June 1, 1907.

CHAPTER 2: "A BROADER PATRIOTISM"

All Tom Paine quotes are from *Thomas Paine: Collected Writings: Common Sense / The Crisis / Rights of Man / The Age of Reason / Pamphlets, Articles, and Letters* (Library of America; 1995 edition, edited by Eric Foner). An extremely useful assessment of Paine's writings, which organizes them by subject matter, is John P. Kaminski's *Citizen Paine: Thomas Paine's Thoughts On Man, Government, Society, and Religion* (Rowman & Littlefield Publishers, 2002). Biographical information regarding Paine is drawn from Foner's *Tom Paine and Revolutionary America*, as well as Harvey Kaye's brilliant *Thomas Paine: Firebrand of the Revolution* (Oxford University Press, 2000); Michael Foot and Isaac Kramnick's *The Thomas Paine Reader* (Penguin Classics, 1987); and Craig Nelson's delightful *Thomas Paine: Enlightenment, Revolution, and the Birth of Modern Nations* (Viking, 2006). Foner, Nelson and I appeared together in June 2009 to commemorate the 200th anniversary of Paine's passing at a fine event organized by Thomas Paine Friends, Inc., in the small Thomas Paine Park that Paul O'Dwyer secured in southern Manhattan. I have written extensively on Paine over the years for the *Nation* and other publications. One article that is reflected in this chapter appeared after the inauguration of Barack Obama: "Obama's Vindication of Thomas Paine," the *Nation*, January 20, 2009.

Howard Fast's lovely historical fiction, *Citizen Tom Paine*, is available in a 1994 edition from Grove Press. Kaye's *Thomas Paine: Firebrand of Liberty* provides invaluable detail about the wrestling over Paine's legacy by the likes of Franklin Roosevelt and Ronald Reagan. Kaye's book is, as well, a tremendous source for insights regarding Paine's continuing influence.

Glenn Beck's book is titled *Glenn Beck's Common Sense: The Case Against an Out-of-Control Government, Inspired by Thomas Paine* (Threshold Editions, 2009). You will not learn much about Paine from it, but there's a lot of Beck. In preparing this chapter, I read Beck's essays, commentaries and transcripts that referenced Paine, and reviewed his reflections on other founders. I also reviewed hundreds of hours of Beck's radio and television broadcasts, a thankless task made significantly easier by the catalogue work of Media Matters, which can be found at http://

mediamatters.org. Beck's "Barack Obama, Socialist?" rant was broadcast April 7, 2010, and readers can find it archived at http://www.foxnews. com/story/0,2933,590532,00.html. Beck's ruminations on Paine are archived at http://www.youtube.com/watch?v=j5qEkWF7HBo and at http://www.glennbeck.com/content/articles/article/198/22914/.

The Social Security Administration's referencing of Paine can be found in publications distributed by the SSA and in its online history initiative—which reproduces the pamphlet "Agrarian Justice" in full—at http://www.ssa.gov/history/tpaine3.html.

Michael Foot wrote extensively about Paine; *The Thomas Paine Reader* he and Isaac Kramnick produced in 1987 is available from Penguin Classics and includes terrific commentaries. Readers will also find writings at the website of the Thomas Paine Society (www. thomaspainesocietyuk. org.uk), with which Foot was for so many years engaged. Finally, "Michael Foot, The Last in a Long Line of Radical Polemicists," a fine article dealing at some length with Foot and Paine, by the historian (and now parliamentarian) Tristram Hunt, appeared in the British newspaper *Observer* on March 7, 2010. Many exceptional reflections on Paine and the radical tradition, including those of historian Catherine Hall, can be found in the a very useful examination on the career of British historian and Paine champion E. P. Thompson by Kaye and Keith McClelland, *E. P. Thompson: Critical Perspectives* (Temple University Press, 1990).

The Eugene Victor Debs quote ("Thomas Paine towered above them all ...") is mentioned in John Eleazer Remsburg's "Thomas Paine: The Apostle of Liberty," a remarkably rich and detailed examination of Paine's influence published in pamphlet form in 1917 by The Truth Seeker Co., one of many presses that attempted in the early years of the twentieth century to renew interest in Paine. Debs's "ignorance alone" quote is from his speech "The Socialist Party and the Working Class," delivered in Indianapolis, Indiana, on September 1, 1904. Quotes from the time of his trial can be found in David Karsner's *Debs: His Authorized Life and Letters from Woodstock Prison to Atlanta* (Boni and Liveright, 1919). Other Debs quotes are from *Writings of Eugene V. Debs: A Collection of Essays by America's Most Famous Socialist* (Red and Black Publishers, 2009). See also Jonathan M. Hansen's *The Lost Promise of Patriotism: Debating American Identity, 1890–1920* (University of Chicago Press, 2003).

For insights on the clashes between Paine and Adams, there are many sources. One of the richest and most enjoyable texts in this canon is Richard Rosenfeld's *American Aurora: A Democratic-Republican Returns; The Suppressed History of Our Nation's Beginnings and the Heroic Newspaper That Tried to Report It* (St. Martin's Griffin, 1998). Kaye's *Thomas Paine and the Promise of America* is another great resource, as is historian Joseph Ellis's review "Founding Father of the American Left," published July 31, 2005, in the *New York Times*.

Matthew Continetti's "The Two Faces of the Tea Party: Rick Santelli, Glenn Beck, and the future of the populist insurgency" appeared in the *Weekly Standard*, June 28, 2010.

Willard Sterne Randall's exceptional biography *Thomas Jefferson: A Life* (Harper Perennial, 1994) provides some fine insights regarding the last days of the author of the Declaration of Independence. Randall's book is also useful for its thoughtful reflection on Jefferson's relations with Paine. I also consulted Randall's *George Washington: A Life* (Holt Paperbacks, 1998) in preparing this section.

Amos Gilbert's 1834 biography of the early nineteenth-century radical agitator Thomas Skidmore, *The Life of Thomas Skidmore*, was reissued in 1984 by Charles H. Kerr, with excellent commentary and a background essay provided by editor Mark A. Lause. Skidmore's "Rights Of Man To Property!" is included.

There are many significant biographies of Fanny Wright, including Celia Morris Eckhardt's *Fanny Wright: Rebel in America*. Barbara Ehrenreich wrote an excellent essay on Wright for *Mother Jones* in the magazine's November 1984 issue. Much has been written about the Working Men's Party; a good place to begin is with F. T. Carlton's "The Working Men's Party of New York City: 1829–1831," from *Political Science Quarterly*, Vol. 22, No. 3, September 1907. The first volume of Philip Foner's *History of the Labor Movement in the United States* (International Publishers, 1947) is, of course, useful, as are the writings of Boydston regarding gender and working class issues in the early republic.

George Evans and the Paineite agitators who got their start in the Working Men's Party and then spawned radical land-reform movements figure in two important books, Jamie Bronstein's *Land Reform and Working-Class Experience in Britain and the United States* (Stanford University

Press, 1999) and Mark Lause's *Young America* (University of Illinois Press, 2005). Most of the best information on Alvan Bovay can be found in the Wisconsin Historical Society archives. I have written extensively on him for a number of publications, including the *Capital Times* newspaper in Madison and the *Nation*. One recent piece, "True Republicans Drawn to Obama: Former Congressman Leach's Endorsement of the Democratic Candidate in Line with the GOP's Original Values," appeared August 27, 2008, in the *Capital Times*.

The groundbreaking essay by John R. Commons, "Horace Greeley and the Working Class Origins of the Republican Party," was published in 1909 in the *Political Science Quarterly*, Vol. XXIV, No. 3. William Herndon's reflection on his law partner, *Herndon's Lincoln*, is available from the University of Illinois Press (2006). The Debs line about how "The Republican Party was once red" comes from a *New York Times* article published May 14, 1920, while the record of his trial—one of the most remarkable in American history—can be found at DEBS v. U S, 249 U.S. 211 (1919).

CHAPTER 3: READING MARX
WITH ABRAHAM LINCOLN

Abraham Lincoln's words have been collected in many forms. For the purposes of this chapter, I relied on *The Collected Works of Abraham Lincoln*, a groundbreaking multi-volume set of Lincoln's correspondence, speeches and other writings. A project of the Abraham Lincoln Association published initially in 1953, this remarkable resource was assembled by the Lincoln scholar Roy P. Basler and an editorial staff that spent five years transcribing and annotating Lincoln's papers. The Lincoln Association has made *The Collected Works of Abraham Lincoln* available online at http://quod.lib.umich.edu/l/lincoln/. For quick reference, the Abraham Lincoln Bicentennial Commission (ALBC), which was established to commemorate the 200th anniversary of Lincoln's birth, has assembled many of the major speeches referenced in this chapter. They can be found at http://www.lincolnbicentennial.gov/lincolns-life/words-and-speeches/. There are, as well, two very fine collections published by Library of America as *Lincoln: Speeches and Writings 1832–1858* and *Lincoln: Speeches and Writings 1859–1865*; Lincoln scholar Don Edward Fehrenbacher's editing is superb, as is his book *Lincoln in Text and Context: Collected Essays* (Stanford University Press, 1988).

The "sad distracted year" is referred in Walt Whitman's poem "1861," as are the other Whitman references noted here. Phillip Shaw Paludan's *The Presidency of Abraham Lincoln* (University of Kansas Press, 1995), the winner of the 1995 Lincoln Prize, provided useful detail, as did Thomas Mallon's engrossing article "In Search of Lincoln's Washington," published in the January/February 2009 issue of *Preservation* magazine.

Horace Greeley wrote a quirky autobiography, *Reflections on a Busy Life* (J. B. Ford and Co., 1868), which has been republished a number of times and is broadly available. William Harlan Hale's *Horace Greeley: Voice of the People* (Harper & Brothers, 1950) is a fine biography, and I quite like *Horace Greeley: Champion of American Freedom* (NYU Press, 2006) by Robert C. Williams. James Ford Rhodes' *History of the United States from the Compromise of 1850* (Harper, 1906) offers excellent perspective on the influence of the *Tribune*, particularly among Free Soil and radical Republican activists. In preparing this book, I also consulted Harry J. Maihafer's *The General and the Journalists: Ulysses S. Grant, Horace Greeley, and Charles Dana* (Brassey's Books, 1998). Dana, Greeley's ablest editor, deserves a contemporary biography, but James Harrison Wilson's *The Life of Charles A. Dana* (Harper Brothers, 1907) is certainly useful. Ultimately, however, my study of the *Tribune*'s politics was best served by the scholarship of Adam Tuchinsky, an associate professor of history at the University of Southern Maine, whose book *Horace Greeley's* New-York Tribune: *Civil War–era Socialism and the Crisis of Free Labor* (Cornell University Press, 2009) is brilliant. Tuchinsky builds on a scholarly tradition that goes back to the important writing of L. D. Ingersoll in *The Life of Horace Greeley* (Union Publishing Co., 1873) and Charles Sotheran and Alice Hyneman Sotheran in their book *Horace Greeley and Other Pioneers of American Socialism* (M. Kennerley, 1915)—as well, of course, as the work of Phil and Eric Foner. Yet, there is something very fresh and energizing about Tuchinsky's work, especially in its nuanced reflection on the varying utopian socialist movements of the 1840s. For more on Greeley and reform movements of the pre–Civil War era, look to the thorough essay by Roy Marvin Robbins, "Horace Greeley: Land Reform and Unemployment: 1837–1862," which appeared in the January 1933 edition of the journal *Agricultural Heritage*.

A number of biographies of Karl Marx touch on his work for the *Tribune*—as does Tuchinsky, of course. But two sources are invaluable: Hale's "When Karl Marx Worked for Horace Greeley," which appeared in the April 1957 issue of *American Heritage* magazine and drew the attention of no less a reader than Massachusetts Senator John F. Kennedy, and *Dispatches for the New York* Tribune: *Selected Journalism of Karl Marx* (Penguin Classics, 2008), with its thoughtful essays by James Ledbetter and Frances Wheen. Wheen's biography *Karl Marx: A Life* (W. W. Norton & Company, 2000) is another great resource. An extensive collection of writings by Marx and Engels for the *Tribune* can be found online at www.marxists.org.

John Waugh's *One Man Great Enough: Abraham Lincoln's Road to Civil War* (Mariner/Houghton Mifflin Harcourt, 2007) is superb on Lincoln's reading habits, and provides genuine insight regarding the sixteenth president's time in the wilderness during the late 1840s and early 1850s. It was during this period that Lincoln made the transition from the old Whig Party to the new Republican Party. Much has been written about Lincoln as a Whig, and especially about his devotion to the ideas and the political career of Henry Clay. Lincoln's eulogy for Clay is an essential document; you'll find it in many places, but I recommend visiting the terrific site of the Miller Center of Public Affairs at the University of Virginia at http://millercenter.org. A recent biography of "the great compromiser," David Heidler and Jeanne Heidler's *Henry Clay: The Essential American* (Random House, 2010), provides insight regarding the Lincoln–Clay relationship. Eric Foner's *Free Soil, Free Labor, Free Men* is useful to those seeking to understand the politics of the era, as is Sean Wilentz's *The Rise of American Democracy: Jefferson to Lincoln* (W. W. Norton, 2005). Lewis Lehrman's *Lincoln at Peoria* (Stackpole Books, 2008) pulls a lot of the threads together.

There is a great deal of excellent writing on the influence of the German '48ers on social movements and left politics in Illinois,

Wisconsin and other states prior to the Civil War. I appreciated the insights in *The German-American Radical Press: The Shaping of a Left Political Culture, 1850–1940* (University of Illinois Press, 1992), by Elliott Shore, Ken Fones-Wolf and James Philip Danky. Jim Danky's thinking with regard to foreign-language and African-American newspapers of this era, and his deep regard for the people and the politics that produced them, has been an inspiration to me for many years. *The Encyclopedia of the American Left* (Garland, 1990), compiled by Mari Jo Buhle, Paul Buhle and Dan Georgakas, is invaluable for its telling of the stories of immigrant radicals. And if you want to read an amazing story of a Marxist commander in Lincoln's Army, find a copy of Karl Obermann's book *Joseph Weydemeyer* (International Publishers, 1947). The most prominent of the '48ers, Carl Schurz, is the subject of a solid study by Hans L. Trefousse, *Carl Schurz: A Biography* (Fordham University Press, 1998) and a number of excellent pieces that appeared in the 1920s and 1930s in the *Wisconsin Magazine of History*: Barbara Donner's "Carl Schurz as Office Seeker" (December 1936) and "Carl Schurz the Diplomat" (March 1937); Carl Russell Fish's "Carl Schurz—The American" (June 1929); and Joseph Schafer's "Carl Schurz, Immigrant Statesman" (June 1928). For a sense of the impact of Henry Bornstein's writing for the *Tribune*, read Merle Curti's "The Impact of the Revolutions of 1848 on American Political Thought," *Proceedings of the American Philosophical Society* (1949; read November 4, 1948) and Tuchinsky.

David Nichols (no relation) offers insight with regard to Lincoln's sour relations with Native Americans in his essential book *Lincoln and the Indians: Civil War Policy and Politics* (University of Illinois Press, 1999), while Daniel W. Homstad's "Abraham Lincoln: Deciding the Fate of 300 Indians Convicted of War Crimes in Minnesota's Great Sioux Uprising," an article published in the December 2001 issue of *American History* magazine adds some detail and nuance to this painful discussion. Greeley's conflicted and at times backward thinking is summed up in the aforementioned biographies, and his own *An Overland Journey From New York to San Francisco in the Summer of 1859* (C. M. Saxton, Barker and Co., 1860). Greeley's wrangling with Lincoln over emancipation has been frequently examined; Allen C. Guelzo's *Lincoln's Emancipation Proclamation: The End of Slavery in America* (Simon and Schuster, 2006) provides a good overview. To my view, however, the full story has yet to be told. I am especially disappointed by the neglect by most historians of the role played by Vice President Hannibal Hamlin and Charles Dana in the debate.

For information regarding Lincoln's dealings with the New York workingmen's groups, I recommend a visit to a remarkable website developed by The Lincoln Institute: "Mr. Lincoln and New York," at www.mrlincolnandnewyork.org. It is, to my view, an essential starting point. The Lincoln Institute's "Mr. Lincoln's White House" website provides details about his presidential schedule and meetings; it's at www.mrlincolnswhitehouse.org.

There are several biographies of Charles Francis Adams that deal with his ambassadorial service and the delicate role he played during the Civil War. I like Martin Duberman's *Charles Francis Adams, 1807–1886* (Stanford University Press, 1968). Adams' diaries are published as the *Diary of Charles Francis Adams* (Belknap Press, 1964); they are also available via the Harvard University Press' broad and ongoing project The Adams Papers. For details regarding Henry Adams and Marx, look to David Partenheimer's "The Education of Henry Adams in German Philosophy" (*Journal of the History of Ideas*, 1988) and of course to the *Collected Works of Henry Adams* (Library of America, 1983).

King's speech on Du Bois is included in Esther Cooper Jackson's *Freedomways Reader: Prophets in Their Own Country* (Basic Books, 2001), which includes a fine essay by Constance Pohl. Du Bois' writings on "the pattern of Lincoln" were first published in *Crisis* magazine in May 1922. Du Bois' *Crisis* essays are collected in many forms. Make a visit to the magazine's website at www. thecrisismagazine.com and read Manning Marable's *W. E. B. Du Bois: Black Radical Democrat* (Paradigm Publishers, 2005).

CHAPTER 4: A LEGAL AND PEACEABLE REVOLUTION OF THE MIND

This chapter is a product, first and foremost, of conversations with Frank Zeidler, the former Milwaukee mayor and great defender of the "sewer socialist" tradition. He published his memoirs as *A Liberal in City Government* (Milwaukee Publishers LLC, 2005), and his papers are housed and well archived in the Golda Meir Library of the University of Wisconsin–Milwaukee. I have written a number of articles detailing interviews and time spent with Zeidler, including "The Last of the Sewer Socialists," which appeared in the *Nation* (July 14, 2006). In the spring of 2010, I delivered the Frank P. Zeidler Memorial Lecture at the Milwaukee Public Library, and Milwaukee Public TV produced a program based on the lecture; it is archived online at http://www.mptv.org/shows/specials/. Historian John Gurda's excellent 2009 lecture on "How the Socialists Saved Milwaukee" can be found there as well.

Several useful books have been written on the political activism of the Milwaukee Social Democrats and Socialists, including Marvin Wachman's *History of the Social Democratic Party of Milwaukee, 1897–1910* (University of Illinois Press, 1945). Melvin Holli's *The American Mayor: The Best and the Worst Big-City Leaders* was published in 1999 by Penn State Press and includes a good deal of information on the "sewer socialists" in general and Dan Hoan in particular. Even more valuable, to my view, are the writings of Sally Miller, whose *Victor Berger and the Promise of Constructive Socialism, 1910–1920* was published in 1973 by Greenwood Press, and Edward Muzik, who completed a fine PhD dissertation on Berger at Northwestern University in 1960. Muzik's "Victor L. Berger: Congress and the Red Scare" (*Wisconsin Magazine of History*, Vol. 47, No. 4, Summer 1964) and Roderick Nash's "Victor L. Berger: Making Marx Respectable" (*Wisconsin Magazine of History*, Vol. 47, No. 4, Summer 1964) were of great use to me, as were the collections of the Wisconsin Historical Society. Eugene Victor Debs contributed the information about his instruction by Berger, in an essay titled "How I Became a Socialist"; it appeared in *Comrade* magazine's April 1902 issue. John Gurda's writings on the Milwaukee Socialists have been published by the Milwaukee Journal-Sentinel over the years; one article that I paid particular attention to in writing this chapter was "Here, Socialism Meant Honest, Frugal Government," published April 4, 2009. An excellent interview with Gurda, conducted by Lisa Kaiser, is available on the website of the *Shepherd Express* newspaper at www.expressmilwaukee.com; it was initially posted May 24, 2009.

Ira Kipnis's *The American Socialist Movement, 1897–1912* (Columbia University Press, 1952) and Howard Quint's *The Forging of American Socialism: Origins of the Modern Movement* (University of South Carolina Press, 1953) provide sound overviews, as does David Shannon's *The Socialist Party of America: A History* (Macmillan, 1955). But I am especially partial to James Weinstein's *The Decline of Socialism in America* (Rutgers University Press, 1984). Jimmy was a fine friend and we had a good-natured debate about his conclusions—in his later years, he would drive from Chicago to Madison for an afternoon of "talking socialism"— but I continue to be dazzled by his scholarship, and I deeply miss his good company.

Individual Socialist leaders and activists wrote extensively on the period of the party's greatest influence, and I relied a good deal on the *Family Letters of Victor and Meta Berger, 1894–1929* (State Historical Society of Wisconsin, 1995), which was ably edited by Michael Stevens, and the many pamphlets written by Berger that I have collected over the years. Berger's *Broadsides* (Social Democratic Publishing Co.,1912), and *Voice and Pen of Victor L. Berger: Congressional Speeches and Editorials* (Milwaukee Leader, 1929) are the best collections of his writings. Emil Seidel wrote *What We Have Done in Milwaukee* (National Office of the Socialist Party, 1911) and *Which Must Go? America or Private Ownership of Railroads?* (Socialist Party of Wisconsin, 1923). Dan Hoan contributed *Socialism and the City: How to Remove Chaos and Put Order and Beauty into American Cities* (Haldeman-Julius Publications, 1931) and *City Government: The Record of the Milwaukee Experiment* (Harcourt, Brace and Co., 1936). Morris Hillquit's memoirs, *Loose Leaves from a Busy Life* (Macmillan, 1934) are as detailed as they are useful.

Benjamin Davis wrote a valuable memoir, *Communist Councilman From Harlem* (International Publishers, 1969), while Simon Gerson wrote *Pete: The Story of Peter V. Cacchione, New York's First Communist Councilman* (International Publishers, 1976). Si's papers, which provide a wealth of information regarding the Communist Party's electoral work, are housed at the Tamiment Library/Robert F. Wagner Labor Archives in the Elmer Holmes Bobst Library, which has organized a terrific guide to the collection. Si's granddaughter Timi, a great activist herself, provided insights regarding his work; and Sean Richman's obituary, "Requiem for a Communist," published June 11, 2005, on Richman's website at www.shaunrichman.org tells Si's story well.

Nick Salvatore's biography of Debs is an essential document, as is Hillquit's "A Tribute to Debs" (*New Leader*, October 23, 1926). There are many fine Norman Thomas biographies; I relied a good deal on Harry Fleischmann's *Norman Thomas: A Biography* (W. W. Norton & Co., 1964), W. A. Swanberg's *Norman Thomas: The Last Idealist* (Charles Scribner and Sons, 1976) and Bernard Johnpoll's *Pacifists Progress: Norman Thomas and the Decline of American Socialism* (Quadrangle Books, 1970). I recall checking the latter book out from the Union Grove Public Library in Union Grove, Wisconsin, when I was twelve. The librarians were bemused, but not particularly concerned.

In writing this chapter, I went frequently to the archives of the *New York Times* and *Time* magazine, both of which covered the campaigning of the Socialist Party and individual Socialists and Communists thoroughly in the period from 1910 to 1960. The coverage was far fairer and more respectful than that afforded contemporary third parties, in part because of the significant influence of the Socialists and Communists but also because media was more serious about covering politics in those days. The *New York Times* coverage of Norman Thomas's 1932 presidential campaign and its aftermath, along with its coverage of the Milwaukee Socialists and Socialist Party activism in New York City and Reading, Pennsylvania, was especially useful in preparing this book, as was its coverage of Communist Party campaigning in New York. *Time* magazine's April 6, 1936, cover story on Milwaukee Mayor Hoan, "Marxist Mayor," is a remarkable article, in that it fairly assesses the contribution of a radical urban leader to the American political debate in a way that would be hard to imagine today.

It is important to note the extent to which reading the archival coverage of Socialist, Communist and leftist campaigning during the early-to-mid-twentieth century is heartbreaking, in that it illustrates how completely elite media coverage of our public discourse has narrowed and degenerated over the past fifty years.

CHAPTER 5: "SIMPLY A STUPID PIECE OF DESPOTISM"

The articles, essays and books by and about Victor Berger that are referenced in the notes on Chapter 4 provided much of the underpinning for this chapter, as did the archived coverage by the *New York Times* of Berger's political and legal battles. Berger's story was front-page news throughout the period. I also reviewed coverage in the *Milwaukee Leader*. All editions of the *Leader* are available—on microfilm reels—at the Wisconsin Historical Society. Finally, I relied on coverage of Berger and the *Leader* contained in the files of the *Capital Times* newspaper of Madison, Wisconsin, with which I have long been associated. The *Capital Times*, a progressive newspaper founded in 1917 to support Robert M. La Follette's campaigns and to defend free speech during World War I, backed Berger's First Amendment fights when few other newspapers did.

Phil Foner's *History of the Labor Movement in the United States (Vol. 8): Postwar Struggles, 1918–1920* (International Publishers, 1988) provides a detailed accounting of the first "red scare." Accounts contained in Howard Zinn's *A People's History of the United States* and Geoffrey Stone's *Perilous Times: Free Speech in Wartime From the Sedition Act of 1798 to the War on Terrorism* (W. W. Norton, 2004) are useful as well. And I commend to readers an account written during the era, *To the American People: Report Upon the Illegal Practices of the United States Department of Justice* (National Popular Government League, 1920), which includes a remarkable essay by the future Supreme Court justice Felix Frankfurter.

I relied on a number of accounts of Emma Goldman's battles with the Department of Justice, including her own writings, contained in *Living My Life* (Knopf, 1931) and *Red Emma Speaks: Selected Writings and Speeches* (Random House, 1972). *Emma Goldman: A Documentary History of the American Years, Volume 2—Making Speech Free, 1902–1909* (University of California Press, 2004) offers useful background, as does Martin Duberman's *Mother Earth: An Epic Drama of Emma Goldman's Life* (St. Martin's Press, 1991). Stone's *Perilous Times* puts the era in perspective. Howard Zinn's *Emma: A Play in Two Acts about Emma Goldman, American Anarchist* (South End Press, 2002) strikes just the right note.

The details of Debs's wrangling with the Feds are well reviewed in his book *Walls and Bars* (Charles H. Kerr Publishing Company, 1927) and in *Eugene V. Debs Speaks* (Pathfinder Press, 1972), which was edited by Jean Y. Tussey. Ernest Freeberg has written a fine book on the case and Debs's imprisonment: *Democracy's Prisoner: Eugene V. Debs, the Great War, and the Right to Dissent* (Harvard University Press, 2009). I also gained from my reading of Anthony Lewis's article "Justice Holmes and the 'Splendid Prisoner,'" which appeared in the *New York Review of Books* on July 2, 2009. The reference for the Supreme Court's decision is DEBS v. U S, 249 U.S. 211 (1919). It can be found online at http://laws.findlaw.com/us/249/211.html.

Joseph Ranney's "Victor Berger: A Reluctant Martyr for Free Speech" can be found on the Wisconsin Court System's website at www.wicourts.gov/about/organization/history/. The reference for the decision in the Leader trial is U.S. EX REL. MILWAUKEE SOCIAL DEMOCRATIC PUB. CO. v. BURLESON, 255 U.S. 407 (1921). It can be found online at http://laws.findlaw.com/us/255/407.html.

CHAPTER 6: FOR JOBS AND FREEDOM

Jervis Anderson's masterful book *A. Philip Randolph: A Biographical Portrait* (University of California, 1986) first introduced me to the great labor and civil rights leader. Other books have been written on Randolph, many of them quite good. But Anderson, the *New Yorker* magazine's ablest chronicler of labor and civil rights history, captured the wholeness of the man and his mission. This chapter is informed by his reporting and insights contained in that book, and in Anderson's fine biography of Randolph's chief lieutenant and closest ally across decades of civil rights campaigning, Bayard Rustin: *Troubles I've Seen* (University of California Press, 1998). Anderson died too young, but he got a measure of the credit due him in a thoughtful obituary, "Jervis Anderson, Writer for New Yorker And Biographer of Rustin, Is Dead at 67," which was written by Robin Pogrebin and appeared January 12, 2000, in the *New York Times*.

I interviewed Rustin late in his life for a piece focusing on his civil rights activism, and we spoke of Randolph at some length. In following the career of former Congressman Ron Dellums, I learned about the remarkable role his uncle, C. L. Dellums, played in forging the Congressman's politics. Dellums spoke often of his uncle and the Sleeping Car Porters. A very fine interview, quoted in this chapter, was conducted February 10, 2000, by Harry Kreisler as part of the "Conversations With History" series of the University of California at Berkeley's Institute of International Studies. It can be found online at http://globetrotter.berkeley.edu/people/Dellums/dellums-con1.html.

Dellum's moving autobiography (written with H. Lee Halterman), *Lying Down With the Lions: A Public Life from the Streets of Oakland to the Halls of Power* (Beacon, 2000), contains some fine historical referencing of the Sleeping Car Porters. A solid history of the union was written by Larry Tye, *Rising from the Rails: Pullman Porters and the Making of the Black Middle Class* (Holt Paperbacks, 2005). John Egerton's *Speak Now Against the Day: The Generation Before the Civil Rights Movement in the South* (University of North Carolina Press, 1995) offers great insight into the contributions made to the civil rights struggle by Randolph, the Brotherhood's southern leaders, and the Highlander Research and Education Center. A winner of the Robert F. Kennedy Book Award, Egerton's book is a great read.

The often difficult relations between the labor movement and African Americans—particularly in the pre-civil rights era—have been well and wisely detailed by Zinn and many other historians. Valuable contributions to the discussion have been made by several relatively recent books, including Robert Rogers Korstad's *Civil Rights Unionism: Tobacco Workers and the Struggle for Democracy in the Mid-Twentieth-Century South* (University of North Carolina Press, 2003). My understanding has been informed and expanded by the important writings of Bill Fletcher who, with Fernando Gapasin, is the co-author of *Solidarity Divided, The Crisis in Organized Labor and A New Path Toward Social Justice* (University of California Press; 2008). Bill and I have appeared together frequently over the years in discussions about labor and civil rights issues, and he is, to my mind, one of the wisest commentators around on the history and the current dynamic of the struggles for economic and racial justice.

Along with those of Fletcher, the writings and oral history comments of Hunter Pitts "Jack" O'Dell tell us a great deal about the way in which the "red scare" of the 1950s attacked both the militant labor and civil rights movements. O'Dell figures in all the great histories of the civil rights movement, including texts such as Taylor Branch's brilliant *At Canaan's Edge: America in the King Years, 1965–68* (Simon & Schuster, 2006). O'Dell's writings are collected in *Climbin' Jacob's Ladder: The Black Freedom Movement Writings of Jack O'Dell* (University of California Press, 2010). With John Munro and Ian Rocksborough-Smith, he is a contributor to a collection of important essays, *Jack O'Dell: The Fierce Urgency of Now* (Center for Study of Working Class Life, 2005). An oral history interview of O'Dell, conducted by Sam Sills on August 5, 1993, gives a great sense of his thinking and is quoted in this chapter. A transcript of the interview can be found at http://historymatters.gmu.edu/d/6924/.

The Rev. Martin Luther King, Jr.'s comments on socialism, Marxism and economic justice are found in *The Papers of Martin Luther King, Jr.*, the groundbreaking series of books published by University of California Press. The King Papers Project is organized by the Martin Luther King, Jr., Research and Education Institute at Stanford University, in cooperation with the King Center, and the King Estate. To learn more about it, visit http://mlk-kpp01.stanford.edu. Michael Eric Dyson's fine book *I May Not Get There With You: The True Martin Luther King, Jr.* (Simon and Schuster, 2000), reflects at some length on King's statements and views regarding democratic socialism. Brian Jones wrote a thoughtful essay on these questions, "Martin Luther King's Last Fight," for the March–April 2008 issue of *International Socialist Review*. A fine reflection on Coretta Scott King's politics and ideology, "Coretta Scott King and the Struggle for Civil and Human Rights: An Enduring Legacy," appeared in the *Journal of African American History*, Vol. 92, No. 1, Winter 2007.

Randolph and his campaigns were, from the mid-1940s on, closely covered by the *New York Times*, and this chapter relies a good deal on the archives of the newspaper. References to Randolph's speeches and campaigns, especially his push for the marches on the 1960 conventions, the 1963 March on Washington and the Freedom Budget are drawn from the coverage in the *Times*. Maurice Isserman's essay on the 1960 marches, "The Protesters of 1960 Helped Change the World," appeared in the *Los Angeles Times* on August 13, 2000. *Ebony* magazine interviews with Randolph during the 1960s provided many useful insights into his thinking, especially the epic 1969 piece, "A. Philip Randolph: Labor's Grand Old Man," which appeared in Ebony's May 1969 issue. In that article he reflected on his connection to the radicals of the 1960s, noting: "I was a young black militant myself, the angry young man of my day. As a Socialist, an advocate of trade unionism and the editor of a radical magazine called the *Messenger*, I didn't agree with anything that was supposed to be respectable, that was supposed to be a part of the American ideal and the American system. I believed that the old political, economic and social order had to be changed and changed immediately!"

AFTERWORD: "BUT WHAT ABOUT DEMOCRATIC LEFT POLITICS?"

Michael Harrington's books, essays, articles and speeches were, as noted above, points of embarkation for this chapter, along with Maurice Isserman's brilliant biographical and political writing. I am indebted to Harrington, Barbara Ehrenreich, Dorothy Healey, Bill Winpisinger, Ken Hoover, Harold Meyerson and others associated with DSOC, DSA, NAM and labor unions that interacted with those groups for insights gleaned during interviews and conversations over these many years. Meyerson's articles on Democratic Agenda, especially his pieces "The Ghost of Democratic Agenda: Echoes of another liberal turning point were felt at last week's Thinking Big conference" (*American Prospect*, February 13, 2009) and "Without a movement, progressives can't aid Obama's agenda" (*Washington Post*, January 6, 2010), were especially valuable to me. And his broad canon is essential to understanding and appreciating the struggles of democratic socialists in recent decades. So, too, are journals such as *Dissent*, DSA's *Democratic Left*, *In These Times* and the old *National*

Guardian, which historically have covered—and in some cases still do cover—the progress of the American left.

This chapter relied on *New York Times* and *Time* magazine archives from the 1960s to the 1980s, a period in which both publications provided reasonably steady coverage of the old Socialist Party, the development of DSOC, Democratic Agenda, DSA and Harrington's general activism. The *Times* used to regularly publish Harrington's op-eds, placing a socialist perspective in the paper and providing the author with a broad forum for advancing frequently radical ideas. *Time* magazine and the *Los Angeles Times* provided reasonably consistent coverage of Tom Hayden's Economic Democracy campaigning, and I am indebted to their archives.

Iowa Congressman Steve King's CPAC speech was published February 20, 2010, in the weekly conservative journal *Human Events* as "CPAC: Remarks of Rep. Steve King." Rob Port's post "Photo Evidence: Michelle Obama Keeps Socialist Books in the White House Library" appeared February 18, 2010, on his website www.sayanythingblog.com. The *Washington Post*'s coverage of the ensuing controversy, in the form of Stephen Lowman's posts "Socialist books in the White House library? A blog provides photo evidence but only part of the story" and "Socialist books in the White House library? Yep—since 1963," appeared later that day on the paper's website. Lowman's articles are archived at http://voices.washingtonpost. com/shortstack/2010/02/socialist_books_in_ the_white_h.html.

More coverage appeared on the sites of *New York* magazine ("More Shocking White House Library Books!" February 18, 2010), the *Christian Science Monitor*'s "Chapter & Verse" blog ("Is Michelle Obama packing the White House with socialist literature? No way! A blogger on a tour jumped to some wrong conclusions about the contents of the White House library," February 19, 2010), the *Los Angeles Times*' "Jacket Copy" blog ("White House library's 'socialist' books were Jackie Kennedy's," February 19, 2010) and the popular "Library Thing" blog ("Cataloged: The 1963 White House Library—Socialist Books Included; February 23, 2010). This chapter's opening owes a debt to all these insightful, and often amusing, assessments of "bookgate."

John Kennedy's speech on Marx's journalism appeared in the Congressional Record as "Remarks of Senator John F. Kennedy at the Annual Awards Dinner of the Overseas Press Club, New York City, May 6, 1957."

It is easily accessed on the site of the John F. Kennedy Presidential Library & Museum, in the "Historical Resources" section, at www. jfklibrary.org. The article to which Kennedy refers is William Harlan Hale's "When Marx Worked for Horace Greeley," *American Heritage* magazine, April 1957. References to the wrangling between JFK and Eleanor Roosevelt rely on letters, diary entries and columns collected, maintained and made readily accessible by the fabulous Eleanor Roosevelt Papers Project, a university-chartered research center associated with the Department of History of the George Washington University. Its website is found at www.gwu.edu/~erpapers/.

Dwight MacDonald's review of Harrington's *The Other America*, "The Invisible Poor," appeared in the *New Yorker* on January 19, 1963. Michael Kaufman's "The Dangers of Letting a President Read" appeared in the *New York Times* on May 22, 1999. Scott Stossel's fine biography *Sarge: The Life and Times of Sargent Shriver* (Smithsonian Books; 2004) provides terrific insight with regard to the "war on poverty" moment, as do Harrington's books and Isserman's *The Other American*. I am also indebted to Michael O'Brien's *John F. Kennedy: A Biography* (Thomas Dunne Books, 2005). The edition of Harrington's *The Other America: Poverty in the United States* with the introduction from Irving Howe was published by Simon and Schuster in 1997.

The McChesney/Foster article "Capitalism, the Absurd System: A View from the United States," appeared in the June 2010 issue of *Monthly Review*. It's brilliant.

Details of the controversy surrounding DSA support of Jesse Jackson came from news reports from 1987 and discussions with Jackson and Steve Cobble, who helped run the 1988 "Rainbow Coalition" campaign.

Joshua Freeman's *Working-Class New York: Life and Labor Since World War II* was published in 2000 by New Press. It's an important and exceptionally useful book, as is Freeman's *In Transit: The Transport Workers Union in New York City, 1933–1966* (Temple University Press, 2001).

I wrote at length about Obama's 2008 campaign for the *Nation* and other publications, and covered many of the incidents and statements recalled in this chapter on my blog, "The Beat," which appears at www.thenation.com. I wrote about Obama's Atlanta talk in July 2008, where he sought to reassure the left, for *Progressive* magazine, in a cover story, "How to Push Obama," for the January 2009 issue. That article and talks given in relation to it at events organized by a number of groups, including the *Progressive*, Progressive Democrats of America, the International Socialist Organization and Haymarket Books, helped to deepen and extend the analysis that closes this chapter.

Much of my writing on the use of the term "socialist" by Republicans has been for the *Nation*, and I contributed a chapter on Palin's excesses to a great book edited by Nation editors Richard Kim and Betsy Reed, *Going Rouge* (OR Books, 2009).

The Rasmussen Reports polling data that is referenced here comes from a study published April 9, 2009, as "Just 53% Say Capitalism Better Than Socialism." The Pew Research Center for the People and the Press survey appeared May 4, 2010, as 'Socialism' Not So Negative, 'Capitalism' Not So Positive: A Political Rhetoric Test."

It was for the *Free Enquirer* newspaper that Frances Wright on November 30, 1830, wrote of "the ridden people of the earth who are struggling to throw from their backs the 'booted and spurred' riders whose legitimate title to starve as well as to work them to death will no longer pass current." John R. Commons, Ulrich Bonnell Phillips, Eugene Allen Gilmore, Helen Laura Sumner and John Bertram Andrews collected Wright's article in a remarkable book, *A Documentary History of American Industrial Society: Labor movement, 1820–1840*, which was published in 1910 by the A. H. Clark Company. The introduction to that book was written by Richard T. Ely, the great University of Wisconsin economics professor and progressive reformer who argued at the turn of the last century that socialist ideas deserved a hearing—and an embrace where they were of value—in America. Ely was not a socialist but, as Arthur Morrow Lewis explained, the professor was a "fair opponent" who had "done much to obtain a hearing for [socialism] among the unreasonable." For that, and for supporting striking printers, Ely was persecuted and threatened with removal from the UW faculty. He fought back against the charge that he had preached "utopian, impractical, or pernicious doctrines," won a trial before the state Board of Regents and established principles of academic and intellectual freedom that were celebrated in the 1960s NBC television series "Profiles in Courage," based on John F. Kennedy's book of the same title.

On Bascom Hill, at the center of the UW campus, a plaque near the great statue of Abraham Lincoln recalls Ely's fight for the right to discuss all ideas—including socialist ones. The plaque reads: "Whatever may be the limitations which trammel inquiry elsewhere, we believe that the great state University of Wisconsin should ever encourage that continual and fearless sifting and winnowing by which alone the truth can be found."

This book is written in the hope that America will engage anew in "that continual and fearless sifting and winnowing by which alone the truth can be found."

Index